FARMINGTON COMMUNITY LIBRARY
FARMINGTON BRANCH LIBRARY
23500 LIBERTY STREET
FARMINGTON, MI 48335-3570
(248) 553-0321
WITHDRAWN

3 0036 01448 2143

AUG 1 4 2023

TANGLED VINES

ALSO BY JOHN GLATT

The Doomsday Mother
Golden Boy
The Perfect Father
The Family Next Door
My Sweet Angel
The Lost Girls
The Prince of Paradise
Love Her to Death
Lost and Found
Playing with Fire
Secrets in the Cellar
To Have and to Kill
Forgive Me, Father
The Doctor's Wife
One Deadly Night
Depraved
Cries in the Desert
For I Have Sinned
Evil Twins
Cradle of Death
Blind Passion
Deadly American Beauty
Never Leave Me
Twisted

TANGLED VINES

POWER, PRIVILEGE, AND THE
MURDAUGH FAMILY MURDERS

JOHN GLATT

ST. MARTIN'S PRESS
NEW YORK

First published in the United States by St. Martin's Press,
an imprint of St. Martin's Publishing Group

TANGLED VINES. Copyright © 2023 by John Glatt. All rights reserved.
Printed in the United States of America. For information,
address St. Martin's Publishing Group, 120 Broadway, New York, NY 10271.

www.stmartins.com

The Library of Congress Cataloging-in-Publication Data
is available upon request.

ISBN 978-1-250-28348-1 (hardcover)
ISBN 978-1-250-28349-8 (ebook)

Our books may be purchased in bulk for promotional, educational,
or business use. Please contact your local bookseller or the
Macmillan Corporate and Premium Sales Department at
1-800-221-7945, extension 5442, or by email at
MacmillanSpecialMarkets@macmillan.com.

First Edition: 2023

10 9 8 7 6 5 4 3 2

For Bea Shapiro and Bernie Freund

Contents

PALMETTO SHORT STORY
ASSOCIATED PRESS—JUNE 28, 1956

BEAUFORT: When two hunting dogs were brought into the state circuit courtroom today in a trial case, 14th circuit solicitor Randolph Murdaugh quipped to the judge: "Defense and prosecution have agreed not to ask them more than three questions each."

PART I

PROLOGUE

Alex Murdaugh's world was falling apart. The highly respected attorney, heir to a powerful legal dynasty that had ruled South Carolina's Lowcountry for more than a century, had run out of places to hide.

The day before, his family's illustrious law firm, founded in 1910 by his great-grandfather, Randolph Murdaugh Sr., had ignominiously fired him for stealing millions of dollars of client funds. Now broke and in the throes of opioid addiction, Alex had decided to die.

He called Curtis "Fast Eddie" Smith, a distant cousin and alleged personal drug dealer, arranging to meet him opposite an old church on Old Salkehatchie Road in Hampton. The odd-job man drew up in his battered old truck to where six-foot-three-inch Alex, known as Big Red for his striking red hair, was waiting by his gleaming black Mercedes-Benz.

Then Alex handed Smith a loaded .38-caliber revolver and ordered him to shoot him in the back of the head and get the hell out of there.

Staging his own death was just the latest chapter for Alex in a roller-coaster of murder plots, financial crimes, and drug addiction, straight out of a Southern Gothic novel. It had captured America's imagination and brought fifty-three-year-old Alex Murdaugh (pronounced Ellick Murdock) and his storied family the unwanted attention they had always avoided.

For more than a century, the Murdaugh family had dominated a huge swathe of South Carolina's luscious Lowcountry, epitomizing power, justice, and big, big money. Three generations of Murdaughs had served as 14th Circuit solicitors (called district attorneys in all other states), turning it into a family business.

Murdaughs prosecuted every crime committed over a sprawling five-county area, from Colleton's rural swamps to the ultra-chic Hilton Head Island beaches in Beaufort County. Feared and revered, Murdaugh solicitors had sent hundreds of people to prison and well over a dozen to the electric chair.

Their powers and influence were limitless. They had lorded it over judges, politicians, and top law officials for eighty-six years, before Alex's father, Randolph Murdaugh III, abruptly retired in 2006, appointing his own hand-picked successor.

The family also ran one of South Carolina's top law firms, specializing in personal injury cases for the common man, which netted them millions of dollars a year. At that time, it was legal for criminal solicitors to also practice civil law—an anomaly that no longer exists.

Deliberately playing down their wealth and privilege for political reasons, the Murdaugh family quietly enjoyed their huge plantation estates, hunting lodges, and waterfront properties, including one called "Murdaugh Island."

It was rumored that family members had made fortunes from moonshine over the years, as well as from massive marijuana-smuggling operations in the seventies and eighties. They appeared to be above the law and impervious to any legal consequences.

In February 2019, everything changed. Alex's nineteen-year-old son Paul drunkenly plowed the family's seventeen-foot fishing boat into a bridge pylon, killing his teenage friend Mallory Beach. With a blood alcohol content three times over the legal limit, Paul was eventually charged with three felony counts of boating under the influence, despite his family's attempts to cast the blame elsewhere.

Then late one night in June 2021, after visiting his dying father in the hospital, Alex returned to Moselle, his 1,770-acre hunting estate, to discover his wife, Maggie, and Paul brutally murdered by the dog kennels. As he stood over their bullet-ridden bodies he tearfully called 911, saying they'd been "hurt bad."

Within hours, the South Carolina Law Enforcement Division (SLED) had reassured the public there was no danger, naming Alex "a person of interest" in the murders. Three days later, his father Randolph III died of cancer after a long illness.

In the wake of the double homicide, SLED reopened a 2015 unsolved killing of gay nursing student Stephen Smith, which Alex's oldest son Buster had been linked to. Soon afterward, SLED opened a criminal investigation into the strange February 2018 "trip-and-fall" death of the Murdaughs' longtime housekeeper, Gloria Satterfield, amidst gossip that Paul had been involved.

The collapse of the Murdaugh house of cards was now well underway.

Exactly what happened after Alex ordered Fast Eddie to shoot him remains unclear.

Initially Alex, who survived the shooting, claimed to have been changing a flat tire by the side of the road when a driver in a truck pulled up, asking if he was having car trouble before shooting him in the head.

Investigators were immediately suspicious. Though his tires were later found to have been slashed, his Mercedes had state-of-the-art run-flat tires and could have been driven another fifty miles. They also found that the knife used to do it belonged to Alex.

A week after the shooting, Big Red fessed up. He admitted to hiring Curtis Smith to murder him, so his surviving son Buster could collect his $10 million life insurance.

Smith had a totally different story. He claimed that after Alex's order, he wrestled the gun away, and during the struggle, it had gone off without any bullet hitting Alex. He'd then panicked and driven off, dumping the firearm on his way home.

Through his team of high-powered attorneys, Alex insisted that Smith had shot him in the head, leaving entry and exit wounds and fracturing his skull. Nevertheless, he was still able to call 911 for help, before being helicoptered to Savannah, Georgia, for emergency treatment. Days later, he checked himself into an Atlanta drug rehabilitation clinic.

"Things were moving really quickly and really negatively," Alex later explained. "My world was caving in. . . . I was in a very bad place."

1

EARLY DAYS

The Murdaugh family has deep, deep roots in South Carolina's fabled Lowcountry. The nonstop drama and colorful exploits of the early members of the Murdaugh family would echo through the generations to come, until the family's tragic fall like a classic Greek tragedy.

Alex's great-great-great-grandfather Josiah Putnam Murdaugh I was born on Christmas Day 1793, in Islandton, South Carolina, just a few miles away from the Moselle hunting lodge where Paul and Maggie Murdaugh would be murdered 228 years later.

Josiah's wife, Mary Ursula Varn, bore him two sons: Josiah Putnam II, in 1830, and Alonzo, in 1857. Two of her relatives, James G. Varn, and his younger brother, the Reverend Little Berry Varn, owned a sawmill in the tiny village of Dixie. In 1872 they sold the right-of-way to the Port Royal and Augusta Railroad for train tracks to go through their land and made their fortune.

The Varn brothers then founded their own town, Varnville, on the north side of the tracks. Over the next 150 years, the booming railroad would play a commanding role in the Murdaugh family saga in so many different ways.

Soon after Varnville was established, Josiah Putnam II married Annie Marvin Davis, the first cousin of Jefferson Davis, the President of the Confederate States. Josiah was appointed Varnville's official moneylender, before making his first fortune in phosphate mining and commercial fertilizer.

He later branched out into real estate, buying up land in neighboring Almeda.

"They ended up with a lot of land after the Civil War," said local historian Sam Crews III, whose family settled in Hampton County around the same time as the Murdaughs. "They were good farmers and sharecroppers but they really believed in education. That was a big thing."

Josiah and Annie had five children; their youngest, Randolph Murdaugh Sr., was born in Varnville on February 28, 1887.

The boisterous young boy was raised on the thriving Murdaugh family farm and educated by private tutors, as were his siblings.

After leaving school, Randolph attended the US Naval Academy in Annapolis. He was all set for a naval career until doctors discovered a heart ailment, rendering him unfit for service.

Randolph then returned to South Carolina to pursue his second choice of going into law. He enrolled at the University of South Carolina (USC), where he was captain of the football team.

He graduated in 1908 with a bachelor's degree, before spending two years at USC's School of Law to get his law degree.

In 1910, the handsome twenty-three-year-old set up his one-man law practice, directly across from the Hampton County Courthouse. His son Randolph Jr. would later boast that even by that point the Murdaugh name was so well-known in Hampton that their law offices never needed a sign outside.

By the time Josiah Putnam Murdaugh II died in August 1912, his youngest son was fast establishing himself as one of South Carolina's most gifted young lawyers.

In 1914, Randolph Sr. married twenty-four-year-old Etta Lavinia Harvey. They had two sons, Randolph Jr., in January 1915, and John Glenn, in August 1918. But three weeks after giving birth to John, Etta caught influenza and tragically died at just twenty-nine.

"Old Mr. Randolph was devastated," said Crews. "[Their son] was just three years old when his mother died so he was a little spoiled."

Several years later, Randolph Sr. would remarry a local woman named Estelle Marvin. Although he was mostly an absentee father, employing nannies to raise his two young sons, he often brought his sons to the courthouse.

While running his thriving law office, Randolph Sr. also started his own short-lived newspaper, *The Hampton Herald*, with a capital of $3,000. He also served as Varnville's official town attorney for a salary of $25 a year, while his brother Mortimer Murdaugh was the tax collector.

In 1920, Randolph Sr. entered the race for the elected 14th Judicial Circuit, encompassing Hampton, Allendale, Beaufort, Colleton, and Jasper counties. Four years earlier, the 14th Judicial District had been severed from the Charleston court system to become South Carolina's only circuit to have five counties, the others just having two or three.

Randolph Sr. won easily, and a Murdaugh would go on to occupy the solicitor's chair for the next eighty-six years.

"He was very well-liked and very smart," said historian Sam Crews, whose great-grandfather, Eugene Peeples, was Hampton County coroner and had worked closely with the new solicitor. "And he believed in doing the right thing."

Over the next few years, Randolph Sr. became a fixture in the Hampton County newspapers, which faithfully chronicled his many legal victories and charity work. He and Estelle regularly made the society pages, showing up at garden parties and judging flower shows.

Randolph Sr. relished high-profile court cases that established him as a statewide figure. He once prosecuted a state governor and made him stand in the prisoner's block while he read out the indictment.

Courtrooms were packed for his colorful murder trials, and no one was off limits as he indicted preachers, police officers, bankers, and corrupt politicians.

His son Randolph Jr.'s earliest memory was following his father to the courthouse. The little boy would often watch the trials and dreamed of becoming a lawyer when he grew up.

Little Randolph attended Varnville High School and then the University of South Carolina, where he played football for the Gamecocks. It was there that he was dubbed "Buster" by USC head coach Bill Laval, because he always "busted the opponent." He would be known as Buster Murdaugh for the rest of his life.

On February 20, 1937, Buster's stepmother Estelle died with her husband at her bedside. She had been in the hospital since the previous September. Randolph Sr. was heartbroken and started drinking heavily.

A few months later, Buster Murdaugh, now at the University of South Carolina's School of Law, married twenty-one-year-old Gladys Marvin of Yemassee, who had recently graduated college.

The couple settled in Varnville, and Buster joined his father's fast-growing law practice, now renamed Murdaugh and Murdaugh.

On October 25, 1939, Gladys bore Buster a baby boy whom they named Randolph Murdaugh III, but it would be another ten years before the couple had another child together.

By early 1940, Randolph Sr. was running unopposed for his sixth term as the 14th Circuit solicitor. His twenty-five-year-old son, Buster, often deputized for him while he was in the hospital for various ailments.

"Young Murdaugh Acts as Solicitor in the Absence of His Father," was the front-page story in *The Hampton County Guardian*'s February 21, 1940, edition.

The following week's *Guardian* carried the headline, "Grand Jury Lauds Solicitor Murdaugh in Term Presentment. Endorses him for Re-Election in Coming Election."

But then tragedy struck.

On July 19, 1940, Randolph Sr. spent the night drinking heavily at a friend's poker party in Yemassee and set out to drive home alone.

At around 1:00 A.M., he was four miles east of Varnville when he stopped by the side of the train track. A few minutes later a westbound Charleston and Western Carolina freight train came hurtling toward him at full speed. As it approached the Camp Branch crossing, Solicitor Murdaugh calmly turned on his engine and drove straight into the middle of the track, stopping directly in the train's path.

Engineer W. W. Bartlett would later testify that by the time he saw

Murdaugh's car it was too late to stop. To his horror, he said, he'd seen the solicitor smile and then wave to the crew seconds before impact.

Randolph Sr.'s body was found fifty yards away from the crossing, and his car was three hundred yards down the track.

A Hampton County Coroner's jury later ruled it an accidental death.

But there was also much speculation the fifty-three-year-old solicitor had committed suicide, as he had been in ill health and depressed since Estelle's death.

2

BUSTER

One month after Randolph Sr.'s death, his son Buster Murdaugh swept to victory in the 14th Judicial Circuit solicitor's election by a margin of sixteen-to-one in Hampton County.

At that time, the solicitor's job only paid $270 a month ($5,400 in today's money), so the vast majority of Buster's income came from his growing private practice and other less legal enterprises.

"When Buster was first practicing, the solicitor was considered a part-time job," explained Beaufort defense attorney Jared "Buzzard" Newman. "So he was a lawyer and did civil cases, like suing people."

On October 1, 1940, Buster sued the Charleston and Western Carolina Railway Company for the wrongful death of his father, demanding $100,000 (almost $2 million in today's money).

The lawsuit, filed in the Hampton Court of Common Pleas, claimed that the train had been traveling "at a high rate of speed" and hadn't signaled its approach with a bell or whistle. It also accused the railroad company of leaving the crossing in "a rough, washed-out, and dangerous condition," therefore placing Solicitor Murdaugh in "sudden and imminent peril."

The case was later settled with an undisclosed payout to Buster.

During World War II, many of Hampton's young men went off to fight in Europe and the Pacific, and a prisoner-of-war camp was built in the town. After the war, the young fighters returned to find new job opportunities on the horizon.

Plywood-Plastics Corporation, later to become Westinghouse, soon opened a factory, bringing jobs to the impoverished area and a much-needed boost to the economy. Coca-Cola opened a bottling plant, and the Cranel B. Herndon Fast Motor Freight Service eventually became one of Hampton's biggest employers.

By the mid-1940s, young solicitor Buster Murdaugh was already making a name for himself. He wooed jurors with his unorthodox courtroom theatrics and magnetic charm. In his early years as solicitor, Buster boasted a ninety-five-percent conviction rate, often cutting legal corners in order to win.

"You could learn more about prosecuting cases in five minutes from Mr. Buster," said one solicitor, "than you could from years in law school."

In his civil practice, he became known as a plaintiff's attorney, who had a good word for everybody and never turned anyone away. Known for his "wit and flaming oratory" inside the courtroom, Buster had a gift for dealing with the ordinary man or woman on the street.

He made it a point to know everyone in Hampton and his other four counties, giving him a major advantage with local juries, who all related to him personally.

Sam Crews's father often accompanied Buster on fishing trips to Hilton Head and always came back with stories.

"Daddy would say, 'Well, don't go to the grocery store with Buster Murdaugh,'" remembered Sam, "'because he knows everyone in there and those that he doesn't know, he'll find out who they are before you leave.' If they didn't [go] fishing that was fine with Buster, because he was working his people. That's who he was."

Always charismatic, Buster moved easily in South Carolina high society, hobnobbing with the rich elite in Hilton Head or Charleston. In 1945 he embarked on a torrid affair with wealthy Philadelphia socialite and heiress Ruth Vaux. The married father was captivated by the fashionable former debutante, affectionately known as Gigi.

Ruth was a direct descendant of Richard Vaux, a lawyer who became mayor of Philadelphia in 1856 and later served in Congress. In 1931 she had made *The New York Times* after receiving blackmail and death threats by an extortionist, demanding $5,000 ($96,000 today). Twice, the money was left on the corner of Thirteenth and Federal Streets with the Philadelphia police discreetly watching. But it was never collected and the case was never solved.

Four years later, Ruth eloped with wealthy financier Henry S. Cram, making the society pages of *The New York Times* and *Daily News*.

In 1943, Cram was drafted to Europe to fight in the Second World War, and Ruth began spending time in Bluffton and Hilton Head, where she first met Buster Murdaugh at a social soiree.

In early 1945, Ruth became pregnant with the solicitor's baby and he gallantly accepted responsibility. When her husband returned from the war, he was furious and immediately filed for divorce.

"[Cram] denied paternity," said Hampton historian Sam Crews III. "It was a matter of honor and he would not allow the child to carry his name. It wasn't like child support was an issue because they were both immensely wealthy."

That November, she gave birth to a baby boy named Roberts Vaux. Buster acknowledged his illegitimate son, who was later accepted by the Murdaugh family but always kept at arm's length.

"They didn't make it public," said Crews, who met Ruth several times. "They would just see [Roberts] and talk to him, but they did not invite him to family gatherings in Hampton [and] would see him at other places in the Lowcountry."

Around the same time, Buster struck up a friendship with an Allendale lawyer named Barrett Thomas Boulware and their families became very close. The two lawyers often worked civil cases together in a lucrative partnership that made both a lot of money.

Later there would be rumors that they were also involved in a major drug-smuggling operation that made them millions.

In December 1948, Solicitor Buster Murdaugh found himself in the difficult position of prosecuting one of Beaufort high society's most scandalous murders, involving members of his own social circle.

Wealthy playboy William Moseley Swain and his beautiful wife were hosting a small drinks party at Belfair, their historic one-thousand-acre plantation estate in Beaufort County. One of the guests was cattleman Victor Strojny, who owned Callawassie Island, with its eleven miles of coastline and fertile salt marshes.

Over cocktails that night, Swain, a renowned sportsman, whose grandfather had founded *The Philadelphia Record*, lent Strojny $600 ($7,000 today).

Toward midnight, the party was winding down and Mrs. Swain retired to bed. A few minutes later, William Swain mysteriously fell down a wooden staircase, fracturing his skull and then dying in the hospital.

Strojny later told Sheriff J. E. McTeer that he had heard a loud noise and went to investigate. He found Swain lying in a pool of blood at the foot of the staircase. Unable to awaken Mrs. Swain, he'd asked the caretaker to call an ambulance.

Sheriff McTeer had arrested Strojny for murder, deciding it was "unlikely" that Swain had fallen accidentally.

Two months later at a preliminary hearing in Beaufort County Court, Solicitor Buster Murdaugh told Judge W. E. Elliott that Swain had been "fatally injured" after "a drinking party." The judge ordered Strojny held under a $3,000 ($35,000) bond, which raised some eyebrows when it was immediately posted by the dead man's widow, also rumored to be his lover.

Buster Murdaugh moved in the same rarified Beaufort social circles as the defendant, whose Callawassie Island was near Chechessee Creek, where Buster owned property.

During the much-anticipated murder trial in November 1949, Solicitor Murdaugh was in the middle of examining Swain's widow on the witness stand, when he suddenly asked the judge to drop all murder charges. In a motion, he explained that because the state did not have enough evidence to convict, it would be "useless" to proceed.

The Associated Press reported Murdaugh's direct examination of Swain's widow, which later went out on the national wire.

"You do not feel that Strojny is guilty, do you?" asked the solicitor.

"No, I do not," replied the small, thirty-five-year-old widow.

"In fact, you offered to help post bond for him, didn't you?" pursued the prosecutor.

"Yes," said the blond witness, primly dressed in black coat and hat.

The judge then dismissed the murder charges and Victor Strojny walked out of court a free man.

As a young boy, Buster's son Randolph III was often in the courtroom to see his father in action. On one occasion little Randolph found himself in the center of one of his father's murder investigations.

Buster would later tell *Carolina Lawyer* magazine how he was out fishing with his small son when the sheriff brought him news that a body had just been discovered.

"[Randolph] couldn't have been more than six or seven," said Buster. "They had recovered a body in a murder case and had the victim's brother in custody."

As the murder suspect would only talk to the solicitor, Buster took his young son with him to witness the confession.

Buster later told the *Carolina Lawyer* that the brother had duly confessed but that little Randolph had been so moved by the suspect's "hard-luck story" that he refused to testify at the trial.

"I told him he could just sit in court then and hold his subpoena," a laughing Buster told the bemused reporter.

Over the next few years, Buster Murdaugh developed an iconic legal persona in courtrooms across the five counties. With his ever-present Red Man chewing tobacco, booming voice, and dramatic flair for acting out murders in front of the jury, he became the scourge of defenders and rarely lost a case. He made sure that every courtroom in the 14th Circuit had a brass spittoon by his wooden solicitor's table, which was surrounded by spit-stained carpet.

"He was a legend, a bigger-than-life presence," remembered Columbia defense attorney Jack Swerling, who often faced off against Buster. "Once, in a murder case, he drew an imaginary box with his finger in front of the jury box and said, 'This is where Johnny is laying in his grave right now.' And when the jury came back with the guilty verdict, they all avoided stepping on that imaginary box Buster had drawn."

Solicitor Murdaugh stacked up his indictments on his table before picking one at random, so the waiting defense attorneys never knew which defendant would be called next.

One of his goriest murder cases came in April 1949, after Buster had convened a grand jury to indict Colleton farmer Wyman Hiott for poisoning and then burying his elderly sister Carrie in a pigpen while she was still alive. Under the solicitor's intense interrogation, the sixty-one-year-old farmer broke down and admitted to killing his eighty-year-old sister, because she "messed the bed so many times."

At trial, Buster acted out Hiott's chilling confession of what happened after his sister succumbed to the poison, even adopting the rural farmer's accent and mannerisms. It was duly reported the following day in the *Florence Morning News*.

"I then went back to her bedroom," said Murdaugh, "picked her up and placed her in the grave, covering her with blankets, then paper, then dirt. At that time she was breathing a little."

Judge J. R. Ross sentenced Hiott to life imprisonment, after the jury recommended "mercy," although Buster had demanded the death penalty.

"I believe you are guilty," Judge Ross told the defendant. "They could have sent you to the electric chair. You were the master of your destiny."

Solicitor Murdaugh had few qualms about dispatching defendants to "Old Sparky." But unfortunately, he played fast and loose with the law and many of his convictions would later be reversed on appeal.

"He was a win-at-all-costs solicitor," said John Blume, a professor at Cornell Law School, who handled appeals for several defendants on death row. "He repeatedly did things that he had to know were improper—primarily in his closing arguments, where he could not keep himself confined to the rules."

One of Buster's favorite closing statements was to tell jurors that if they voted not guilty, they would be directly responsible for turning loose other rapists and murderers.

The 14th Circuit solicitor was later officially censured by the South Carolina Supreme Court for "egregious jury arguments," after sending fourteen men to death row.

Solicitor Murdaugh also found himself in hot water with his civil law practice. One client accused him of mishandling mortgage loan funds and sued him for $50,000 [$605,000 today]. This led to an official investigation by the Hampton Bar Association that could have led to his disbarment.

On October 2, 1949, the state bar association's grievance committee held a ten-hour-long closed meeting in Columbia to decide Murdaugh's fate. After hearing testimony from two Hampton County bankers, Moses Tucker Laffitte and Frank A. McClure, the committee found the 14th Circuit solicitor innocent of all charges.

A victorious Buster told the *Florence Morning News* that he welcomed the investigation and was delighted with the result.

In early 1950, Gladys Murdaugh fell pregnant again and Buster became the proud father of a daughter, Brenda. Whether or not Gladys was aware of Buster's then–five-year-old son Roberts with Ruth Vaux remains a closely guarded family secret.

Soon after the birth, Buster and Gladys moved to 115 Carolina Avenue in Varnville, where they would raise their family.

Buster was close friends with almost every judge on the 14th Circuit. He regularly held lavish parties at his new house, inviting influential local politicians and members of law enforcement. It was a close-knit boy's club whose members looked after one another.

"Buster had a few people he kept close and away from harm," explained Kim Brant, a Hampton businesswoman who knew the Murdaughs. "When he was unhappy with a certain person, it was their job to handle it."

Another Hampton resident, who wished to remain anonymous, said the tough law-and-order solicitor could also look the other way when it came to his friends.

"As a little girl," she said, "I remember Daddy saying, 'Go to Buster

Murdaugh, he'll make it disappear.' It was always that good ol' boy system."

Buster's social and professional connections were most impressive. He was a 32nd Degree Freemason and a Shriner, but it was his staunch Democrat party credentials that gave him power in the Columbia Statehouse. His political support was a valuable asset to any state congressman seeking election.

At that time, the Lowcountry was strictly segregated, and the local white business community relied on the solicitor to keep everything rolling smoothly.

"The Caucasians were very supportive of him," explained Greenville attorney Henry Philpott, who later attended law school with Buster's son Randolph III. "They felt he kept a lid on things."

In the early 1950s, the Murdaugh Law Practice expanded, recruiting future 14th Circuit judge Clyde Eltzroth and Robert Peters as partners. Renamed Murdaugh, Eltzroth & Peters, the Hampton County law firm would continue to grow exponentially over the next decade.

Buster Murdaugh knew everyone in Hampton County. He always had a friendly handshake and a good word to say to anyone on the street, engendering goodwill. So when the juries were picked for personal injury cases in tiny Hampton, all the jurors knew Buster and were open to handing out hugely outsized payouts to his clients. Over the years the "Hampton Jurors," as they became known, would instill fear in large corporations.

Buster Murdaugh's most notorious murder case spanned almost a decade and riveted the entire state. John D. Bowers had annihilated his entire family during a drunken rage. Known in the press as the Estill Baseball Bat Slayer, the forty-three-year-old storekeeper had a long history of severe mental illness.

In December 1948, he calmly waited until his wife, Mae, seven-year-old son, Wayne, and four-year-old daughter, Sandra, returned home from a movie before savagely beating them all to death with his baseball bat.

Bowers broke down and confessed to Solicitor Murdaugh, and after undergoing treatment in the South Carolina State Hospital in Columbia, he was declared mentally fit for trial. The solicitor told *The Hampton County Guardian* that Bowers was "a dangerous person" who would kill again if he was ever returned to society and "resumed the use of alcohol."

According to Murdaugh, it would be "just another case to me," and he intended to demand that the jury give Bowers "the chair and nothing else."

On Wednesday, October 25, 1950, Bowers was tried at the Hampton County General Sessions for the murder of his little daughter. He pleaded not guilty.

"[This trial will be] one of the most sensational in this section of the country in recent years," Buster informed local reporters outside the courtroom.

During the one-day trial Solicitor Murdaugh repeatedly brandished the baseball bat in front of the jury to vividly demonstrate the vicious killings.

"John Bowers has to be removed from society by electrocution, if Hampton County is to be made a safe place in which to live," he told jurors in his closing argument. "If he is ever released on society and kills again," he shouted, "no one is responsible but yourselves."

After eight hours of deliberation, the jury found Bowers guilty of killing his four-year-old daughter, Sandra, with a recommendation of mercy.

Judge Woodrow Lewis sentenced Bowers to hard labor for the rest of his life in the state penitentiary in Richland County.

Ten years later, Bowers was back in the Hampton courtroom for two separate trials, this time for the murder of his wife and son. At the first in 1961, nine-year-old Sam Crews III, whose parents were close friends of the Murdaughs, served as a jury boy, running errands for $5 a day. After the solicitor did his obligatory baseball bat demonstration for the jury, he handed it to Sam and began coaching him for Little League.

"It was in the middle of the trial," Sam remembered, "and he was telling me how to get in the stance."

For the next few minutes, the little boy playfully swung the bat in front of the jury, until the furious judge summoned his mother to come and take him home.

At both trials, Bowers was found guilty of murder and further sentenced to two life imprisonments to run concurrently, after the jury denied Solicitor Murdaugh's furious demands for the electric chair.

3

TRIALS AND TRIBULATIONS

Now approaching middle age, Solicitor Buster Murdaugh was starting to groom his young son Randolph III to take over from him
one day. The young, cherubic red-headed boy had long been a constant
presence around Hampton County Court, often accompanying his father
to investigate crimes.

"I can't remember not wanting to be a lawyer," he later told *The Win-
chester Star*. "I followed my father around the courtroom. I'm talking
about, hell, when I was six years old."

In 1955, the towns of Hampton and Varnville were consolidated, creating
the Wade Hampton High School on the borders of each. It was named in
honor of the former South Carolina governor Wade Hampton, who was also
a Confederate officer and slaveholder.

After attending Varnville Elementary School, fifteen-year-old Randolph III was among the first intake of students at the new Wade Hampton School. He was already dating Elizabeth "Libby" Jones Alexander, the
high school sweetheart he would later marry.

In their senior year, the teenage couple were anointed Wade Hampton's "Most Athletic," with Randolph becoming the school's first "four-
letter athlete," earning varsity letters in baseball, basketball, football, and
track, and Libby running for homecoming queen.

In his graduation photograph, Randolph has a wide, confident smile
alongside his yearbook quote: "China Doll—Cut it Rocky!—football
hero—bright red hair—lawyer."

He was later interviewed by *The Post and Courier* newspaper about his future aspirations.

"I would like to follow in my father's footsteps," Randolph III was quoted as saying, "and work towards a law degree."

As the teenage Murdaugh prepared to enter the University of South Carolina, his father was facing the biggest crisis of his career, clearly demonstrating the family's long history of corruption. In an eerie foreshadowing of what would happen more than half a century later, Buster's criminally reckless behavior had finally caught up to him.

He had now held the 14th Judicial Circuit solicitor position for sixteen years, although it was an open secret that he was in cahoots with the local bootleggers, feeding them information about any threatening police activity in their area.

"People were making moonshine and Buster helped them," said Hampton historian Sam Crews III. "It was only ten years after the end of the war and we had an employment problem. The only downside was that Buster . . . got caught."

Newly elected South Carolina governor George Bell Timmerman had vowed to root out corruption, passing a new set of laws that any police officers or other officials under criminal investigation must resign. And he'd turned his attention to the highly lucrative illegal whiskey industry thriving in the Palmetto State.

In late June 1956, Solicitor Murdaugh, Colleton County Sheriff G. Haskell Thompson, and two local magistrates were indicted by a federal grand jury, accused of a two-year conspiracy to violate the Internal Revenue Service liquor laws.

Murdaugh was accused of taking payoffs from bootleggers in return for inside information on upcoming police raids. Additionally, he was charged with attempting to bribe a grand juror.

It was alleged that the Lowcountry's chief prosecutor had masterminded the "Colleton Whiskey Conspiracy" involving thirty-two moonshine stills that pumped out 90,000 gallons of illegal liquor during the two-year federal investigation.

Assistant United States attorney Arthur G. Howe described it as *the* most important case ever tried in South Carolina.

"It reaches to the crux of our government and our way of life," he told reporters. "From the swamps of Jackass Pond into the Colleton County Courthouse."

On September 7, Buster Murdaugh was forced to resign as 14th Circuit solicitor, and Governor Timmerman immediately replaced him with Beaufort attorney G. G. Dowling.

In his fiery letter of resignation, Buster branded it "a conspiracy," welcoming the opportunity to clear his name at the earliest opportunity.

"This action causes me the deepest sadness," he told the governor. "The security, honor, and happiness of my wife and children face destruction; my personal integrity and liberty are at stake."

The former solicitor then initiated a campaign of intimidation, going all the way up to the United States prosecutor handling the case.

"Government witnesses were threatened," revealed a Department of Justice (DOJ) report into the controversial Murdaugh case, released the following November. "Attempts were made to influence them by promises of reward for themselves or members of their family."

The sensational two-week trial began on Monday, September 17, and Buster faced a long prison sentence if convicted.

The government's star witness was Colleton County deputy sheriff Riddick Herndon, who had made a deal with prosecutors to testify against Murdaugh and Thompson.

In explosive testimony, Herndon told the court he had personally witnessed Buster Murdaugh and the former sheriff split a $500 ($6,000 today) payoff for arranging a lighter sentence for bootlegger George W. McPeake, who had been caught operating an illegal whiskey still.

The deputy also testified that after pressure to stop illegal whiskey making in Hampton County, Solicitor Murdaugh had come up with a plan for Sheriff Herndon to stage "friendly raids" on local bootleggers.

During his testimony, Herndon quoted Murdaugh as saying, "For

God's sake, make the raid even if you have to warn them in advance, catch them, and set up fines. I'll take care of them."

On the tenth day of the trial, Buster Murdaugh took the stand to defiantly proclaim his innocence.

"Battle of Wits Marks Murdaugh Court Appearance" was the headline in the next day's *Post and Courier*.

Reporter Jack Leland, who was covering the trial, wrote that it was such a "tense verbal skirmish" between Murdaugh and the prosecutor that Judge Walter E. Hoffman offered to get them boxing gloves so they could duke it out later.

During cross-examination, Buster was asked about previous testimony that one of the indicted bootleggers was a longtime hunting and fishing friend of his.

"We're not in the same social class at all," replied Murdaugh dismissively, after conceding they had hunted together. "I've never visited him at his home nor he in mine."

In closing arguments, Assistant Attorney General Irvine C. Belser Jr. pulled no punches.

"This man Murdaugh used to be called 'Righteous Randolph,'" he told jurors, "but now it's 'Bootlegging Buster.' If you want a solicitor who takes bribes, counsels bootleggers, and takes part in deceiving a grand jury . . . then bring an acquittal."

On October 1, despite all the evidence against him, a jury acquitted the former solicitor on all charges, although Sheriff Thompson was convicted, receiving a seven-year jail sentence and a $3,000 fine ($31,000 today).

Judge Hoffman was furious at the jury's decision and reprimanded Buster Murdaugh for his "unethical practices." He especially "deplored the fact" that Buster, already the unopposed candidate in the upcoming 14th Judicial Circuit solicitor's election on January 1, 1957, would soon be back in power.

One week after the verdict, Buster's first cousin Alex G. Murdaugh was indicted by a federal grand jury for jury tampering. It carried a maximum sentence of five years' imprisonment and a $5,000 fine ($53,000 today) if found guilty.

At his December 1957 trial, Alex denied all charges and was acquitted of all charges.

On January 1, 1957, Buster Murdaugh was back as 14th Judicial Circuit solicitor after a six-month hiatus, as if nothing had happened. Perhaps feeling empowered by the acquittal, he was even more outrageous than he had been before his trial.

In one notable case, the defense attorney had told the jury that his client was "cloaked in a veil of innocence." This was like a red rag to a bull for Buster.

Just before closing arguments, Solicitor Murdaugh was spotted carefully hiding evidence under his jacket. At a moment of high drama in his closing, Buster strolled up to the jury box and said, "Let's see what's behind that cloak."

Then with a flourish he reached into his coat and pulled out a sawed-off shotgun and a pistol, hurling them across the tiled courtroom floor and hitting the jury box.

"[Buster] was a hell of a trial lawyer," remembers Beaufort defense attorney Jared "Buzzard" Newman. "He could get away with things you couldn't do now. He'd throw evidence across the courtroom if he wanted to make a point. He had a flair for the dramatic."

After his close shave with the law, Buster Murdaugh reinvented himself as a South Carolina pillar of justice. In November 1957, he helped found the South Carolina Trial Lawyers Association, one of the state's most enduring and respected legal associations. Its stated mission was, "to advocate for those who are harmed by the actions of others no matter how powerful, wealthy or well-connected . . . and to uphold the highest standards of ethical conduct and integrity in the legal profession."

Over the next sixty-five years, three generations of Murdaughs would serve on its board of governors, including Buster's grandson, Alex, who in 2014 would become president of the South Carolina Association for Justice, as it became known.

On June 3, 1961, Randolph Murdaugh III married Libby Alexander, after graduating from the University of South Carolina with a BS in business administration.

Sam Crews's mother, Betty Ruth, a close friend of the couple, was invited to the wedding. It was the social event of the year in Hampton and was spoken about for years afterward. The reception was held at the groom's parents' house in Varnville.

"It was one of the biggest weddings [the Murdaughs] ever had," remembered Sam. "But it wasn't considered ostentatious. They had been high school sweethearts and everybody liked their story."

After their honeymoon, the newly married couple moved to Columbia, where Randolph became the third generation of Murdaughs to attend the USC School of Law.

"I was very fond of Randolph III," remembers Greenville attorney Henry Philpott, who was in the same class. "He was a privileged young man, nice-looking [with] reddish hair and very tall."

Philpott was well aware of Buster Murdaugh's "flamboyant" reputation, but says his son was far more reserved.

"Randolph was quietly spoken," said Philpott. "He was not real loud or obnoxious and dressed pretty much like all the other guys. He was a very nice fellow."

Although everyone in Hampton was aware of the Murdaugh family's dynastic power in South Carolina's Lowcountry, it was never mentioned.

Randolph III started law school with his best friend, Rodney Peeples, whom he had grown up with in Hampton. It was rumored that Buster had put Peeples, who came from a poor family, through law school in return for helping his son get a law degree.

"They seemed to be really tight-running buddies," said Philpott. "You'd see one, you'd see the other and they were both Kappa Alpha."

* * *

Now back at the helm of South Carolina's 14ᵗʰ Judicial Circuit, Buster Murdaugh strengthened his grip on the Lowcountry. He organized weekly poker nights and weekend hunting expeditions at his luscious Green Swamp hunting preserve on the Savannah River in Jasper County. He invited leading members of law enforcement, judges, game wardens, and bankers, who were only too willing to enjoy his generous hospitality.

"And here is where Buster Murdaugh's power came from," explained longtime Hampton resident Kim Brant. "That's where the relationships were forged. They all socialized, played poker, drank, and ate well."

After a rowdy night of poker and drinking, Buster's guests would sleep it off in one of his Green Swamp cabins before donning their camouflage for a day of hunting deer, dove, or wild turkey.

Buster also hosted lavish parties at Murdaugh Island, his river house on the water at Chechessee, inviting the Palmetto State's rich and powerful.

"That was the party place," said Brant. "They socialized on the river and invitations were coveted."

Sam Crews III viewed the Murdaughs as the Kennedys of the Lowcountry, minus the glitz and glamor.

"They weren't as high profile because they didn't push themselves," said Crews. "They were a bit more behind the scenes than the Kennedys."

Careful not to publicly flaunt his wealth, Buster Murdaugh adopted the persona of an everyman, accessible to everyone whatever their status. He was charismatic and loved charming people with his tall tales of winning trials and buying jurors, often leaving listeners scratching their heads. A much sought-after dinner guest, Buster would have the room in fits of laughter with stories about jurors falling asleep and how he'd woken them up with some outrageous court antic.

"He was an entertainer," explained Crews. "He liked a little drama and humor, and he'd say, 'That jury cost me $10,000 to get that one done.' You didn't know whether they were true or not but they were hilariously funny. He knew how to make people feel good."

4

The Cock of the Walk

In January 1964, Randolph Murdaugh III graduated from the USC School of Law and he and Libby moved back to Hampton County. Three months earlier, Libby had given birth to a baby girl they'd christened Lynn Elizabeth.

They settled down in a palatial house at 65 Park Street in Varnville. Built in 1955, the 3,800-square-foot ranch-style brick house boasted five bedrooms and four bathrooms. The neighborhood soon became a privileged enclave known as The Pines. Palmetto State Bank owner Charles Laffitte and his wife LaClaire lived there, as did several judges, the mayor, a game warden, and the police chief.

Randolph joined Murdaugh, Eltzroth & Peters, and his father appointed him the only badge-carrying assistant solicitor on the 14th Circuit, although it was an unpaid position.

The Murdaugh father and son were a formidable duo in the courtroom, often trying cases together. Over the next few years, they jointly prosecuted many criminal cases, as well as personal injury suits that racked up big money for the family firm.

In April 1969, a controversial new South Carolina blue law banned all statewide sporting events on a Sunday. The inaugural Heritage Classic Golf Tournament had already been scheduled on Hilton Head Island, and was to be the first PGA Tour event ever played in South Carolina.

The organizers were livid when they learned of the ban, but Buster assured them he would "look the other way" and it could go ahead as planned. It was good politics and generated a lot of goodwill for the Murdaughs in the affluent Hilton Head area.

At a time when rural Democrats dominated Lowcountry politics, Buster Murdaugh and his son, now known by all as Randy, were fast becoming a political force to be reckoned with. Local candidates at every level courted the Murdaughs for their blessings and support, especially judicial candidates who would later owe them favors.

The Murdaugh father and son were natural politicians. Since the 14th Circuit solicitor was an elected position, Buster was constantly campaigning for reelection. He was a master of public relations and would often donate money to needy Hampton residents who had lost property in a fire or couldn't pay hospital bills. The mostly impoverished electors would later show their gratitude by giving generous payouts when they served as jurors for the Murdaugh law firm's personal injury cases.

Solicitor Murdaugh regularly visited Wade Hampton High School to address civic classes and arranged student tours of the courthouse, which would always finish up with one of his rousing speeches.

"I heard Buster one time give a talk," recalled Sam Crews, "about how hard it was to be a politician and run for solicitor at the same time."

He said it was a challenge having to prosecute young men while staying friends with their parents.

"So he had to convince a jury that their son murdered somebody," said Crews, "but you also have to convince the parents that he's helping them by taking [their son] off the streets. [Buster] was good at that."

In 1971, a young Pat Conroy, soon to become one of South Carolina's greatest writers, had a memorable encounter with Buster Murdaugh. Conroy was in Hampton County Court suing the Beaufort County School District, after being fired from his teaching job for refusing to use corporal punishment on pupils.

During his trial, the twenty-five-year-old Conroy became aware of the portly middle-aged man with receding red hair, sitting in the jury box smoking a large cigar. Every so often Conroy, defending himself against the school district attorney, said something that made the man in the jury box "laugh his ass off."

While they were waiting for the verdict, the man called him over and introduced himself as Buster Murdaugh. Years later Conroy would memorialize their brief courtroom encounter in his 2013 memoir, *The Death of Santini*.

"Smoking a cigar [Buster Murdaugh] said, 'I'm the cock of the walk in this part of South Carolina, and, boy, you really know how to put on a show. You scared the living hell out of those bastards. But you're going to lose your ass.'

"'What if I'd had you as a lawyer?'" I asked. Buster took a puff of his cigar and blew a pillow of smoke in my direction before saying, 'You'd be teaching in that little school of yours tomorrow morning. But you ain't going to be teaching ever again. Let me send you to law school; then you come back and work for me. I'll make you the goddamnedest lawyer you've ever seen.'"

Over his long career as 14th Circuit solicitor, Buster Murdaugh sent nineteen men to the electric chair, something he was extremely proud of. He frequently lectured juries in death penalty cases that if they allowed the defendant to escape the electric chair, then the state might as well abolish the death penalty.

Many of his death penalty cases involved Black men shooting white men, but Buster's most controversial one was the other way around and made national headlines for years.

In May 1970, eighteen-year-old Wallace Youmans was walking by a small grocery store in a Black neighborhood in Fairfax in rural Allendale County when he was ambushed by six white men and shot to death. The killing was in retaliation for an attack on a white man a week earlier.

No charges were ever filed by Solicitor Murdaugh, who oversaw all Allendale criminal investigations.

Two years later on his deathbed, a Fairfax policeman with a guilty conscience confessed to the Youmans murder. He revealed that he and five others, including a magistrate and another police officer, had taken vigilante revenge. They had agreed to kill the first Black man who walked past the store.

The Charlotte Observer subsequently published a series of articles on the Wallace Youmans case, which led to the investigation being reopened. Solicitor Buster Murdaugh told *The New York Times* that although he knew who the murderers were, he did not have enough evidence to prosecute them.

In April 1974, following the intervention of the US Justice Department, a grand jury finally indicted the magistrate and four others on first-degree murder charges.

"A grand jury was convened by Mr. Murdaugh," reported *The New York Times*, "but he said that the decision to prosecute had not been as a result of newspaper pressure."

At trial, a jury of seven African Americans and five Caucasians acquitted two of the defendants, and all charges against the other three were dismissed.

In 1973, Murdaugh, Eltzroth & Peters expanded, taking on two new partners, Clyde Eltzroth Jr., known as Jack, and John E. Parker. The humble son of a Hampton music teacher and motel owner, Parker would cleverly exploit South Carolina's venue laws to create one of South Carolina's most profitable law practices.

"Those [venue] statutes govern where suits are brought," explained Jay Bender, the former media professor at the University of South Carolina. "If you had any property in a county, you could bring suit against a corporation in that county regardless of where the injury might have occurred. And the railroads running through South Carolina often got sued in Hampton County by lawyers from the Murdaugh firm. And they were quite successful."

At that time, it was quite legal for Solicitor Murdaugh to prosecute criminal cases while acting for plaintiffs in civil ones.

"It's pretty well accepted in South Carolina," explained attorney Henry Philpott. "And down there it was just a very urban area, so it probably would have been hard to pay [Buster] enough to be an attorney. He'd have been on food stamps if he hadn't had some kind of side work."

That same year, Buster Murdaugh, who'd also acquired the nickname "Big Daddy," arranged for the South Carolina General Assembly to officially create the paid position of assistant solicitor for the 14th Judicial Circuit for his son Randy. Under the state code of laws, the qualifications for the new job were the same as a solicitor, with half the annual solicitor's salary but the same expenses.

"The assistant solicitor shall be appointed by and serve at the pleasure of the circuit solicitor," read the new law, "and shall perform such duties as may be assigned to him by the solicitor."

Randy also received an assistant solicitor's badge, which guaranteed all manner of perks in the five counties, especially with law enforcement.

On October 1, 1966, Libby bore Randy Murdaugh a son they named Randolph IV (Little Randy). Eighteen months later, on May 27, 1968, their second son Richard Alexander (Alex), who would ultimately bring down the Murdaugh dynasty, was born. John Marvin followed in October 1970 to complete the family.

Six feet four inches tall with bright red hair, Randy was a striking presence in the courtroom. In his spare time, he loved to hunt and fish, often taking along his two elder sons. They hunted deer, doves, and wild turkeys and went skeet shooting.

As the assistant 14th Circuit solicitor, Randy Murdaugh was being paid a meager stipend and would always defer to his grandiose father. But the young man was a quick study with a photographic memory and soon became a highly effective prosecutor in his own right.

"He's an excellent trial attorney," said defense attorney H. W. "Woody" Gooding. "Randy has this unbelievable ability to remember the facts in a case without taking many notes, and is pretty flamboyant on cross-examination."

Randy and Libby Murdaugh were now regulars in the Lowcountry newspaper society pages, hosting extravagant parties for their powerful friends in their exclusive Pines enclave.

Randy Murdaugh had grown up in his father's influential social circle, with its innate system of power throughout the lower five counties of

South Carolina. He now stepped out on his own by hosting fully catered Thursday poker nights in The Pines, which soon became a Hampton County institution.

"They built a big party house out back and had a kitchen," said Kim Brant. "A cook came down every Thursday night and put on a spread. And all the judges, law enforcement, and game wardens would play poker, drink alcohol, and eat until the wee hours."

Randy also initiated monthly potluck men's barbecues, which over the years became something of a Hampton institution, generating much goodwill.

"They entertained beautifully," recalled Sam Crews III, who attended many Murdaugh parties. "They'd have a big barbecue and hunting weekends for highway patrolmen that worked in the circuit."

Randy also held court at Harold's Country Club in Yemassee. The restaurant and bar was conveniently situated by exit 38 on I-95, where the Hampton, Jasper, Beaufort, and Colleton counties intersect. Randy turned it into his personal clubhouse and his photograph still hangs over the bar.

And as the years passed, with each new generation of the Lowcountry's movers and shakers growing up together and going to Wade Hampton High School, strong bonds were formed between all the different branches that ran the five counties.

"The Murdaughs had built a relationship with law enforcement and it hasn't been illegal," explained *Hampton County Guardian* editor and lifelong Hampton resident Michael DeWitt. "You're working side-by-side on cases but you're also hunting and fishing together. You're enjoying some good barbecue together."

5

TROUBLE IN PARADISE

On Thursday, November 18, 1976, Hampton County woke up to a shocking headline in *The State* newspaper: "Civic, Church Leader Mrs. Murdaugh Dies."

Underneath was a full obituary for Randy Murdaugh's young wife Libby, announcing her sudden death at their Varnville home the previous day.

The very next day, the embarrassed newspaper admitted it had all been a hoax and Mrs. Murdaugh was "alive and well."

In a printed correction entitled, "Setting It Straight," *The State* publisher, Columbia Newspapers, Inc., announced it was working with the South Carolina Law Enforcement Division (SLED) to find the culprit.

Libby Murdaugh's fake obituary was the talk of Hampton County for weeks. Everyone had their own theories as to why it had happened. Some said it was planted by Libby to punish Randy for having a mistress, while others maintained she was having an affair and Randy had ordered her lover to leave town.

"There might have been a little marital problem at the time," said Sam Crews. "[Randy] was working real hard and staying out of town a lot . . . and she went to counseling."

As part of her therapy, says Crews, Libby had to write her own obituary, but was not supposed to send it to the newspapers.

Always headstrong, Libby was determined not to be a stay-at-home mom like many of her society friends. She was now working full-time as an English teacher at Wade Hampton High School. Several generations of local children would be taught English by Libby, instilling much love and respect for the Murdaugh family in Hampton.

"One of my kids had Mama Murdaugh as a school teacher," remembered Hampton Library branch manager Chrissy Cook. "They did a lot of good for Hampton."

In 1975, Clyde Eltzroth Sr. was elected 14th Judicial Circuit judge and officially resigned from Murdaugh, Eltzroth & Peters. Solicitor Buster Murdaugh's former partner would now be judging the death penalty cases that he prosecuted. Apparently any conflicts of interest this created were never raised.

The tall, red-faced judge still kept his office at the Murdaugh family law practice in the Warren Building, across the street from the Hampton County courthouse where he had his new chambers. And the longtime friends soon found themselves at opposite sides of a Beaufort courtroom for one of the most high-profile murder cases in South Carolina history.

On April 12, 1978, a thirty-three-year-old Black woman named Betty Gardner was hitchhiking in Beaufort County when she was picked up by four young white men from Pennsylvania in a green Pontiac.

Cousins John Plath, twenty-four, and John Arnold, twenty-two, and their girlfriends, Cindy Sheets and Carol Ulman, who was just eleven, took Gardner to a rural dirt road. There they sexually assaulted and strangled her with a rubber hose before stabbing her to death. Then Arnold carved the letters "KKK" into her body.

Several months later, Arnold admitted to killing Gardner and he and the other three were arrested after her body was found in the woods. Solicitor Buster Murdaugh then granted Cindy Sheets and Carol Ulman full immunity in exchange for testifying against Arnold and Plath.

The sensational case generated much publicity in the Beaufort press, and the defense filed a motion for a change of venue, claiming the coverage had been "inflammatory."

Judge Eltzroth denied the motion, ordering the case to be heard in Beaufort County.

"Prosecuting the case will be Randolph [Buster] Murdaugh, a powerful political figure in South Carolina and 14th Judicial Court Solicitor for 40 years," reported the *Hanover Evening Sun*. "Attending the trial will be a capacity crowd of reporters, writers for national mystery magazines, and authors planning books."

It went to trial on January 22, 1979, with Solicitor Murdaugh demanding the electric chair for Arnold and Plath, who were charged with murder and rape. In his dramatic opening remarks, Solicitor Murdaugh constantly referred to defendant Arnold as "Mad Dog," describing the crime as "*the* most terrible, inhuman, degrading, and nauseating case" of his long career.

"This is going to be a right gory case," Murdaugh told the jury, "but it's my duty to present all the facts. This is as cold-blooded a killing as has ever been performed in Beaufort County or the state of South Carolina."

The prosecution's star witness was seventeen-year-old Cindy Sheets, whom Buster questioned under direct examination. At one point, the solicitor stunned the jury when he ordered her to stand up and wrap a section of rubber hose, which he had brought into court as a prop, around his neck. As Judge Eltzroth looked on approvingly, his pet Labrador retriever, Spook, curled up under his bench, Solicitor Murdaugh paced back and forth in front of the jury box with the hose around his neck.

"I'm going to leave it here," Murdaugh announced at one point, "because we're still going to be talking about it."

Then he continued questioning his witness with the hose wrapped around his neck for dramatic effect. Sheets testified that they became angry that the hose wasn't killing Gardner fast enough, so Plath started jumping up and down on her neck. Then Arnold began stabbing her with a pocket knife but she still would not die.

"By this time, Murdaugh was lying down on the floor of the courtroom playing the role of the dying woman," recalled attorney C. Scott Graber, who defended John Arnold, "while the girl and a sheriff's deputy pulled the ends of the hose."

During his dramatic closing argument, Solicitor Murdaugh reminded the jury how Arnold had "snickered" during the trial.

"It's a joke to him," exclaimed Murdaugh. "He doesn't think y'all got the guts to kill him."

The jury subsequently found the two defendants guilty of all charges and sentenced them to death, after the solicitor vowed to "never bring another death penalty case in Beaufort County" if they voted for anything less.

Ten years later, the South Carolina Supreme Court overturned the convictions. By that time, Buster's son Randy was the 14th Circuit solicitor and retried the case, with the jury again finding the men guilty.

Arnold and Plath spent nearly twenty years on death row before being executed by lethal injection in July 1998.

In 1979, attorney Paul Detrick joined the Murdaugh family law firm and a year later it was renamed Peters, Murdaugh, Parker, Eltzroth & Detrick (PMPED). And in the early 1980s, new state ethics laws made it illegal for solicitors to prosecute criminal cases and run a civil law practice at the same time.

"That made a difference to the Murdaughs," said Sam Crews III, "and it all came to a screeching halt [because] they had a very strong practice."

It was at that point that the law firm branched out, opening an office in Ridgeland with several more soon to follow. By the mid-1980s, PMPED was one of the biggest law firms in South Carolina, with more than a dozen top-notch attorneys to handle their highly lucrative personal injury business.

Approaching his seventieth birthday and nearing retirement, Buster Murdaugh had recently hired his illegitimate son Roberts Vaux, who had graduated from the South Carolina School of Law seven years earlier, as an assistant 14th Judicial Circuit solicitor, working alongside his half brother Randy.

Jared "Buzzard" Newman was a young deputy in the Beaufort sheriff's department and would often see Buster in court while waiting for cases to be heard.

"We called him the Old Man," said Newman. "I was a witness at a couple of the cases that he tried. He was really dramatic [and] some of the stuff he did you couldn't do in court these days."

In February 1983, the Murdaugh family's longtime friend and business associate Barrett Boulware Sr. and his twenty-seven-year-old son Barrett Jr. were arrested after seventeen tons of marijuana was seized on their shrimp boat near the Bahamas. The Boulwares and seven other suspects were arrested as part of George H. W. Bush's South Florida task force to stamp out rampant marijuana drug smuggling at all levels.

"Our investigative efforts will be as stringent on bankers and business-men who profit from crime," explained then–Vice President Bush, "as on the drug traffickers, the pushers, the hired assassins, and others. There will be no free lunch for the white-collar criminal."

A federal grand jury indicted the father and son on two charges of conspiracy to possess and distribute 34,000 pounds of marijuana into the United States.

Like the Murdaughs, the Boulwares lived well, owning property all over the Lowcountry. And over the years both families had done numerous property deals together and it was rumored that several small islands they jointly owned in Beaufort were drop-off points for illicit drugs coming into America.

Then just days before the Boulwares' trial, the government's star witness, shrimp boat captain Franklin C. Branch, died under suspicious circum-stances.

"[He] was apparently making his way to the Wonder Bar in St. Joe Beach," reported the *Tallahassee Democrat*, "when he walked into the path of an oncoming vehicle."

A few days later, all federal charges against the Boulwares were dropped, although the four other co-conspirators were convicted and faced twenty years in a federal prison and fines up to $140,000 ($405,000 today).

When the government announced plans to reindict the Boulwares, US District Judge Falcon B. Hawkins prohibited them from doing so.

"I think it's wrong for Mr. Boulware to sit out there and wonder," ruled the judge, "if the next grand jury is going to indict him, or the next one, or the next one."

And there were many questions about whether the powerful 14th Judicial Circuit solicitor, Buster Murdaugh, had somehow pulled legal strings on his friend and business partner's behalf.

6

GROWING UP A MURDAUGH

As heirs to the Murdaugh dynasty, Richard Alexander Murdaugh and his brothers, Randolph IV, also known as Randy like his father, and John Marvin, were raised with a sense of entitlement. From their earliest days, their father taught them to hunt and fish, instilling in them a love of the outdoors. Although mixing with Hampton County's mostly impoverished sons and daughters at Wade Hampton High, the Murdaugh boys lived in the lap of luxury and were given anything they wanted.

Strikingly handsome with his bright red hair, Alex was a friendly little boy who always had his own set of friends. He was especially close to a young Black boy named Jordan Jinks, who was a couple of years younger. The son of a Yemassee town council member who worked closely with Alex's father, Jordan often played with Alex in the backseat as their dads drove to meetings together.

Growing up, Randy and Alex would play with the local Hampton County boys. Alex often led the other kids into scrapes and always called the shots.

"My kids grew up with them," said Ernestine Glynn, who still works for the Hampton County School District. "They played with my kids and they'd get dirty and muddy and nasty. You would think they were orphans."

Even as a little boy, Alex lacked something in his emotional makeup. He could charm anyone but totally lacked empathy, only relating to himself. If someone was not in his gang, he had no time for them what-soever.

"He was a bully," one of his Wade Hampton schoolmates told *The Hampton County Guardian*, "and he abused the lower-class kids."

Alex also had problems with his studies at Wade Hampton and found it hard to concentrate for any length of time. Later he became convinced that he had suffered from attention deficit disorder (ADD), which went undiagnosed or treated.

Alex and his brothers regularly attended their father's parties, where alcohol was freely served. Everyone in the Murdaugh family was a heavy drinker, and getting drunk was seen as a badge of honor.

"All Murdaughs are alcoholic," said Suzy Murdaugh, a relative on her father's side. "Three generations back they ran moonshine. So we come from a long line of alcoholics."

So from an early age, little Alex was drinking beer and spirits, before moving on to freely available drugs such as marijuana and cocaine.

Although underage, with little parental supervision, he would go out drinking late at night around the bars in Hilton Head. Late one night the boisterous teenager got into a drunken brawl after someone insulted his grandfather.

Beaufort Police were called and Deputy Sheriff Jared Newman arrived at around 3:00 A.M. to find a drunken Alex staggering around a parking lot covered in bruises.

"So I get his ID and it says, 'Richard Alexander Murdaugh' and he's about seventeen years old," said Newman. "And I'm like, 'Holy crap!' This is the solicitor's kid."

When the other person involved said he did not want to press charges, Deputy Newman told them both to go home.

"I yelled at them," he said, "and that was about the end of it."

In 1984, sixteen-year-old Alex, now six feet three inches tall, followed his elder brother Randy to Wade Hampton High School. He already had a bad reputation for arrogant behavior and looking down on others.

"He just thought he was better than anyone else," said a former classmate, who did not want to be identified. "He would be like, 'My name's Alex Murdaugh. I can do what I want to [because] my daddy's the solicitor and my granddaddy was, too.'"

As his mother Libby was on the school board and the family were generous donors, the mischievous teenager was never punished or even reprimanded by his teachers.

So Alex grew up believing that his Murdaugh heritage and name provided his get-out-of-jail-free card for life, and he took full advantage of it.

"This is what Alex has always done," said Sally Hernshaw (not her real name), who was in Alex's elder sister Lynn's grade. "Alex has always been trying to get away with things, and then getting out of them because of his father and his grandfather's reputation."

Naturally athletic, Alex was on the school's varsity football mighty Red Devils team his sophomore year, as well as the baseball team.

During his senior year, Alex started dating an attractive local girl called Susie Seckinger, who would later marry Russell Laffitte—whose father, Charlie, owned Palmetto State Bank and was a close friend of Buster Murdaugh.

The 1986 Wade Hampton High School yearbook captures their blossoming romance on no less than three separate pages. On the "Memories in Motion" page, the young couple are pictured "strolling through Wade Hampton," with Susie staring lovingly up at Alex, towering above her. A couple of pages on, they are seen posing in garden chairs as the school's "Best All Around," and they are also pictured together on the "Sponsors" page.

Alex Murdaugh is the star of the "Superlatives" page, with an array of awards, including "Best All Around," "Most Athletic," and "Wittiest," alongside a photograph of him posing with a pretty classmate and a stuffed doll in his bedroom.

In his graduation picture, Alex wears a tuxedo and black bow tie with a big grin and the smug look of an accomplished car salesman.

On November 1, 1986, Alex's grandfather Buster Murdaugh announced his retirement. He had served forty-six years as 14th Judicial Circuit solicitor, minus the six months missed for his bootlegging conspiracy indictment. The Murdaugh family would erase that minor inconvenience from his history, proudly claiming him as the longest-serving prosecutor in the history of the United States.

"I'm tired," he told the *Associated Press*. "Anybody that's been in that office for as long as I have has paid their homage to society. I think I might fish and hunt for a while and then I might practice law or be an assistant solicitor."

The seventy-one-year-old solicitor craftily timed his resignation so it fell in the second half of his four-year term. That enabled South Carolina democratic governor Richard Wilson Riley to conveniently appoint his son Randy to succeed him without needing a special election.

"They had a transition of power," explained veteran Beaufort attorney Jared "Buzzard" Newman. "Buster ran for his last [four-year] term and waited two years and a day to resign. There was no question that was going to happen."

On January 1, 1987, Governor Riley swore in Randolph Murdaugh III as the third generation of Murdaughs to hold the 14th Circuit solicitor's position.

To commemorate the transfer of power, *The State* newspaper carried a profile of the "legendary" solicitor under the headline, "Like Father, Like Son."

Buster was asked how he felt about all the rapists and murderers he had dispatched to the electric chair over his long career.

"My job was over when the jury convicted them," he replied. "I've had some real bad ones but I've never had any desire to see anyone electrocuted. I hear it's a pretty gruesome thing."

7

BIG RED

In the fall of 1986, Alex Murdaugh moved to Columbia to begin his studies at the University of South Carolina's School of Law. He was following in his father's, grandfather's, and great-grandfather's footsteps. Well over six feet tall with fiery red hair, the handsome eighteen-year-old was immediately nicknamed "Big Red," but being a Murdaugh engendered a lot of ill will among the other students.

"I met him at the freshman orientation," recalled Matt, who didn't want his surname used. "He was a jackass. He just thought he was better than everybody else. If you were in his group and he was buddies with you, then it was all good. But if you weren't . . ."

Alex moved into a well-situated campus apartment which soon became known for its wild parties. He also joined the elite Kappa Alpha Order fraternity, chaperoned in by his alumnus father. It claimed to be the world's oldest and largest professional fraternity, and in the years to come, he would become one of its leading members.

But political science studies took second place to Alex's love of drunken hell-raising, and he soon needed all his Murdaugh credentials to stay out of jail.

"Everybody on campus knew him because he was just cocky and loud," said Matt. "He would blatantly say, 'We can do whatever we want because we won't get in trouble.'"

A few months after he arrived in Columbia, Alex and a group of his friends went barhopping on a Saturday night. They got home well after midnight and Alex started racing his Jeep around campus at high speed. Somebody called 911, leading to a wild police chase up a flight of stairs and down a hundred-yard ramp until Alex came to a grinding halt outside a dormitory's concrete barrier. Then he jumped out of the Jeep and fled into the night.

The next day, after sobering up, Alex was ordered to the police station for questioning. But as soon as the powers-that-be realized he was Solicitor Randy Murdaugh's son, he was allowed to leave with no further action taken.

"Alex got in trouble for it very briefly," said Matt, "but then it immediately went away. Had it been me I would have gone to jail. But he was Alex Murdaugh."

In his second year at the university, Alex started dating a pretty blond student named Margaret Kennedy Branstetter, who was a year below him. They first met at a football game and Alex was immediately smitten by the Kappa Delta sorority girl everyone called Maggie.

The granddaughter of a hardworking barber from Horse Cave, Kentucky, Maggie's childhood was light-years away from Alex's privileged one. Her parents, Terry and Kennedy Branstetter, had been high school sweethearts before eloping to Tennessee to marry because they were underage.

After they married, Terry went to college and received three post-grad job offers from IBM, Ford, and DuPont. He took the DuPont job, and he and Kennedy moved to Nashville, where Maggie was born on September 15, 1968.

When Maggie was twelve, her father was transferred to Unionville, Pennsylvania, and she was enrolled in Unionville High School.

"Her parents were very proper," remembered Lisa Hineman-Moore, who was good friends with her. "We had our little cliques and we ran after boys and did a little partying."

At Unionville High, Maggie always dressed well and adopted a preppy look. She also took great pride in downing a six-pack of beer in a night.

"She was from the South," said Hineman-Moore, "and the Southern dream for a girl at that time was . . . find a husband, get married, and have kids."

In the late 1980s, DuPont transferred her father to Cooper River, South Carolina, and Maggie became a student at the University of South Carolina, where she met Alex Murdaugh.

According to Alex's older sister, Lynn Elizabeth Goettee, he "actively pursued" Maggie, who initially shunned his advances. Eventually she agreed to attend his Kappa Alpha fraternity formal in Savannah and they were soon dating.

In the summer of 1989, three generations of Murdaughs appeared on the cover of the prestigious *Carolina Lawyer* magazine. Photographed outside Hampton County Courthouse, Randolph "Buster" Murdaugh Jr., Randolph III, and Alex's brother young Randolph IV, now in his second year of law school, were clearly trying to establish the family as South Carolina's legal Mount Rushmore.

Under the headline "A Heritage in the Law," Buster cast himself less as a child of privilege than as having worked his way up from nothing.

"He settled comfortably into the leather chair behind his desk and unwrapped a cigar," began the profile by writer Gary C. Dickey, "Buster propped his feet on the desk and motioned towards his son with the unlit end of his cigar."

"While my father always appeared to be hard-nosed when he had to be," said Randy, "he always had the innate ability to show compassion when there was some redeeming characteristic to the individual on trial.

"He is an excellent judge of character and he seldom makes a mistake. The purpose of prosecution is to end crime. Some crime can be stopped by a slap on the wrist—some requires incarceration. And some can only be stopped by electrocution."

Then the family patriarch lit his cigar and began waxing lyrically as he attempted to rewrite Murdaugh family history. He now claimed that his own father, Randolph Sr., had lost everything in the Great Depression.

"When I left to go to [law] school at Carolina," said Buster, "he was flat broke."

The former solicitor told Dickey he'd gotten into law school on a football scholarship, and was so hard up he "worked a full schedule in a variety of jobs in addition to his law studies." His day had begun at 7:00 A.M. working for the State Highway Department, and after morning classes he had a second job at the State Insurance Commission.

"One quickly detects a strong bond among all of the three generations bearing the name Randolph Murdaugh," wrote Dickey, "and the admiration of each for the other is apparent."

In 1991, Alex Murdaugh and Maggie Branstetter both graduated from the University of South Carolina with bachelor's degrees. Then Alex entered the South Carolina School of Law like his father, grandfather, and great-grandfather before him, to study for the bar, join the family law firm, and maybe even become the 14th Judicial Circuit solicitor one day.

He became best friends with his new roommate Cory Fleming, socializing with their own close-knit set, which also included Carmen Mullen, later to became a 14th Judicial Circuit judge.

The athletically built red-haired giant also became the fourth generation of Murdaughs to play football for the USC Gamecocks. Maggie Branstetter faithfully attended all his matches, laying out elaborate football game-day spreads of food for their elite circle of friends.

Maggie's parents, Kennedy and Terry Branstetter, liked Alex and thoroughly approved of the match. The young Southern girl had been swept off her feet by the mystique and power of the Murdaugh name, and was already preparing for her new status in life.

That August, an angry group of protestors picketed the Beaufort County Courthouse to protest Solicitor Randy Murdaugh's "unfair practices," vowing to oust him at the next election. Holding placards denouncing the solicitor, they accused the "Murdaugh Dynasty" of deliberately refusing to prosecute certain homicide cases for political reasons. They vowed to follow him to every courthouse on the 14th Circuit to embarrass him.

When asked for his reaction by *Island Packet* reporter Tony Moreno,

Murdaugh shrugged it off, noting that his job as prosecutor was not always popular.

Protest leader Phil Mattie said his fifteen-year-old son had been killed in a hit-and-run accident after a Hampton County deputy sheriff refused to give him a lift, telling him to "hitch a ride." Mattie wanted the officer charged with manslaughter but Murdaugh had refused to prosecute him.

"The protesters shared stories of loved ones killed unjustly," wrote Moreno, "and all said that Murdaugh failed to see that justice was done in each case. The reasons are mostly political, they claim, and are part of the Murdaugh 'Dynasty' that has held the solicitor's office for more than seventy years.

"Mattie said people have been afraid of the Murdaughs, but they are rallying to unseat him in the 1992 election. He said he knew it would be unpopular to square off against the family."

A year later, Randy ran unopposed in the 14th Circuit solicitor's election to win a new term.

In late February 1993, Alex Murdaugh went on a drinking binge around the bars of Hilton Head Island with a large group of friends. At that time, the elite resort was known as Snow Island because cocaine was everywhere, and Alex's group had had their share.

Just after midnight they arrived at Cadillacs Strip Club for more drinks and a show. The bartender refused to serve them because they were so rowdy, and twenty-four-year-old Alex, a second-year law student, started a violent brawl, injuring two bouncers.

"They appeared intoxicated so I refused to serve them," the bartender later told police. "The redheaded gentleman became abusive and I asked him to leave."

When Alex refused, angrily demanding beers, the bartender called over two bouncers to eject him from the club. As they escorted him out, Alex challenged them to a fight. He then started "riling up" his drunken group and a dozen of them "bum-rushed" the bouncers.

"They began to push and shove . . . and became extremely violent," said one of the bouncers. "All of the men were highly intoxicated and I did not know who had bottles or weapons."

Somebody dialed 911 and deputies from the Beaufort County Sheriff's Office arrived, taking Alex and two of his friends into custody.

But once Alex announced that his father was solicitor, a patrolman was assigned to personally drive him back to his family house in Varnville, sixty miles north of Hilton Head.

A month later, all charges against Alex Murdaugh were quietly dismissed.

On Saturday, August 14, 1993, Alex and Maggie were married at the Second Presbyterian Church in Charleston. Alex's best friend, Cory Fleming, was a groomsman. It was a lavish affair attended by hundreds of guests, who watched the bride and groom tie the knot in *the* South Carolina wedding of the year.

After a large reception at Hibernian Hall, the bride and groom left to honeymoon in Jamaica, before settling in Columbia so Alex could finish studying for his law degree.

In the summer of 1994, Richard Alexander Murdaugh graduated from the South Carolina School of Law with a juris doctorate degree, and in November he was admitted into the South Carolina Bar Association. In his graduating class were good friends Cory Fleming, Carmen Mullen, and Chris Wilson, who would all remain close.

He and Maggie moved to Beaufort, where Fleming had just started working as an assistant solicitor for Alex's father. Alex got his first legal job working for James H. Moss's law firm, and he and Maggie rented a house on Cat Island, just outside Beaufort.

Solicitor Murdaugh appointed his son Alex a badge-carrying 14th Judicial Circuit assistant solicitor. He began prosecuting criminal cases in the Beaufort courtroom, mainly handling simple drug possession cases.

"We'd see each other at court appearances," said then–assistant solicitor Jared Newman. "He was gregarious and would come up and say,

'Hey Buzzard, how are you doing? Let's go and get a liquor drink after court.'"

In February 1995, Muhammed Ali came to Hampton to testify as a character witness on behalf of the controversial Hilton Head doctor, Dr. Rajko Medenica, who was treating him for his Parkinson's disease. The Murdaugh law firm PMPED was representing Thomas and Gayle Taylor, who had claimed in a malpractice suit that Dr. Medenica's blood-cleansing procedure called "plasmapheresis" had destroyed Gayle's kidneys.

The trial was well into its third week when the boxing legend testified that he totally trusted Dr. Medenica's treatment, calling him the greatest doctor in the world. Then he happily posed for photographs in Hampton Courtroom before leaving town.

As the trial dragged on, the jurors' daily stipend ran out and they were left without income. Several asked the judge to be excused, jeopardizing the future of the entire trial. And it appears that the Murdaughs saw an opportunity to win favor with the jury by quietly paying them their lost wages.

"My husband sat on the jury for a month and his job was not paying him at all," said Hampton Library branch manager Chrissy Cook. "Then the Murdaughs stepped in and paid him out of their own pockets to stay. They were so good to my family. We were raising two children at the time and not having any money was rough."

The trial continued with the Hampton jury finally awarding the Taylors a massive $14 million judgment against Dr. Medenica after just one hour of deliberation, giving PMPED a huge payday.

A photograph of Muhammed Ali posing at Hampton County Courthouse was then ceremoniously hung in the PMPED Offices, to commemorate another win by a Hampton jury.

On April 11, 1996, Maggie Murdaugh gave birth to a baby boy at Beaufort Memorial Hospital. He was named Richard Alexander Murdaugh Jr. after his father, but would always be known by his great-grandfather's nickname, Buster. Alex asked his best friend Cory Fleming to be godfather.

Alex and Maggie had now settled down in Beaufort and the ambitious young lawyer was eager to make inroads into Lowcountry politics. That year he was elected Chairman of the Hampton County Democratic Party, a position he would hold for the next ten years. Following in his family's tradition, he raised money and hosted benefits and other events for Murdaugh-favored Democratic candidates.

"[The Murdaughs] worked very hard," said Hampton County administrator Rose Dobson Elliott. "They give back to their community. They will loan their property, their houses, or whatever, for some type of fundraiser."

Alex was also voted onto the board of the prestigious Arnold Fields Community Endowment, which honored South Carolina African Americans' contributions to history and culture.

Big Red was a natural politician, inheriting his grandfather Buster's gift of connecting with ordinary people, when he wished to. He was gregarious with great people skills and never came across as snobby.

"He always spoke to you no matter who you were," said Hampton librarian Chrissy Cook. "Everybody knows the Murdaughs and they did a lot of good for Hampton."

And as the charismatic young Murdaugh scion stepped into his preordained role in the Lowcountry, he seemed like the perfect fit to take his prominent family into the twenty-first century.

"Alex was the one we all thought would have replaced his dad as solicitor," said Jared Newman. "Alex was the brash, no-BS politician, put his arm around you and remembered your name. He's been a good guy to me."

But some were skeptical about Alex and his family's true motives, believing their benevolent altruism to be self-serving.

"The Murdaughs had a long history of being Democrats," said Hampton businesswoman Kim Brant, who was active in the party for many years. "They posed as being big Democrats, but they were also funding money to Republicans. It just depends on who's in power."

8

SUCCESSION

On Thursday, February 5, 1998, Randolph "Buster" Murdaugh Jr. died at the age of eighty-four at the Hampton Regional Medical Center. His wife, Gladys, had passed away the previous June.

The *Associated Press* marked his passing with a full profile, lauding the "second-generation circuit solicitor" for his "wit and flaming oratory." Retired 14th Judicial Circuit judge Clyde Eltzroth, who had also been Buster's law firm partner, called him "the finest trial lawyer I ever saw."

"He was a fine gentleman and a very gentle man," said Eltzroth. "I never knew him to refuse help to anyone who asked."

His funeral was held the following Sunday at Hampton Cemetery. Among the mourners was his now fifty-two-year-old secret son, Roberts Vaux, who kept a low profile.

"He went to his father's funeral," said Sam Crews III, a longtime Murdaugh family confidant. "He met with the family for a little private service and then he left [before] the public funeral."

A few months later, Alex Murdaugh moved his family to Hampton to join PMPED as a staff attorney, soon to become a partner in his family law firm. His older brother, Randy, had started there seven years earlier. Their younger brother, John Marvin, who liked to refer to himself as the family's black sheep, had opted out of law entirely, opening his own rental center for construction and residential equipment.

Maggie hated the prospect of bringing up a family in the deeply rural county with a population of just 21,000 after the sophistication of Columbia and Beaufort. But Alex insisted she come to Hampton, as he wanted to exploit his Murdaugh name as much as possible.

"He told her that a condition of the marriage was living in Hampton," explained Sam Crews III. "And it's hard to get a wife to come to Hampton. It's a small town."

The headstrong young mother had trouble assimilating into the bleak town, with its lack of culture, fashionable boutiques, and gourmet restaurants.

"Maggie made no bones about that fact that she was too good to live there," said Kim Brant, whose sister was a close friend of hers. "The people were all inferior to her circle of friends. She was not content to be in Hampton, but she was content to be married to Alex Murdaugh. She thought she had a real prize there."

On April 14, 1999, Alex and Maggie's second son, Paul Terry Murdaugh, was born to complete the family. It was a difficult birth and Maggie reportedly suffered from postpartum depression.

Soon after the birth, Alex hired a housekeeper named Gloria Satterfield, whose sister Ginger Hadwin had been in his Wade Hampton High School class. From the beginning, Maggie welcomed Gloria into the Murdaugh family, relying on her to bring up Buster and Paul, as she had few maternal instincts.

"[Paul] was barely walking when she started working for them," said Ginger, "and he called her 'Go-Go' and she called him 'Paul-Paul.'"

The thirty-eight-year-old housekeeper, who also had two sons of her own, called her new boss "Mrs. Maggie" and worked six days a week, only taking Sunday off to go to church.

"She was the babysitter," said Kim Brant. "She cooked. She cleaned. She did the laundry and ironed for them. She was the au pair and did everything."

Brant believes that Maggie never really bonded with Paul as a mother should because of her depression.

"Paul was always a little different," she explained, "and they didn't have that bond that most mothers and children have. I think that situation in the very, very early months is why he came to be the way he was."

In September 2000, Alex and Maggie moved into 515 Holly Street, a newly built house in the center of Hampton. The 6,752-square-foot single-family house had four bedrooms and three bathrooms, and Maggie extravagantly furnished it with expensive furniture and fittings. They also installed a saltwater pool, as Buster suffered from acute eczema.

For the last year, Walmart had been in secret negotiations with Solicitor Randy Murdaugh to buy a large plot of his land in Varnville and build a superstore that would transform Hampton County and create hundreds of new jobs. The land in question also included his recently deceased parents' house at 115 Carolina Avenue, where Randy had grown up.

After the Walmart sale went through, Randy had the old house moved brick by brick to land the family owned in Almeda, and then rebuilt for him and Libby to live in.

Then Walmart pulled out of the deal after discovering that under the state venue laws, so deftly exploited by PMPED, the company could be sued for alleged personal injury cases occurring anywhere in South Carolina.

So ironically, only the Murdaughs benefitted from the big box retailer's failure to come to Hampton by selling off their Varnville land at a huge profit. It is estimated that the city of Varnville lost over two hundred potential jobs, $8 million in investment, and thousands of dollars in tax revenue. A Family Dollar store now sits on the original site of Buster Murdaugh's house.

In early January 2001, Solicitor Randy Murdaugh arrived at the Beaufort County Courthouse to prosecute one of the most high-profile murder cases of his career. He had now been solicitor for fourteen years and had already dispatched half a dozen souls to the electric chair.

Now balding with wispy reddish-white hair, the tall, bespectacled solicitor dressed like a country gentleman, with loose-fitting herringbone suits and colorful ties. He was known as a "skillful prosecutor with an uncanny memory."

A year earlier, Randy had indicted sixteen-year-old Sarah Nickel from Okatie, South Carolina, along with two male friends, for the brutal murder of her mother. It made national news because the horrific stabbing was alleged to have been a satanic ritual. All three teenagers were charged with armed robbery and murder.

In February 2002, Solicitor Murdaugh announced that he would only be asking for life imprisonment and not the electric chair for the teenage girl.

"I've never asked for the death penalty for a sixteen-year-old," he explained. "But that's not to say I wouldn't in some other case."

Just before the trial, Randy brokered a plea deal with Sarah's two friends to testify against her in return for a thirty-year sentence.

During the trial, Solicitor Murdaugh made full use of his late father Buster's flair for the dramatics. At one point, he brandished Sarah's dead mother's blood-soaked T-shirt in front of the jury, while the pathologist described her injuries in graphic detail.

In his cross-examination of the petite blonde defendant, the solicitor read out extracts of her diary where she railed against her mother.

Solicitor Murdaugh's fiery closing to the jury would have made his father proud.

"Ladies and gentlemen of the jury," he began. "I feel like I need to get my walker to come up here. And I am old and I'm tired and I'm worn out and I know y'all are. And I promise you I'll be brief."

He then urged the jury to use their common sense and that although her two accomplices had actually "beat, stabbed, and strangled" the defendant's mother, Sarah was just as guilty as they were.

"We know that this was a vicious, brutal, a nasty murder," he told the jury as he waved Sarah's diary in front of them. "We know that Sarah Nickel hated her mother . . . and she is guilty of murder."

After the jury found Sarah Nickel not guilty of her mother's murder, but guilty of armed robbery, Judge Brown sentenced her to thirty years in prison. She will not be eligible for parole until 2026.

9

"The House That CSX Built"

The law firm that Alex's great-grandfather, Randolph Murdaugh Sr., had started almost ninety years earlier as a one-man operation had achieved success beyond his wildest dreams. After successfully fine-tuning the South Carolina venue laws, PMPED was raking in millions of dollars a year, and opening a third office in Walterboro.

Over the last five years, the increasingly lax interpretation of the state's venue laws had brought a flood of big-money personal injury cases to the Murdaugh family law firm in tiny Hampton County.

Things had become so bad that the highly respected American Tort Reform Foundation (ATR) had recently branded Hampton County as a "Judicial Hellhole." It cited how in South Carolina a lawsuit could be filed wherever a corporation "resides," which was being interpreted as anywhere that a defendant "own[s] property or transact[s] business."

"To compound matters," found the ATR report, "trial court judges in Hampton County, in particular, appear to have shunned their traditional discretion to transfer a case when it serves the convenience of witnesses and the interests of justice. This practice allows cases to remain in the 14th Judicial Circuit, even when it would be more logical for the specific case to be heard in another area of the state, such as where the alleged injury occurred or witnesses reside."

In July 2002, *Forbes* magazine printed a damning exposé of PMPED, singling out Johnny E. Parker and the absurdities of South Carolina law. And it shone a national spotlight for the first time on how Parker had so

"deftly" exploited a state law that had "turned him and his small, impoverished county into a litigation machine."

It highlighted the recent case of a woman who had suffered head injuries after she rolled her GMC Safari van in Tennessee. PMPED then filed
a personal injury suit in Hampton County, which was ninety miles from
where she lived and 350 miles from where the accident happened, and
despite the fact that GMC was based in Michigan and that Cooper Tire &
Company was in Ohio.

"The legal nexus," explained *Forbes*. "Products made by GM and Cooper Tire are sold in Hampton."

The article revealed that a massive 610 civil suits had been filed in
Hampton in 2001, twice as many as in other South Carolina counties.
With little regard for the faceless corporations being sued, Hampton ju-
ries were giving huge awards in the millions to PMPED clients.

Forbes argued that the biggest corporate loser of all was the Jackson,
Florida–based CSX national rail carrier. Ironically it was the direct descendant of the Charleston and Western Carolina Railway Company, which
Buster Murdaugh had successfully sued after his father's apparent 1940
suicide.

CSX Transportation tracks literally dissected Hampton County, with
trains stopping at various points to load or unload freight, so the rail
company was an easy target.

Hampton jury awards against CSX were staggering. In 2001, PMPED
netted a $12.5 million verdict against the rail carrier, after a man died
walking across a track that was obscured by overgrown vegetation. With
so many huge payouts in Hampton County, other companies would settle
immediately to avoid having to argue their case there.

"It's an uphill battle for most defense lawyers there," said James E.
Lady from Charleston, who had represented CSX and other companies in
Hampton courtrooms. "These cases are being valued at between two and
three times what they would elsewhere."

In May 2002, an astonished *Forbes* reporter witnessed Judge Rodney
Peeples, whom Buster Murdaugh had reportedly put through law school
many years earlier, adjudicate a $13 million lawsuit brought by PMPED.

After hearing arguments from both sides, the gregarious judge, sitting right in front of portraits of Randolph Sr. and Buster Murdaugh, handed out freshly picked strawberries from his garden to all the lawyers before joining them for a seafood lunch.

At the end of the day, Judge Peeples shook Johnny Parker's hand and blew a kiss to defense attorney Celeste Tiller Jones.

Parker later labeled allegations of legal laxness as "propaganda," claiming that defense lawyers could always ask for a change of venue.

"We don't live in a world where people don't have relationships," he said.

The *Forbes* exposé pointed out that ultimately the biggest losers were Hampton County residents, who were struggling to survive with a median income of just $26,300, nearly $13,000 below the national average.

In February 2005, the supreme court of South Carolina took note of all the embarrassing publicity and closed the venue shopping loophole. This drastically reduced the amount of out-of-town cases coming to Hampton County.

But PMPED hardly missed a beat, scoring a record $31 million verdict from Ford Motor Company a year later.

By then the law firm had built a new grandiose three-story red-brick edifice in the colonial style, occupying an entire block for its seventeen attorneys. Dubbed "The House That CSX Built" by wisecracking locals, it lay directly across from Hampton County Courthouse, which had just undergone a major renovation, thanks to a million-dollar donation from PMPED.

Now a full partner at PMPED, Alex Murdaugh was learning from the best how to manipulate the legal system to his full advantage. He handled personal injury cases as well as working as a part-time solicitor on criminal cases.

Although outwardly friendly and caring, Alex had zero empathy for his clients, who had frequently suffered horrible injuries. Still, he was an excellent lawyer and well respected by his personal injury clients, who felt comfortable in his hands.

But he soon came to see them as nothing more than a license to print money, and many would not even realize he had robbed them blind.

10

THE BUDDY SYSTEM

In early 2003, Charles Hendricks (not his real name) and his wife moved to Hampton County and opened a mini-mart. He soon realized how things worked around there.

"The Murdaughs are basically everything," he said. "This is a small town and everybody knows everybody. You can get away with anything around here if you know the right people—you scratch my back and I'll scratch yours."

Over the years, Hendricks made it a point to cozy up to the town's power brokers.

"I'm included in the buddy system," he said. "I know the local police. I know the local judge. I know the sheriff's department. If I get in trouble I call them up, 'Hey, let's go.'"

Soon after opening his store, he was ticketed for selling alcohol to a minor, and after a quiet word with the sheriff, the charges were dropped.

Several years later he was not so lucky after being rear-ended by an out-of-town woman in his parking lot. Three years after the accident, she hired PMPED to sue him for huge damages and seize his store.

"She filed a lawsuit against me," said Hendricks. "Alex Murdaugh was at the deposition I had to give and said, 'Hi, how are you doing,' and was pleasant enough."

The case was eventually dismissed after Hendricks's insurance company lawyer proved the woman was at fault. But had he lost, PMPED would have taken everything he had.

"The Murdaugh law firm will sue you until you're naked," said Hendricks. "They even tried to sue me for property I don't own."

According to Hendricks, corruption in Hampton County is rampant and everybody can be bought at the right price.

"Basically, in this town if you go to jail for a serious crime [like] murder," he maintained, "you most likely get out the next day. You pay somebody off for bail, and the judge knows you and lets you out."

Alex's father, Randy, had now been solicitor for almost two decades and was looking to retire and devote himself full-time to PMPED. His wife, Libby, had recently left her teaching job at Wade Hampton after thirty-one years and was now on the school board.

In early 2005, Solicitor Murdaugh sat down in his modest solicitor's office with author Rosalyn Rossignol, who was writing a book on the Sarah Nickel case. His office was situated in an old storefront with a sign in the window reading, "Solicitor's Worthless Check Unit."

In her 2017 book, *My Ghost Has a Name*, Rossignol describes the Murdaugh patriarch as "a disheveled-looking man [sitting] at a makeshift desk" wearing a brown-and-white plaid flannel shirt.

"I'm the third solicitor in my family," he informed Rossignol. "My father held this office from 1940 to 1986, and his father from 1930 to 1940."

Asked about his caseload for the five counties he presided over, Randy estimated that about seventy percent of them involved drugs, especially crack cocaine.

"I mean people buying, selling, stealing," he told her, "and committing other crimes to get their hands on it or on the money to buy it."

Solicitor Murdaugh told her that crack had changed the entire culture of the Lowcountry, and he'd become cynical after everything he'd seen over his long career as solicitor.

"We had [a] girl," he said. "Tortured a paraplegic man. Tried to kill him for two days. Injected him with air, put him in the trunk of a car with the motor running for forty-five minutes, shut him in a refrigerator, stoned him, and stabbed him."

Warming to the topic, he then recounted several other horrific local cases he had prosecuted over the years.

"There was [sic] two boys came down from Philadelphia," he continued, "kidnapped a retarded girl, had sex with her every way known to God and man, then killed her. A Hardeeville man cut off his wife's head and put it in the bed with her, stuck it under her arm."

As their sons Buster and Paul grew up, Alex's wife Maggie became more and more unhappy. She confided to close friends that she felt out of place in Hampton, often leaving for lavish shopping trips to Charleston with her sister, Marian Proctor.

"Maggie was always in the mix to go to Charleston to shop or dine," said Kim Brant, who knew the Murdaughs. "She pressured Alex to buy a beach house."

In January 2003, Alex Murdaugh bought 3606 Big Bay Drive on beautiful Edisto Island for $415,000. The luxurious 2,144-square-foot beach home had four bedrooms and three bathrooms and was by Big Bay Creek, perfect for Alex's growing collection of boats. There were palm trees in the garden and a sundeck. From then on, Maggie would take her sons to spend the summer there.

Unlike the other Murdaugh wives, Maggie never worked, except for a brief period when she opened a gift store called "Branches" on Hampton's Lee Avenue. With her housekeeper, Gloria Satterfield, dutifully bringing up Buster and Paul, Maggie had a lot of free time on her hands, and often lunched with friends at Coconuts restaurant in the center of Hampton.

Alex was now making good money at PMPED, and he and Maggie lived the good life. They started buying expensive cars and going on extravagant hunting vacations, always taking their two young sons. And their increasingly public displays of wealth began to set them apart from the previous generations of Murdaughs, who had always downplayed their assets.

"We didn't recognize the Murdaughs as being prominent, wealthy people," said Kim Brant. "They were just like us and didn't flaunt their wealth. They drove the same cars and didn't want to attract attention.

But Alex and Maggie had to have the best of everything and it didn't go unnoticed."

On December 31, 2005, Randolph Murdaugh III officially retired at the age of sixty-six, and his handpicked successor, Duffie Stone, was sworn in as 14th Judicial Circuit solicitor. Over his eighteen years as solicitor, Randy had tried more than two hundred murder cases, once convicting two murderers in the same week.

He would now return to his family's far more lucrative private practice in Hampton, joining his sons, Randolph IV and Alex.

"In three years, I'd be too damn old," he told reporters.

It marked the end of an era and the Murdaugh family's almost eighty-seven years in possibly *the* most powerful judicial positions in South Carolina. Randy had run unopposed in five elections and sent almost a dozen people to the electric chair.

His successor Duffie Stone immediately appointed him Prosecutorial Consultant for the 14th Circuit, trying its most violent and habitual offenders for a $2,500 monthly stipend. Over the next decade, Randy would be lead prosecutor in eight cases of rape and murder, often assisted by his son Alex.

Many were surprised that Randy did not appoint one of his sons to succeed him as the fourth generation of Murdaugh solicitors.

"If anyone was going to be solicitor after Randolph in the family, it would have been Alex," said former assistant solicitor turned defense lawyer, Jared "Buzzard" Newman. "But I don't think he wanted it. He was making too much money."

Maggie Murdaugh felt very insecure about Alex's faithfulness, well aware of his family history of affairs and adultery. So whenever her husband hired a new secretary, Maggie would do research on her to see whether she could be trusted with her husband.

Struggling with motherhood, she relied more and more on Gloria Satterfield. Her loyal housekeeper was so strapped for cash she lived in a trailer, spending more time with Paul, now seven, and Buster, ten, than she did with her own two sons, Tony and Brian. A religious woman, Gloria considered the Murdaughs her extended family and felt very honored to be in their lives.

"Maggie adored her because she made her life easier," said Murdaugh family friend Sam Crews III. "She was helping Maggie with Paul, who was always a problem child from day one."

The angelic-looking red-headed boy had a vicious temper and was already showing signs of mental instability, violently lashing out at the least provocation.

"I saw him snap at least once," an unnamed Murdaugh family member told the *New York Post*. "He told his aunt Nancy to go f*** herself. I was on his case about it but he said he didn't give a shit. He did not take authority well."

Kim Brant, who knew the family, remembers Paul and Buster being spoiled rotten. Maggie would let them do anything they wanted, then throw up her hands and tell Gloria to rein them in.

After a couple of drinks, Maggie would relax and deliberately try and shock people, knowing there would be no comeback because she was a Murdaugh.

"She'd let her hair down," said a Murdaugh family friend, "and drop some f-bombs and tell you to piss off if she felt like it."

And Buster and Paul began to imitate their mother, who fully encouraged them to use foul language.

"At four years old they cussed like sailors," said Brant, "and Maggie thought it was funny. [She] instilled in them from a very young age that they were better than anybody else because they were Murdaughs. The same rules don't apply to you that apply to these other people. 'You're a Murdaugh! You're a Murdaugh!'"

Gloria Satterfield also cleaned for Kim Brant's sister and would always arrive with shocking new Paul and Buster stories.

"There was always drama at that house," said Brant. "Paul would go outside in his underwear and snake boots and call his brother a 'motherfucker.'"

The housekeeper also told far more disturbing stories of Paul killing small animals such as frogs, squirrels, or lizards. Later, he would report-edly run over dogs with the family Jeep and take their collars as trophies.

"One day Paul came in and said, 'I need a damn knife,'" Brant remem-bered. "And Gloria said, 'Paul-Paul, what do you need a knife for?' And he replied, 'I'm going to kill that motherfucking lizard!' This is when he was just out of diapers and not even in kindergarten yet."

Like Alex when he was a boy, Buster and Paul were allowed to drink alcohol from a very young age by their parents, who always kept a cooler of beers in the kitchen. The boys grew up viewing Alex and Maggie as playmates rather than authority figures, with alcohol freely dispensed on the hunting and fishing trips they all went on.

"Maggie thought that if Paul went to the refrigerator and got a beer that was funny because he was just a little boy," said Brant. "It was cute."

When they were very young, Maggie enrolled both boys in a preschool playgroup to learn how to socialize with the local children. It included Kim Brant's niece and nephew, who soon came home with tales of how wild and undisciplined the Murdaugh boys were.

"Paul and Buster played rough and called each other motherfuckers," explained Brant. "And they hadn't even started school yet. They liked to fight and squabble and Paul often had a knife."

When the other parents heard about the dangerous games played by the Murdaugh boys, they became so concerned for the safety of their children that they pulled them out of the playgroup.

PART II

11

THE SEEDS OF DESTRUCTION

On September 20, 2007, a distant cousin of Alex Murdaugh named Curtis Edward Smith was in a logging accident, severely injuring his spine and knee. Although they had hardly known each other before, when Curtis became one of Alex's PMPED clients, it would have lasting consequences for both of them.

The forty-seven-year-old former National Guardsman came from the poor end of the sprawling Murdaugh family. His mother, Emmaline Murdaugh Smith, was married to a Marine, and Curtis was born on Parris Island, South Carolina, where his father was stationed.

The oldest of three brothers, Curtis lived in North Carolina and Mississippi before the family settled down in 1983 in Walterboro, South Carolina. He attended high school there before dropping out in the twelfth grade to work for a forklift company.

After a short-lived marriage that produced a daughter, Smith started working on oil rigs in Mississippi and the Gulf of Mexico. He eventually moved back to Walterboro and bought a logging truck, spending the next two decades operating his own logging truck and doing other work in the timber industry.

Then in September 2007, while working for the American Forest Management, he fell into a ditch and was seriously injured, eventually ending up in Alex Murdaugh's PMPED office.

"I was hurting," he later testified. "I had three discs removed in my back and got rods and screws in every place of them. It's not fun."

He underwent two surgeries and was prescribed a cocktail of Oxycontin, oxycodone, and Valium for the pain, soon becoming addicted.

For the next year, he carried on working as a logging company supervisor, until his claim for workers' compensation was approved and he quit and went on disability.

Soon afterward, Smith began doing odd jobs for Alex Murdaugh, and they became friends. The powerful attorney would later confess that Fast Eddie, as he was nicknamed, became his personal drug dealer, selling him all manner of hard drugs. They would also allegedly manufacture and deal drugs together. Although Murdaugh hid his increasing dependence on drugs and was fully functional in the courtroom, it would become increasingly difficult for him to straddle both worlds.

In the early hours of Friday, July 3, 2009, an arsonist set fire to the Murdaugh home at 515 Holly Street while Alex, Maggie, and the children were asleep upstairs. Firefighters rushed to the scene and managed to quickly extinguish the fire with minimal damage.

The Hampton Police Department immediately launched an arson investigation, aided by the State Law Enforcement Division (SLED) arson team, the Varnville Police Department, and the Hampton County Sheriff's Office.

"We suspect that . . . someone spread some kind of accelerant around the house and tried to set it on fire from the back door," Hampton Police chief Perry McAlhaney told *Bluffton Today*. "Luckily, for some reason it didn't spread through the house."

According to Kim Brant, whose cleaning company was called in to fix the damage, the fire was set by a disgruntled contractor upset with Maggie and Alex.

"They wouldn't pay him because they were upset with his work," said Brant. "So he went back and set a little fire."

In 2021, Alex would confide to his sister-in-law Liz Murdaugh that he first became addicted to pills around the time of the fire, blaming it on all the marital friction it created.

"It generated some bitter damn feelings," he told her. "Maggie had a hard time when we moved to Hampton. There's no doubt it started then."

With a growing drug appetite and a need to finance it, Alex Murdaugh turned to crime. After years of working personal injury cases for PMPED, netting the company untold millions, the assistant solicitor devised a scheme to funnel some of it into his pocket. He would use his inside knowledge of exploiting the old venue law to strong-arm insurance companies into coughing up big sums of money.

He enlisted the help of Cory Fleming, then a partner with the Beaufort law firm Moss, Kuhn & Fleming, and Russell Lucius Laffitte, vice president and later CEO of the Hampton-based Palmetto State Bank, owned by his family. The successful banker, a lifelong friend, was now married to Alex's high school girlfriend, Susie Seckinger.

Over the next decade, with their assistance, Alex would steal millions of dollars from some of the neediest people in Hampton.

His first known victims were two little sisters whose mother and brother had both died in a horrific car accident. On July 16, 2005, Angela Plyler, thirty-seven, was driving her Ford Explorer on I-95 in Hampton County when a tire blew out. The vehicle skidded off the road, rolling over several times before hitting a row of pine trees. Angela and her fourteen-year-old son, Justin, were instantly killed; twelve-year-old Alania and eight-year-old Hannah, who were in the back seat, were both seriously injured.

Later the sisters were referred to Alex Murdaugh at the PMPED law firm through a family member. He jumped at the chance to handle the wrongful death case.

On November 8, 2005, Alex Murdaugh and another PMPED attorney filed lawsuits in Hampton County against Bridgestone Corporation, Firestone, and the Ford Motor Company. When Alania first met Alex at a deposition in Charleston, she was impressed.

"I felt very comfortable . . . and protected," she recalled. "I remember he looked at me and said, 'We're going to make this right, and make those people pay for what they've done.'"

In November 2006, Alex introduced Alania and Hannah to his friend

Russell Laffitte, explaining that since no one in their family could be trusted with the large settlement they would soon receive, Laffitte should act as their conservator.

"Alex informed me that Russell's a good guy," said Alania. "They grew up together and he was one of his good friends. I liked Alex's personality and his go-getter mentality, so I thought we were in good hands. I trusted him."

In 2007, the Plyler sisters were awarded a settlement in the millions. Over the next nine years, Murdaugh and Laffitte would plunder it relentlessly.

"They placed their trust in Alex Murdaugh, his law firm, banker Russ Laffitte, and Palmetto State Bank," plaintiff attorney Eric Bland would later maintain, "to guide them . . . through the remainder of their childhood into adulthood."

As the sisters grew up, they had to ask Laffitte, who they viewed as a father figure, to sign off on anything they needed, such as clothes and basic school supplies. They were never told that they were entitled to $24,000 a year from the settlement money without a judge's permission.

Meanwhile, Murdaugh allegedly stole $990,000 from their settlement, and Laffitte, $355,000. Laffitte allegedly also used the sisters' trust money to give Murdaugh hundreds of thousands of dollars in unauthorized bank loans, although his own Palmetto State Bank accounts were frequently overdrawn.

"Russ Laffitte and Alex Murdaugh plundered their conservator accounts," said Bland, "and treated it like their own personal slush fund."

The innocent, underage Plyler sisters were the first victims in what investigators believe soon evolved into a huge multimillion-dollar criminal enterprise, involving the scions of two of Hampton County's oldest and most prestigious families.

Alex Murdaugh's next victims in December of 2009 were a poor Black family involved in a horrific car crash after their car tires blew out. Twenty-one-year-old Hakeem Pinckney, an all-around athlete at the South Carolina School of the Deaf and Blind, who had led his school to a national football championship, was paralyzed from the neck down and left a quadriplegic.

While on a ventilator and fighting for his life in the ICU, his mother

Pamela, who had been driving the car, sought out Alex Murdaugh, whom she knew by reputation. He immediately agreed to file personal injury suits for Hakeem, his sister Shaquarah, and cousin Natarsha Thomas, all passengers in the car. Then Alex suggested the family hire Cory Fleming to represent them in a lawsuit and Russell Laffitte to take care of any monetary settlement, without mentioning his close ties to both of them.

Later a heartbroken Pamela Pinckney would explain how Alex Murdaugh had won her family's trust, after looking them in the eye and saying he would look after them.

Murdaugh then filed lawsuits through PMPED on behalf of Hakeem and Natarsha against the Michelin tire company. These were both settled in early October 2011, but the Pinckney family were never told that he had won them over $600,000 in compensation.

Four days after the settlement went through, Hakeem's ventilator was mysteriously unplugged. It took thirty minutes before anyone noticed, as the alarm was not working. Hakeem was rushed to a nearby hospital, but it was too late. He died later that day.

"I received a call from the . . . facility that Hakeem had taken a turn for the worst and was being transported to hospital," his mother later wrote in an affidavit. "When I arrived at the hospital, the doctor on duty told me that Hakeem had been off of the ventilator . . . for more than thirty minutes . . . when they found it unplugged."

Two months later, in early December, the PMPED's client trust account at Palmetto State Bank received two insurance settlement checks for both personal injury cases: one for Hakeem Pinckney's estate for $309,581.56, and the other for $325,000 to go to Natarsha Thomas for her injuries.

But instead of paying them, Palmetto Bank's Russell Laffitte, now appointed conservator, allegedly used his bank's computer system to launder both checks into money orders and cash for Alex and several members of his family.

There were further checks from the Michelin tire company: one in January 2012 for $60,000 to Hakeem Pinckney's estate, and a $25,250 one to Natarsha Thomas in August 2012. Both were again allegedly funneled by Laffitte through Palmetto State Bank directly into cash for Alex Murdaugh.

Murdaugh and Fleming apparently used part of the settlement money to charter a private plane to take them and an attorney friend to the 2012 College World Series in Omaha, Nebraska.

Then in October 2014, completely unaware of all the previous insurance payouts, Pamela Pinckney enlisted PMPED to sue the Pruitt-Health facility for Hakeem's wrongful death. Alex Murdaugh helped prepare all the paperwork for the suit, which hasn't been decided yet.

Alex Murdaugh finally acted on his cousin Curtis Smith's personal injury case, exactly three years after his logging accident. He initiated a personal injury case against American Forest Management with his father Randy under the PMPED umbrella.

The complaint was filed on September 17, 2010, in the Colleton County Court of Common Pleas, where the former solicitor's good friend, 14th Judicial circuit judge Perry M. Buckner, presided. It demanded punitive damages, accusing the company of reckless and willful negligence by not properly marking the ditch into which Smith had fallen while cutting timber.

"The plaintiff," it read, "in the process of performing his duties, attempted to jump over a ditch but failed to do so . . . injuring his spine, knee, and other parts of his body."

It claimed that Fast Eddie's injuries had required doctors, hospitalization, and medical necessities that he had paid for out of his own pocket.

"As a result of these injuries," it claimed, "the plaintiff is totally and permanently disabled from gainful employment [and] has suffered and will continue to suffer great pain, humiliation, and mental anguish."

"Do you have any other relatives in Colleton County by blood or marriage?" a defense lawyer asked Smith at one hearing.

"Yes," replied Smith, "Murdaughs."

"Say that one more time?"

"Murdaugh!" he repeated.

On May 30, 2012, American Forest Management agreed to settle with Curtis Smith for an undisclosed sum, in order to avoid going to court and facing a Hampton jury.

12

THE NEXT CENTURY

On Tuesday, September 28, 2010, PMPED celebrated its one-hundredth anniversary by throwing a party for all Hampton County residents. The Murdaugh family's company, founded by Randolph Sr. in 1910, used the centennial to triumphantly polish its reputation as the legal giant standing up for the little guy.

"We have continuously represented the run-of-the-mill people," Randy Murdaugh told *The Augusta Chronicle*, "the ones who are injured, the ones who can't afford to handle litigation. We have helped those people from the very beginning."

In the laudatory article, *The Augusta Chronicle* pointed out that although PMPED had won many multimillion-dollar verdicts over the years, it was most proud of making a difference in people's lives.

PMPED president Johnny E. Parker boasted that all their victories against the CSX railroad that had made their fortune had also benefitted the community by making safer train crossings.

"We basically put ourselves out of work," he explained. "People aren't getting killed by trains quite so much these days."

Then Randy Murdaugh issued a public invitation to every Hampton County resident to come to the "House That CSX Built" to celebrate.

"I'm extremely proud that the firm has lasted this long," said Randy, "but I am most proud that I have two sons who are mighty fine lawyers. We hope you will come and enjoy yourselves and help us celebrate our one-hundredth anniversary."

* * *

In late 2010, Maggie Murdaugh, now forty-two, opened a Facebook account. She enthusiastically embraced social media, giving ordinary people an insight into her family's privileged lifestyle.

She especially enjoyed posting photos of Alex and the boys—now dubbed the "Crazy Brood"—after a hard day's hunting, posing with all the dead deer, ducks, doves, and other animals they had slaughtered.

On November 7, she posted a photograph of her fourteen-year-old son, Buster, in full camouflage hunting gear, proudly holding the horns of a freshly killed deer.

In 2011, following his father and grandfather, Buster began his freshman year at Wade Hampton High School. He played basketball but was an average student and not academically inclined. But in a 2011 yearbook photo the chubby-faced, red-haired fifteen-year-old looked every inch a Murdaugh.

The Murdaughs were genuine Hampton County celebrities and everyone at Wade Hampton knew who he was and treated him with kid gloves.

"Buster was a good kid," said Ernestine Glynn, who works for the Hampton County School District. "He was going to law school."

Stephen and Stephanie Smith joined Wade Hampton High School in their sophomore year and were both in Buster Murdaugh's class. The fifteen-year-old twins lived in tiny Brunson with their father, Joel, who worked for the South Carolina Highway Department in Hampton. He and their mother, Sandy, were divorced.

Fastidiously groomed with long blond hair, Stephen was openly gay in homophobic Hampton and often picked on.

"There were mainly guys that called him names," said his friend Eleanor Lee. "It's not a thing that they accept."

A caring boy who dreamed of becoming a doctor, Stephen mostly kept to himself.

"He didn't have a best friend," said Eleanor. "I was always there [and] I always had to back him up."

Although Buster had played Little League baseball with Stephen, a straight-A student, he publicly avoided him. Whether or not they had a secret relationship would later be the cause of much speculation. Indeed, Stephanie would claim her brother had told her about "a fling."

"[Buster] was high class and we were middle class," explained Stephanie, "so we never socialized."

Maggie dutifully attended all of Buster's games to cheer him on. She seemed happy at last and genuinely enjoyed socializing with the other parents at sports and social events.

"Maggie lived for her kids," said her friend Bubba Mixson, whose eldest son was in Buster's class. "She was at every school function. She was such a sweet person. She never met a stranger."

Most weekends Alex and Maggie would take their sons to watch South Carolina Gamecocks games, and college sports dominated Murdaugh life.

"You'll see Alex with the family at a Carolina football game," said Kim Brant. "But aside from that they don't mix and mingle much."

In mid-November 2011, Maggie posted a photo of twelve-year-old Paul, leaning on a fence with a huge grin on his freckled face.

"What a good-looking Murdaugh!" commented one of Maggie's friends. "I bet he's a charmer like his daddy!"

Alex and Maggie were now living the high life with money he had siphoned off from his personal injury case payouts. They chartered private jets for their extravagant hunting and fishing trips all over the world. And they always flew first class with no thought about where the money had come from.

"They lived high with private planes," said family friend Sam Crews III. "The fishing trips were just over the top. I went duck hunting with them several times."

Alex took his family for two-week sailing vacations to Key West or the Bahamas, always staying at the classiest resorts. There was duck hunting

in Argentina and pheasant hunting in North Dakota, as well as prearranged luxury tours to some of the world's finest hunting preserves.

After returning from one foreign dove hunt, Alex's father Randy complained that his arms and shoulder hurt after firing off sixteen hundred
rounds of ammunition in a couple of days. Because it was against the
law to bring the dead doves back to America, Alex had the meat cooked
locally and served at nightly family feasts.

Little Paul, as everybody called Alex's youngest son, was now at North
District Middle School, where he was having problems. He hated going to
school and seemed only interested in hunting and fishing.

"Paul could do anything," his father once said, "but he had to be interested in it. He had a really hard time focusing."

Maggie took him to doctor after doctor before he was diagnosed with
attention deficit hyperactivity disorder (ADHD). He was prescribed an
array of different medications to help him become more stable, finally
settling on Adderall.

"Different medicines for ADHD had different side effects on Paul,"
Alex would later explain to his sister-in-law Liz Murdaugh when she had
the same problem with her son, Randolph. "It was a real struggle getting
the right fit and it took a long time. The big one we struggled with . . . was
losing his appetite. He never wanted to eat when he was on that medicine.
And if he took it late he couldn't sleep."

In eighth grade, Paul was expelled from North District Middle School
for beating up another pupil. Despite his grandmother, Libby, being on
the school board, Paul was then banned from following his grandfather,
father, and brother to Wade Hampton High School.

"He was not welcome in the Hampton School District after the eighth
grade," said a local teacher with knowledge of the subject. "They didn't
want him [even though] his grandmother was on the school board and
his parents had also been intimately involved in every aspect of Wade
Hampton."

Alex eventually managed to get his troubled son into the private
Thomas Heyward Academy in neighboring Jasper County. The school

was thirty-six miles from Hampton, and Maggie would drive Paul to school in the morning and collect him after school.

But it didn't take long for Little Paul to get a reputation for being arrogant with a sense of entitlement.

"I just remember him [proclaiming]," said Taylor Dobson, who knew him growing up, "'My last name's Murdaugh [and] I can do whatever I like.'"

After allegedly robbing the Pinckney family of $1,325,000 in insurance payouts, Alex Murdaugh felt emboldened and targeted his next victim.

Two years earlier, in January 2011, Donna Hay Badger, a thirty-five-year-old mother of six, had died in a traffic accident involving a UPS truck. Her grieving husband, Arthur, who was also injured, asked Alex Murdaugh to help him get compensation so he could support his large family.

Murdaugh immediately filed a personal injury suit and soon got a big payout, but Arthur Badger saw none of it. Alex had persuaded Badger to appoint his banker friend Russell Laffitte as the personal representative of his wife's estate, and then they went into action.

The fourteen thefts began in February 2013, with a $388,687.50 check made out to Palmetto State Bank and disbursed from the PMPED client trust account. Laffitte, acting as Donna Badger's estate's personal representative for "a sizable fee from the settlement," then allegedly steered the money into Alex Murdaugh's account, who used it to buy a money order "payable to a business associate."

Over the next fifteen months, a million dollars' worth of checks meant to compensate Arthur Badger landed in Alex Murdaugh's account. He used them to purchase various money orders for a "family member" or "business associate," or turned them straight into cash.

In January 2014, two compensatory checks totaling $85,000 were rerouted from Palmetto State Bank's PMPED client trust account into Murdaugh's personal one. A month later, he did it again with two more totaling $203,000.

It would be another ten years until Arthur Badger, who struggled to bring up his six children and should have been a millionaire, would learn that his trusted friend and attorney Alex Murdaugh had robbed him blind.

On April 15, 2013, Alex Murdaugh bought 4147 Moselle Road in Islandton for just five dollars, from longtime family friend Jeannine Boulware. The Murdaugh and Boulware families had been close for years, going back to the 1940s when Old Buster Murdaugh tried cases on the 14th Judicial Circuit with the late Thomas McCullough Boulware.

But after the rumors that the Murdaughs had been involved in a large drug-smuggling operation with Barrett Boulware Sr. and Jr. in the early eighties, they had kept a low profile in their ongoing business dealings.

The mysterious five-dollar sale was for Moselle, a sprawling 174-acre hunting lodge set in the forests and swamps straddling the border of Hampton and Colleton Counties. Two years earlier, Barrett Thomas Boulware Jr. had built a 5,275-square-foot house with four bedrooms and three bathrooms. It had pine floors throughout and a large game room. Nearby was a 1,140-square-foot guest house and large dog kennels.

The stately entrance to the main house lay behind two ornamental red brick walls with a large metal gate between them. The towering green trees lining the main driveway created the illusion of gazing down a tunnel toward the main house.

The expansive hunting preserve bordered the swampy banks of the Salkehatchie River, with more than two and a half miles of river frontage for freshwater fishing and kayaking. And there was also a twenty-acre dove field, a fully stocked fishpond, and a rifle shooting range.

The transfer deed included a caveat that the five-dollar Moselle sale was for the exchange of a $730,000 "like-kind replacement property," as the two families owned numerous tracts of land around the Lowcountry. It was also to avoid capital gains.

On October 7, Alex Murdaugh wrote out a check to his cousin, former client, and handyman, Curtis Smith, for just under $10,000. They had come to an arrangement for Smith to launder the check into cash for Alex. Over the next eight years, Murdaugh would write a further 457 checks to his distant cousin totaling almost $2.5 million. They would all be for less than $10,000 so they wouldn't be flagged by Murdaugh's various banks and reported, as required by law.

Prosecutors would later reveal that most of the money was used to manufacture and distribute "illegally obtained narcotics" all over South Carolina, involving multiple drug-dealing accomplices.

Alex Murdaugh and his powerful group of friends from law enforcement, politics, and the legal profession often threw ultra-private parties at various locations. Besides the freely available alcohol and drugs, they employed the services of a high-class madam, who supplied girls for the guests to choose from.

In late 2014, Lindsey Edwards, an attractive blond call girl employed by the madam, attended one of Alex Murdaugh's parties at a beach house on the Isle of Palms.

"It was apparently a guy's weekend," she later told *FITSNews'* founding editor, Will Folks. "There were a bunch of guys drinking and doing drugs."

The half a dozen girls spent the first hour socializing with the guests, drinking cocktails, and snorting cocaine. As they were running low on the marching powder, the madam sold them a couple of eight balls she had brought with her.

As the night progressed, the men picked out the girls they liked and Lindsey found herself alone with the red-haired Alex Murdaugh, whom she found very charming and a perfect gentleman.

"He told me his name and that he was a personal injury lawyer out of Hampton," she told Folks. "I was like, 'Oh, that sounds really familiar, I live in Beaufort.' And we kind of connected on that."

After making small talk about their favorite Beaufort restaurants, Alex took her into a nearby bedroom for sex.

"My expectations were still pretty high," she said. "I've already done this a good hundreds of times at this point. He seems like a really nice person."

But as soon as the bedroom door closed, Alex dropped his charming persona and violently attacked her.

"He went into a completely different personality," she recalled emotionally. "You could see it in his eyes. I don't know if it was the cocaine but his pupils just got so much bigger . . . solid black."

Then he put both his hands around her neck and started choking her until she couldn't breathe. She desperately tried to fight back and scratch his wrists, but her six-foot-three-inch, two-hundred-and-fifty-pound attacker was far too strong.

"I thought at that moment I was going to die," she said. "And it was also while being violently penetrated."

As soon as Murdaugh was done, Lindsey grabbed her clothes off the floor and ran into a bathroom, locking the door. Then she composed herself and went back into the living room where her madam was chatting with the other guests.

Lindsey said she wanted to leave immediately, but her madam said they had to wait until the other girls had finished servicing their clients. So Lindsey went outside and told their bodyguard what had happened. He was very sympathetic and went straight into the house to tell the madam about Murdaugh's vicious attack.

"She dismissed it," said Lindsey. "She just didn't care."

Later the madam told Lindsey that Alex Murdaugh was so important that he got "special privileges."

A couple of weeks later, the bodyguard drove Lindsey to an appointment at an Extended Stay hotel in North Charleston. As she got out of the car, her madam told her the client was Alex Murdaugh. Lindsey said she did not want to be left alone with Alex again, because he was too violent. But the madam ordered her to go inside, driving off to take the other girls to their appointments.

"I was essentially alone," she remembered. "I went up to service him and [it was] just violent penetration and ripping hair out of my head."

After he'd finished, Lindsey fled the room and hid in the stairwell until her madam arrived to collect her.

Lindsey had several more violent encounters with Alex Murdaugh, including being slapped across her face and having a washcloth shoved into her mouth, before she quit the tawdry business in disgust.

13

TIMMY

In early June 2014, Buster Murdaugh graduated from Wade Hampton High School and his parents were ecstatic. Maggie posted a series of photographs on Facebook of Buster at his graduation ceremony in a mortar board and gown receiving his high school diploma.

The First Family of Hampton County also took a full-page advertisement in the 2014 school yearbook to celebrate their eldest son's achievements.

> **BUSTER MURDAUGH**
> **CONGRATULATIONS!**
> **Thank you for all your school**
> **Years that have filled our lives with love, laughter, and many**
> **Wonderful memories. We are so proud of you!**
> **We love you,**
> **Mom, Dad, and Paul**

And the doughy eighteen-year-old had a dozen photographs in the yearbook's senior pages, covering everything from his sporting achievements to his social life. For his favorite quote, Buster channeled Babe Ruth: "Never let the fear of striking out get in your way."

Stephen and Stephanie Smith were also in Wade Hampton's 2014 graduating class, although they hardly merited a mention.

"You can have all the money in the world . . . but one thing you will never have . . . is a dinosaur," was Stephen's Homer Simpson–inspired favorite quote. He added that he was most likely to "Become a medical physician or rule the world."

There was also a double-page spread entitled, "The Faces of Those Who Make Us Great!" with Buster's photograph alongside Stephen's, who stares mournfully into the camera.

In late July, Hampton was dealt a crippling body blow when the town's biggest employer, Nevamar, announced it was closing and moving to Maine. Sixty years earlier, it had arrived as Plywood-Plastics, before being taken over by Westinghouse and then International Paper, and finally Nevamar. The huge manufacturer of laminate surfaces planned to lay off 250 workers by the end of the year, in the already high unemployment area.

It would be the end of an era and the plant's loud steam whistle, which had sounded every fifteen minutes since World War II, would soon be a distant memory.

"We will survive," Hampton mayor John Rhoden told *The Hampton County Guardian*. "It will be a big blow to the big businesses here, down to the small mom-and-pop."

With a 7.4 percent unemployment rate, Hampton County was already well above the state average. Many residents had already left Hampton for better job opportunities elsewhere, with a three percent population drop to 20,400 in just four years.

"That was a big blow to this community," said local historian Sam Crews III. "That hurt everything and the schools started going down."

After the Nevamar plant closed, Hampton sank further into poverty, with many of the young unemployed turning to street drugs and petty crime.

"There's a lot of drugs in this community," said local business owner Charles Hendricks. "Not the high-end drugs but meth and opioids, and it's brought a lot of crime."

Several weeks later, R. Alexander Murdaugh, as Alex now referred to himself in professional circles, was elected president of the highly prestigious South Carolina Association for Justice (SCAJ). The renamed South

Carolina Trial Lawyers Association had been founded almost sixty years earlier by his grandfather, Buster Murdaugh.

Murdaugh, who would later confess to being an opioid addict by this time, was officially declared president-elect at the SCAJ's Annual Convention in Hilton Head.

"SCAJ is an organization built around putting people first and helping others," he declared. "I'm excited to volunteer my experience and my Hampton County roots to help advocate for the great people of our state."

The twelve-hundred-member-strong association billed itself as "the leading voice for plaintiff's attorneys in the Palmetto State," and would take Alex's influence and credibility to a frightening new level.

Ironically, SCAJ's stated mission read: "We are advocates for those who are harmed by the actions of others no matter how powerful, wealthy, or well connected."

R. Alexander Murdaugh would now be speaking for all South Carolina's plaintiff lawyers, and his regal pronouncements would carry much weight in the legal community.

After moving into Moselle, Alex and Maggie stepped up their entertaining, hosting lavish parties and quail-hunting weekends for local law enforcement, politicians, and others they wished to impress, inviting their wives along as well.

And his love of the good life was clearly on show with Alex's fast-expanding waistline.

The next generation of Murdaughs now carried on the family tradition with parties of their own. Buster, now eighteen, was interning at PMPED while preparing for law school, and fifteen-year-old Paul would invite their friends to weekends at Moselle. And although they were all underage, there was always cold beer in the deer cooler, with Alex and Maggie often joining in the festivities.

"They threw parties every weekend," said Taylor Dobson, a Wade Hampton classmate of Buster's. "That was the party spot in Hampton.

A lot of fights, alcohol, and drugs thrown in there all at the same time. Things can go way out of control when you mix all that together."

There were also parties on one of several boats Alex owned by the sandbars of Beaufort River or on their grandfather's luxurious Cheches-see waterfront property, Murdaugh Island.

"During the summer," said Connor Cook, who grew up with the Mur-daugh boys, "it was an every-weekend thing. We [went] to all of them."

Paul was already a heavy drinker and taking heavy medication for his ADHD. He often veered out of control, getting into fights and scaring people with his strange, unpredictable behavior.

"I've been to parties at the [Murdaugh] home," said a friend, Eleanor Lee. "There was always a fight. It seemed like he had a lot of anger."

Friends noticed that whenever Paul got drunk he became like Dr. Jekyll turning into Mr. Hyde. First his eyes became "as wide as half-dollars" without blinking, and his fingers would then spread out like they were stuck, as he waved his arms erratically and became belligerent.

His friends christened his drunken persona "Timmy."

"It started one night at Mr. Alex's house in Moselle," remembered Connor Cook's cousin, Anthony. "I don't remember who came up with [Timmy], but it's just a different name because he turns into a completely different person. So when they can tell he's drunk, somebody will say, 'Here comes Timmy! We got to go!'"

Paul would strip down to his boxer shorts when he got really drunk, no matter how cold it got. Then he would parade around half naked as he shotgunned beers for the rest of the night, before passing out.

One drunken New Year's Eve, Timmy suddenly took off and drove his truck right into the middle of a field and stopped. Someone had to go after him and drive him home.

"He's a crazy drunk," said Morgan Doughty, who would become Paul's girlfriend. "He does weird things."

For spring break 2015, one of Paul Murdaugh's wealthy friends rented a condo on the golf course at Edisto Beach as their party HQ. Although it was very close to Alex and Maggie's beach house, Paul spent the entire week there drinking with his cronies.

"They destroyed the condo and caused $40,000 of damage," said Kim Brant, who knew the owner. "Then they drove a golf cart into the lagoon."

Paul's friends even posted Vine videos of them wrecking the condo. It showed them shotgunning cans of beer as they swung from kitchen cabinet doors and squirted ketchup and mustard all over the walls.

When the owner saw all the damage, she threatened to sue, but Alex Murdaugh and the other fathers quickly settled to hush things up.

Feeling empowered as the new president of the South Carolina Association of Justice, Alex Murdaugh threw himself into politics and now had the financial clout to do so.

In February 2015, Russell Laffitte's Palmetto State Bank had granted him a $500,000 line of credit, secured by real estate. Three months later, that credit line was withdrawn, leaving Murdaugh with a negative balance of almost $52,000. Immediately the bank agreed to raise his line of credit to one million dollars.

In June 2015, with next year's presidential election on the horizon, Alex and Maggie donated $2,700 to the Hillary Clinton campaign. The Murdaugh family was also active at the city and state level, giving thousands of dollars to senate and city council races.

They also held fundraisers at Moselle for many local candidates, as well as local charity events. Viewing himself as a Lowcountry kingmaker, Murdaugh was always the genial host, shaking hands, making small talk, and being his charming self.

Later, when James Smith, his pledge brother at the Kappa Alpha Order fraternity, became the 2018 Democratic Party nominee for governor, Alex and Maggie hosted three Moselle fundraisers for his campaign.

"Every time I called on Alex," said Smith, "he would always do more than I ever asked."

Like his father and grandfather before him, Alex Murdaugh was a savvy political operator, buying the right people who would then owe him a favor.

"His influence, especially in the Lowcountry, was unmatched," said Michael Mule, a Charleston-based GOP political consultant. "The guy knew how to play the political game here. In politics, far too often, money means power."

14

STEPHEN SMITH

After graduating from Wade Hampton High School, amidst rumors of a romantic relationship with Buster Murdaugh, Stephen Smith enrolled at the Orangeburg-Calhoun Technical College to become a registered nurse. He had always dreamed of becoming a doctor and was working hard toward it.

He was also exploring the gay lifestyle, and his twin sister, Stephanie, often helped him prepare for a night out on the town.

"His hair had to be perfect," said Stephanie. "His makeup had to be perfect. He didn't miss a beat."

The twins lived with their father, Joel Smith, in Brunson, South Carolina. He worried about his son's safety, as homosexuality was frowned upon in the Lowcountry.

"My dad was afraid for Stephen's life," said Stephanie, "because of the fact that he was gay and we lived in a small town full of rednecks."

After starting college, Stephen's father got him an old SUV for the one-hour commute to Orangeburg, South Carolina. He drove to and from school with two girlfriends of his, Britany Dandridge and Rachel Tuten.

For the first semester, everything seemed fine and he came straight home after classes to do his homework. But then everything changed.

On January 29, 2015, Stephen Smith celebrated his nineteenth birthday by going clubbing in Charleston with friends. While he was dancing at a gay disco he met forty-seven-year-old Marc Bickhardt, who had a young son.

"He was shaking his booty," remembered Bickhardt. "I went there with a friend and that's where we first met. We didn't do anything because he had to leave."

Over the next several months, they stayed in touch on social media, exchanging texts and photographs. Then in April, they went on a date and began a relationship. For privacy, Bickhardt bought him a cell phone and agreed to pay the monthly bill. He would also give him money.

"I know he was Stephen's sugar daddy," said his twin sister, Stephanie, whom he confided in. "But Stephen never spoke of him . . . so he wasn't important."

Stephen and Marc went to the beach together on dates or hung out at Bobcat Landing in Bamberg. Once Stephen badly sprained his ankle and then told his parents that it happened at home.

"He was lying," said Stephanie. "He didn't come home until two or three in the morning."

Later, Bickhardt would claim that he and Stephen became engaged that spring and planned to marry. Stephanie totally rejects that, saying Stephen would definitely have told her if it was true.

At the end of May, Stephen Smith failed his exams and had to take a special summer course in order to rejoin his class for the next semester. He seemed to lose all interest in his medical studies and started playing hooky and smoking marijuana. He spent most days at his mother's house taking selfies in her Jacuzzi tub on his iPad and then posting them online.

"He was acting a little secretive," said Stephanie. "That's when he started coming and going as he pleased."

Stephen befriended another student in his first responder class named James. They went to rap parties together before having a falling out, and Stephen started spending more and more time in gay chat rooms, using the alias Noah Rivers.

"It was more of a friend thing," said Stephanie. "He didn't really want anything too close and personal with these people. But I always told him . . . he was going to mess with the wrong people and something was going to happen."

Then Stephen began receiving gifts from men he had met in the chat rooms. One day his sister was cleaning his bedroom when she found a pile of packages addressed to Noah Rivers.

"There were dildos . . . and porn magazines and all of that," said Stephanie. "He told me that somebody was buying stuff for him . . . and I just ignored it from there [on]."

Marc Bickhardt would later tell investigators that Stephen was working for a Hilton Head escort service under the name "Brian," making up to $3,800 a night.

His mother, Sandy Smith, didn't take Stephen seriously when he suddenly announced that when his education grant ran out he had other ways of making money.

"We used to joke [that] he was going to be a stripper and . . . work for an escort service," Sandy later told police, "to make money to pay for his school."

In the last week of June, Gavin Wakefield (not his real name) arranged to meet Stephen for a date after seeing his ad on Craiglist. After a series of texts, Gavin, the divorced father of an eighteen-year-old daughter, invited Stephen over to his house for sex. Stephen was working at Hampton's Watermelon Festival, but after finishing his shift, he drove over in his newly acquired 2007 yellow Chevrolet Aveo, arriving around eleven o'clock at night.

Wakefield would later describe it to investigators as a "consenting adults encounter," with no money changing hands.

"It was a one-night stand," he explained. "We mutually enjoyed each other's company. I was just concerned that he left [my house] kind of late and he had an hour drive to head back to his home."

The next morning Wakefield texted Stephen to make sure he got home safe.

"He just said he had a good time," said Wakefield, "and that he was willing to meet me again sometime in the future."

On Saturday, July 4, Stephen Smith went swimming at Bobcat Landing with friends. Around 2:00 A.M. he had an altercation with someone and police were called. Stephen texted his sister, Stephanie, to come and get him, saying he'd gotten into an argument and police were on their way.

Later he told Marc Bickhardt that a guy with a Guns N' Roses Tattoo had "harassed" him for being gay and messed with his car locks and battery.

Three days later, Stephen called his twin sister from an Exxon gas station in Brunson, complaining his car had gone "crazy" and wouldn't start.

"I came to his rescue because I was the mechanic of the family," she said. "Somebody had unscrewed his battery connections and his oil drain plug was loose."

Stephanie tightened the battery and got his yellow Aveo car going, before following him back to their father's house.

Once there Stephen took a shower and put on a short-sleeve black shirt, tan khaki shorts, and blue athletic shoes, saying he was going to school.

"He left at exactly six o'clock," said Stephanie. "And that was the last time I ever saw him."

15

THE PRIME SUSPECT

At 3:57 A.M. the next morning, Ronnie Capers, who owns a Hampton towing company, was driving down Sandy Run Road near Crocketville when he saw something lying in the middle of the road. At first he thought it was a dead deer, but as he approached he realized it was a man's body. He drove past and called 911 at the next stop sign.

"Hampton County 911, where's your emergency?" answered the Hampton dispatcher.

"I'm just going along Crocketville Road," he replied. "I see somebody laying out."

As there was no Crocketville Road in Hampton County, it took the dispatcher some time to realize he actually meant Sandy Run Road.

"He's lying in the road," said Capers. "I ain't moving him . . . but somebody's going to hit him! Somebody's going to hit him!"

"OK, we'll get an officer out that way to see what's going on," said the dispatcher, hanging up.

At 4:40 A.M., Deputy Michael Bridges of the Hampton County Sheriff's Office arrived to investigate. It was a hot, humid night and there was no lighting on the lonely two-lane highway surrounded by dense woods.

Initially, he did not see anything with his headlights in the pitch-black darkness, and was about to leave when he took a second look. Then he saw a young man's body lying in the middle of the road, with his arms outstretched and a gaping head wound.

Deputy Bridges summoned EMS, who arrived five minutes later, and called the coroner. The blond-haired victim appeared to have been shot. He had a seven-inch gash on the right side of his forehead, and his head had caved in from a heavy blow of some kind.

Within minutes, the South Carolina Highway Patrol, the Hampton County Sheriff's Office, and two firefighter units arrived. The South Carolina Law Enforcement Division (SLED) Crime Scene Investigation team was also called in to process the suspected crime scene.

There were no tire marks or any traces of another vehicle, such as debris, paint scrapes, or broken headlights found near the body. The victim's loosely tied shoes were still on his feet, a sign that it was not a hit-and-run. Officers found a cell phone and car keys in the pocket of his khaki shorts.

The scene was then secured by yellow crime scene tape and a rectangle was spray-painted in orange paint around the body, before it was covered in a sheet until the coroner arrived.

"After photographing the area, the sheet was removed," SLED CSI officer James B. Tallon later wrote in his report. "A hole in the skull was located above the victim's right eye. It . . . was still unclear at this time if this hole was caused by a projectile."

Officers searched the area for cartridge cases, but none were found.

As soon as Trooper David Rowell saw Stephen's body and his terrible head injury he suspected foul play.

"Nothing at the scene appeared that it was a vehicular accident," he later explained. "He had no abrasions, no torn clothes. His shoes were still on his feet and his cell phone was still in his pocket. The only injuries . . . were to his head."

At 6:25 A.M., Hampton County coroner Ernie Washington arrived and immediately ruled it a homicide.

"He pointed out the wound to be a gunshot wound and showed me the entry point," South Carolina Highway Patrol investigator Sergeant Moore later wrote in his report. "Assistant Coroner Kelly Greene then began to show me photographs they took, again pointing to the entry point to the head and also a defensive wound to the hand. I then asked for clarity if they were sure it was a homicide and their response was yes."

Coroner Washington ordered the body to be transported to the medical examiner's office for autopsy, and the South Carolina Highway Patrol officially handed the investigation over to SLED.

Three miles away on Bamberg Highway a yellow Chevy Aveo had been found abandoned, with its gas cap open and hanging on the side. The doors were locked and although the battery was working, it would not start, having run out of gas. The car keys found in the dead man's pocket unlocked the door.

After getting a search warrant, investigators found Stephen Smith's wallet containing a driver's license with his photograph and formally identified him.

The fact that Smith had left his wallet in his car after running out of gas should have raised red flags. It made no sense that he would not have taken his wallet and money with him to walk home. But it would be years until investigators would follow up on that.

At 9:18 A.M., after a simple walk through the death scene, SLED crime scene agents inexplicably released it to the Hampton County Sheriff's Office without any further investigation.

Although a suspected homicide, Stephen Smith's death would never be investigated as one. The usual sketches were made and digital photographs taken, but there was no evidence gathered or blood splatter analysis performed.

At 10:30 A.M., the Hampton County Coroner's Office officially notified Stephen Smith's parents that he was dead. A few hours earlier, his mother, Sandy, had heard on the radio that a body had been found on Sandy Run Road. She immediately called Stephanie and learned that Stephen had not come home the night before.

"It was devastating to hear that news," said Sandy, who initially thought Stephen had been shot. "They laid him in that road like a piece of trash."

Shortly afterward, Alex Murdaugh's older brother Randy called Stephen's father, Joel Smith, offering to represent the family pro bono if they wanted to pursue a personal injury claim. It's a mystery how he found out so early, before the victim's name had even been released.

"Randy Murdaugh was the second person to call my dad after the coroner," said Stephanie. "And he said he wanted to take the case and it would be free of charge. My dad's a little iffy."

Sandy later told investigators that over the next few weeks she received a barrage of calls from Randy Murdaugh, requesting all of Stephen's electronic devices.

Randy declined to comment on any of these accusations.

At 11:30 A.M., Stephen's autopsy was performed by pathologist Dr. Erin Presnell at the Medical University of South Carolina in Charleston. It was attended by two SLED officers. Presnell found no traces of a gunshot wound. She also took a rape kit.

The pathologist ruled that Stephen Smith's death was the result of "blunt head trauma sustained in a motor vehicle crash." Her report stated that the victim had been struck by a vehicle mirror.

The autopsy was completed at 1:43 P.M. and the two crime scene agents took the evidence back to SLED's Forensic Services Laboratory. SLED told the South Carolina Highway Patrol that Stephen's death warranted further investigation, but that went unheeded. Stephen's remains were already on the way to the Peeples-Rhoden Funeral Home in Hampton.

When Sergeant Moore, who had been told by Coroner Washington that it was a homicide, discovered it had now been downgraded to a hit-and-run, he was livid. He immediately called the coroner, who had already authorized the pathologist's determination, asking why he had changed his mind.

"I then reminded him that earlier that morning they were certain it was a gunshot wound," he wrote, "and he told me he had to go by the opinion of the doctor."

But the dogged investigator refused to let it go. He called the funeral home and said he was sending an officer straight over to pick up the deceased's clothes.

"He stated it was in a paper bag with the body," wrote Sergeant Moore. "I asked them to immediately stop whatever preparations they were making to the body and cover him up, and we would come and get the clothing."

Sergeant Moore then called Dr. Presnell to find out why she had ruled Smith's death a hit-and-run. The pathologist was adamant there was not a gunshot wound, explaining that no bullets or fragments had been found during the X-ray.

"It didn't look like a bullet wound in her opinion," wrote Sergeant Moore. "Since the body was found in the roadway, she could only theorize that it had to be a motor vehicle that caused the death. I then asked her why she was ruling it as a motor vehicle accident, and what she thought caused the head injury. She told me that it was not her job to figure that out, it was mine."

Within hours of Stephen's death, the Hampton rumor mill was rife with talk that Buster had been in a gay relationship with Smith, and the Murdaugh boys were somehow responsible for his death. It was said that the powerful Murdaugh family was already calling in favors to make it all go away.

Corporal Michael Duncan, who headed the South Carolina Highway Patrol's Multi-Disciplinary Accident Investigation Team (MAIT) and had been at the death scene, believes it was definitely murder that had been covered up.

"It was a disaster from the start," he said. "I've never had a case . . . shrouded in so much secrecy. There was a rape kit done which to me is unusual. If it's a hit-and-run, why are we doing a rape kit?"

Early Thursday morning, the South Carolina Highway Patrol sent out two press releases to local media, appealing for any witnesses to come forward. They also issued flyers that were handed out to motorists on Sandy Run Road.

The initial release carried the headline "Fatal Hit-and-Run" in which "a pedestrian was struck and killed." But then it was changed to the more sinister "Fatal Incident."

At 9:00 A.M., MAIT investigator Sergeant Moore arrived at the Peeples-Rhoden Funeral home in Hampton to examine Stephen Smith's body. Earlier he had dispatched officers to Sandy Run Road to look for any debris from another car, but they found nothing.

At the funeral home, Sergeant Moore was joined by Corporal Duncan and SLED agent Brittany Burke. After taking photographs of Stephen's body, they closely inspected it.

"There's no body trauma other than to the head area," Corporal Duncan observed in his audio notes at the time. "He does not appear in my opinion struck by a vehicle—possibly something else."

The agents all agreed that the blunt force trauma to the head did not appear to be caused by a motor vehicle, and were baffled as to why it had been dismissed as a hit-and-run so quickly. All relevant evidence in the case was also contaminated, especially Stephen's car, which could have contained vital clues.

"We were never given the opportunity to see the car in its original state," said Corporal Duncan. "I examined the car a few days later in a compound lot that sat there pretty open. There was no chain of custody done with the clothes. We were trying to piece a puzzle together when [we didn't] have a whole lot of pieces."

From the beginning, Sandy and Stephanie Smith were certain their son's death was murder and not a hit-and-run. Since they were small, the twins had walked up and down Sandy Run Road, less than six miles from where they lived, often playing hide-and-seek in the surrounding woods.

Just the week before his death, Stephen had run out of gas on Sandy Run Road and called Stephanie to pick him up. It was late at night so he hid in the woods for safety, as Stephanie and their dad drove up and down the road looking for him.

"He's like, 'You passed me!'" remembered Stephanie. "'You passed me again!' And we [told him] 'Come out of the woods.' But he wanted to make sure it was us before he would. That's the type of person he was."

Sandy believed her son had been murdered because he was gay, and that his body was left in the road to be hit by an early morning logging truck.

"It was a hate crime," she told *Fox Carolina News.* "That's what it was."

At 5:32 P.M. that afternoon, WSAV-TV posted a story on their website with the headline "Hampton Community Wants Answers in Fatal Hit-and-Run Case."

"Investigators in Hampton County are still piecing together clues," it began, "after a young man was found dead along a rural road. They say it appears to be a hit-and-run that killed nineteen-year-old Stephen Smith on Sandy Run Road. Friends and family of Smith hope a suspect can be identified."

The story featured interviews with several of Smith's friends, who were devastated by the news.

"What kind of monster could do this to somebody?" asked his Wade Hampton classmate Felicia Walling. "I remember the Friday nights we used to go and hang out at the skating rink with . . . all of our best friends."

The story said the highway patrol was now leading the investigation, and investigators believed that Smith died instantly and didn't suffer.

"I was so shocked. I was so angry," said another classmate, Betty Ferguson. "But I guess things happen for better reasons, and at least he's in a better place."

On Saturday morning, Stephen Smith's obituary was published online by the Peeples-Rhoden Funeral Home.

"The Angel of death has visited again and a Godly life ended on Wednesday morning," it began. "Mr. Stephen Smith was taken from our sight. We know he is at rest with our Heavenly Father."

At 5:00 P.M., the family held a wake at the funeral home. According to Sandy's wishes Stephen was dressed in his new scrubs, which had only arrived in the mail the day before. It was open casket, as she wanted everyone to see his horrific head injury.

Halfway through the wake, Marc Bickhardt suddenly appeared, announcing that he was Stephen's boyfriend and making everyone uncomfortable.

"My dad told me to take him in there to go and see Stephen," Stephanie later told investigators. "And I said, 'Brace yourself. It don't look like him.'"

On his way to the casket, Bickhardt suddenly stopped to call someone on his cell phone.

"Yes, Stephen's dead!" was all he said before hanging up.

"Then we walked to the casket," Stephanie said, "and he looked and [asked], 'What was it?' I said, 'A hit-and-run.' And then he [said], 'No, he was beat to death!' And I looked at him [and said], 'How would you know?'"

Then, after asking if Stephen had been "sexually assaulted," Bickhardt left.

On Sunday afternoon, Stephen Smith's funeral was held at the Sandy Run Baptist Church, followed by burial in the Gooding Cemetery. The next day Marc Bickhardt, who had attended the funeral, posted an emotional tribute on Facebook.

"I met you and we both fell in love," he wrote, "and immediately I moved to Hampton to be with you. Your young life was cut short and we were going to get married . . . when you graduated. My heart is bleeding and I don't know that I could ever love again."

16

THE COVER-UP

The South Carolina Highway Patrol's MAIT investigation team were now interviewing everybody associated with Stephen Smith. They were treating his death as a homicide, although they had to tread carefully as it was officially a hit-and-run.

None of Stephen's friends thought it was an accidental hit-and-run either, and Hampton's fertile gossip grapevine was working overtime about whether the Murdaugh boys were involved. And as investigators started interviewing Stephen's friends, Buster's name came up repeatedly.

"Because the Murdaugh name was brought up so much we wanted to gather as much information [as we could]," said Corporal Duncan, "so if we get the opportunity to interview them we can confront them with [it]."

One of the first interviews was with Marc Bickhardt, who had been spotted by police hanging around Sandy Run Road where Stephen's body had been found.

Interviewed at his home by MAIT investigator Michael Duncan, Bickhardt claimed to have been in constant cell phone contact with Stephen on the night he died. Around 3:30 A.M., Stephen told him that he had run out of gas and was walking home.

"The calls kept dropping," Bickhardt told Duncan. "I was worried about him."

Bickhardt said he had last seen Stephen on July 4 when they'd gone swimming together. He feared "foul play was involved," and that Stephen's escort agency was involved.

Then the investigator asked if he would be willing to take a lie detector test.

"I'll do it," said Bickhardt. "Let's do it. Set it up. I'm telling you I didn't do this. We were about to get married. I will go to the end of the earth for him but I did not kill him."

On Thursday, July 16, Stephanie Smith went out shopping for the first time since her brother died and was stunned by all the rumors about her brother's death. In one Hampton store, "a bunch of people" told her that Buster Murdaugh had done it with some friends.

"I was mind-boggled at that," she said. "What? It makes no sense. We went to school with Buster and he's never said anything bad about Stephen."

And her mother was also hearing the exact same talk.

"Everybody keeps . . . saying it was the Murdaugh boys," said Sandy Smith.

The next day, MAIT investigators Duncan and David Rowell interviewed Stephanie at the Hampton County DMV Office. She told them how Stephen had suddenly become "very secretive" two weeks before his death and she had no idea why.

"He started acting a little funny," she said. "He started coming home late."

"Is it possible that he could have met somebody online over the past two weeks," asked Duncan, "when he started becoming a little more secretive?"

"Yeah," she replied.

The investigator then asked if Stephen had ever advertised himself in gay chat rooms.

"Yeah," Stephanie replied. "He put himself out there."

"So he let people know he was available?"

"Yeah, but he's never received money from anybody except Marc."

Then the MAIT investigator leveled with her, admitting they had no leads, and asked her to keep it to herself.

"I'm going to be honest with you," said Duncan. "We're at a loss. There's nothing. I don't feel like it was a hit-and-run. It's more a death investigation basically. It could be a homicide."

He then asked her to spread the word around the town "rednecks" that the highway patrol investigators had solid leads about Stephen's killer, in the hopes someone would talk.

"Put a little bluff out there," he told her. "Shake the tree a little bit. Have them feel like we're homing in on something."

Investigator Rowell said Buster Murdaugh was a person of interest, and they were having to tread very carefully.

"Maybe people out there know stuff," he told her, "that are not directly involved in it. If they feel we're close to solving this thing, they're going to come forward and tell us what they know . . . to clear their name."

Stephanie then told the investigators how Buster's Uncle Randy had called immediately after the coroner to offer his legal services free of charge.

"It's kind of weird," she said. "No lawyer . . . says it'll be free and you can have whatever money you want."

Duncan told her that they would only solve the case by putting pressure on people Stephen was hanging around with or locals that didn't like his lifestyle.

"I don't care what kind of lifestyle he led," said Duncan. "That has nothing to do with it. He's somebody's family member and that's the way I see it."

A few days later, Sandy Smith's sister Pam Chaney contacted a law firm in Savannah, Georgia, to handle a personal injury case on behalf of the Smith family.

"We talked to them," she said, "and the minute you mentioned Murdaughs [they said], 'We can't take the case.' Everybody's scared of the Murdaughs [and] nobody wants to talk against them."

Over the next few weeks, highway patrol MAIT agents made little headway in the investigation. Although they were in possession of Smith's iPhone, they were unable to unlock it. However, they did manage to download his iPad, discovering a cryptic message he'd sent an unknown person the night he died: "Frankly I want to go home. The heat is killing me."

On July 22, Trooper Todd J. Proctor, now leading the investigation, went to the Medical University of South Carolina to interview pathologist Dr. Erin Presnell, who had ruled Smith's death a hit-and-run. He arrived without an appointment and found the pathologist to be openly hostile.

"She began in a negative tone . . . that she was very busy," Proctor later wrote in his MAIT report. "She could not even begin speaking with me without the coroner's consent."

When Proctor informed her that he had spoken to Coroner Washington the previous day she called him a liar, but backed off when he offered to call him there and then.

"I asked her why she stated [it was a hit-and-run] in the report and her answer was, 'Because he was found in the road.' She had no evidence other than that."

The trooper then asked if someone could have caused the head injury with a baseball bat, and she said "No."

"When I probed further," he said, "saying what about someone in a moving car with a bat, she stated, 'Well, I guess it's possible.'

"I could see that this conversation was not going to yield any positive results. As I was leaving, she stated that the report was preliminary and it was my job to figure out what it was [that] struck him, not hers."

The next day Coroner Washington faxed Trooper Proctor the final autopsy report, saying he didn't agree with Presnell's findings that Stephen's injuries were caused by a motor vehicle.

The coroner added that Dr. Presnell had told him she would be willing to change her autopsy report to read however he wanted it to.

Two weeks later, Stephanie Smith texted Corporal Duncan that she had heard through a third party that Buster Murdaugh had been in a relationship with her brother. For the next four days, Duncan worked on the lead, tracking it down to a Wade Hampton classmate named Brenden Strother.

"I just heard that Buster did it," he told Trooper Duncan. "I mean everybody knows who Buster is and his family . . . so it was kind of shocking."

Stephanie Smith was also making inquiries of her own and arranged for Trooper Proctor to interview another of their Wade Hampton class-mates, Taylor Dobson. Proctor first contacted him by phone, but Dobson was so nervous to talk about the Murdaughs that he insisted on a face-to-face meeting.

On September 2, almost two months after Stephen Smith's death, Trooper Proctor drove to Beaufort from his Charleston office to interview Dobson. He began by saying "no big name in Hampton" worried him, although he knew others had been intimidated and told to keep their mouths shut.

"Typically you don't see the highway patrol working a murder and that's what this is," he told Dobson. "There's no doubt. We're not classify-ing this as anything other than a murder."

Then Taylor recounted what he had heard secondhand, originating from Buster Murdaugh's best friend, whom he named.

Buster and a couple of friends had left Moselle after midnight in search of food. He was driving his Ford F-150 truck down Highway 601 near Crock-etville when he spotted Stephen's yellow Chevy by the side of the road. He had driven past at first, before seeing Stephen walking along the road. Then they made a U-turn to "mess" with him.

"They stuck something out of the window and it hit him," said Dob-son. "In the head or the back."

Dobson said he was a grade ahead of Buster at Wade Hampton, where they'd played baseball together and occasionally hung out. He'd also been to pool parties at Moselle and the family had always been good to him.

"I've known the Murdaugh family pretty much my whole life," he said. "Hampton's not a very big town."

Taylor had also heard that Buster was on drugs at the time of the in-cident.

"Whether that's true or not, I don't know," he said. "It's just strictly hearsay," adding that another mutual friend had attended many Mur-daugh parties at Moselle, where drugs were freely used.

Then Trooper Proctor asked who else was in the truck with Buster.

"The only name that was given to me was 'Murdaugh,'" said Taylor. "And, of course, everyone's kind of shy to say it out [loud], because of the power of the Murdaugh name in Hampton County. It was like that all through school—[very] hush-hush."

Dobson speculated that perhaps they hadn't intended to kill Smith, but then freaked out and tried to cover it up by driving the body to Sandy Run Road.

"I just think it was them being stupid," he explained. "They picked on him and then it turned into, 'Oh crap! We've done something [bad] and we have to cover our tracks.' I'd hate to say that it fit the mold, but with the right amount of alcohol or drugs . . ."

The trooper then told him that the Murdaughs knew they were under suspicion. "Buster was on our radar long before you were," he said. "Even for a small town [like] Hampton it's weird."

Toward the end of the interview, Dobson said he was certain that the Murdaugh family had several generations of legal power to protect their kind.

"I mean you know the name," he said. "They're lawyers. Buster's grand-daddy was solicitor, yadda, yadda, yadda."

The highway patrol's MAIT investigation soldiered on for the next three months, with more and more people mentioning Buster Murdaugh's name.

On Monday, October 1, Joel Smith died at home after a brief illness. Friends said he died of a broken heart after his son Stephen's death.

By November, lead investigator Todd Proctor had interviewed ten people who had all mentioned Buster's name. According to the final MAIT report, an investigator called Buster once, but he refused to answer. And then, to the investigators' frustration, word came down from the very top not to pursue it further.

"We were told to hold off," Trooper Duncan later explained. "If we're going to confront somebody, [we're] only going to get one opportunity with the household name like that."

Local historian Sam Crews III closely followed the Stephen Smith case and is convinced the autopsy was fixed.

"And I think that's horrible," he said. "The Murdaugh boys came up immediately. They went to the same school. Were they friends? Yes. Do I know of a sexual affair? I mean I don't know anything about it. I've just heard."

That Thanksgiving, with no apparent progress in the investigation of her son's death, Sandy Smith went public to try and get things moving. Without mentioning names, she told *The Hampton County Guardian* reporter Matt Popovich that Stephen was killed by former classmates from "prestigious" families, who would do anything to protect their children.

"Mother of Slain Teen Says 'Hit-and-Run' May Be a Hate Crime," was the *Guardian* headline. "Please come forward with tips."

The newspaper also published a sidebar story entitled, "It's time to do the right thing, Hampton County."

"I just want to know what happened to my son," Sandy pleaded in the emotional interview. "I am going to do whatever it takes to get justice."

She said Stephen had been killed for being gay and she knew exactly who was responsible.

"Stephen told his twin sister that he had 'a fling' with the boy," she said. "He also told me that he and the boy had a deep-sea fishing trip planned for July. Stephen died on the eighth of July."

She complained that because highway patrol investigators were not getting anywhere, she had gone to South Carolina governor Nikki Haley, who had promised to look into it.

"I want to know who took my son from me," she said. "People need to realize that these murderers are still out there and it could be their child next."

17

THE HIGH LIFE

In the summer of 2015, Alex Murdaugh opened an account with the Bank of America under the name "Richard A. Murdaugh, Sole Proprietor doing business as Forge," solely to steal clients' money. He cunningly mimicked the name of the real financial holding company, Forge Consulting LLC, relying on its fine reputation to allay suspicions of impropriety.

The Atlanta-based firm, with an office in Columbia, works with plaintiffs' attorneys to distribute structured settlements, used when a beneficiary is a minor or incapacitated. A client's insurance payout is then placed in an interest-accruing account to be paid out over time instead of a single payment.

Ironically, as president of the South Carolina Association of Justice, Alex Murdaugh worked closely with Michael Gunn, the head of the real Forge Consulting's Columbia office, who had no idea of the bogus account.

From then on, Alex would siphon many of his client insurance payoffs directly into it for his own use.

He started using his illicit Forge account in August 2015, while representing Deon Martin in a personal injury case. Over a thirteen-month period, he had Martin write two checks to his fake account, totaling $383,000, telling him it would go into a trust set up for him. These came from a fictitious $500,000 insurance payout, invented solely to pay himself a $200,000 commission.

Prosecutors would later accuse Murdaugh of depositing the checks and then using the money to pay off his credit card bills, withdraw cash, and write personal checks.

"This account was nothing more than an illusion," explained South Carolina Attorney General's Office prosecutor Creighton Waters, "a fabrication that what he was getting in various settlements were going to a legitimate settlement consultant, when in reality they were going into an account that he controlled."

Several weeks after opening his Forge account, Alex and Maggie Murdaugh chartered a plane and flew to Los Angeles for a lavish weekend. Using stolen money from his trusting clients, Alex made no secret of the opulent lifestyle his family was now enjoying. And Maggie proudly cataloged their travels on Facebook, to burnish the Murdaugh image.

On September 1, she posted a photograph of them outside the Staples Center.

"This generation of Murdaughs are the jet set," said Hampton native Kim Brant. "They're in New York partying, they're in Columbia, and they're out West and all over the place. Just living their best life and posting it on Facebook."

The first week of December, Maggie posted a family photograph aboard one of Alex's boats. They looked the epitome of a close, happy family. Later that day, they were pictured dressed to the nines at a Carolina Yacht Club black-tie event.

That Christmas, Alex and Maggie hosted the extended Murdaugh family at Moselle for a hunting party. Maggie duly posted a family photograph showing Alex in shorts and his father Randy at the wheel of their golf cart hunting truck. John Marvin sits on a beer cooler holding a rifle next to his two young children.

In late January 2016, Alex and Maggie flew to New York on a private jet for the weekend. They stayed at the ultra-chic Mandarin Oriental Hotel on Columbus Circle, where rooms cost up to $4,000 a night.

"New York!!!" was Maggie's caption on Facebook to a photograph of her and Alex on a night out with friends at the exclusive New York Athletic Club. The highlight of the trip was a black-tie reception at the elite Metropolitan Club, where Maggie donned an elegant black jeweled halter gown and Alex wore his tuxedo.

"Whatta Knock Out," commented one of Maggie's friends. "Gorgeous People in the House! Xoxo."

Two days later, Maggie posted a photo of her and Alex boarding a private jet, captioned, "On the way home!"

"Rockstars!" commented one of Maggie's followers.

While Alex and Maggie Murdaugh lived it up in Manhattan, highway patrolman Trooper Todd Proctor got a search warrant from Verizon Wireless for Stephen Smith's cell phone. It was a last-ditch attempt to get hard evidence and bring the person responsible for Stephen's death to justice.

"The individual was found deceased in the middle of the road with severe head trauma," Proctor wrote in his warrant. "The investigation has led to this individual not being struck by a vehicle and possible foul play."

If anything of significance was found on Stephen's phone, it has never been made public. The investigation into his death went cold, to the intense frustration of his family.

"They thought Stephen was a nobody and we didn't matter," Sandy Smith later told *Fox Carolina News*. "But I wasn't giving up. Somebody was going to listen."

Over the next few months, Alex threw himself into local and national politics, as he was plundering his PMPED clients for millions. His greed and hubris were limitless.

On March 3, he publicly lobbied President Barack Obama to appoint a Palmetto State judge to replace the late Justice Antonin Scalia.

"Our organization is devoted to fighting for fairness under the law, and upholding the rights guaranteed us by our constitution," wrote President R. Alexander Murdaugh in a press release entitled, "SC's Top Legal Group: Restore Supreme Court to Full Strength."

Two weeks later, the SCAJ president cheekily unveiled his new "Payment for Potholes" program. It would connect South Carolina residents who are seeking compensation for damage to vehicles caused by crumbling roads directly to him.

"As trial lawyers," he wrote in a SCAJ press release, "we are leaders of our communities. We felt this safety issue was too important to ignore, so we are lending our expertise to those impacted by the current roads crisis."

By mid-April, President Murdaugh had turned his attention to proposed legislation to repeal local government rules against gender discrimination for public restrooms. Labeling it "unconstitutional, unenforceable, unnecessarily invasive, and downright discriminatory," Murdaugh warned it would also be "incredibly damaging" to South Carolina's economy.

"The bottom line is," he wrote in an official SCAJ press release, "we don't need politicians to tell us how and where we can use a restroom."

With Alex Murdaugh's "impeccable credentials," it was only natural for his childhood friend Jordan Jinks to seek his help after being severely injured in a traffic accident. The two had remained in touch over the years, with Jinks doing odd jobs for Alex in exchange for legal advice.

Over the next two years, Murdaugh used his bogus Forge bank account to launder $150,000 of Jinks's $830,000 personal injury settlement for his own use. He told his trusting lifelong friend that the money should be put in a trust for medical bills. Then Alex allegedly forged Jinks's signature and put the money into his fraudulent Forge account, using it for cash, credit card payments, and personal checks. He also paid himself a further $325,000 in fees from the settlement.

In June, Murdaugh told Johnny Bush that he had spent $100,000 of his settlement money on "accident reconstruction" for his case. Instead, it is alleged, he wrote a $95,000 check to his Forge account for Bush's fictitious "structured funds."

Three months later, he persuaded Manuel Santis-Cristiani to write out a check for $70,000 from his personal injury settlement to the Forge account. Although it was supposed to be for a structured settlement, Alex spent it on himself. A week later, he used the same treacherous ploy with Jamian Risher, convincing him to place $90,000 into the Forge account.

Later he flew a chartered jet to New York for another lavish weekend, billing Risher $5,500 in fictitious expenses he claimed to have incurred working on his behalf.

Over the next few years, Alex would allegedly steal millions more from many other clients, using his Forge account for fictitious structured settlements and then spending the money on drugs and living the high life.

After graduating from Wade Hampton, Buster Murdaugh had enrolled at the elite Wofford College in Spartanburg, South Carolina. As part of his liberal arts course, Buster had to write an essay on his favorite photograph. He chose a picture of Hampton County Courthouse.

"I chose this picture," he wrote, "because the courthouse plays an important role within my family. My entire family is in the law business, so I have spent a fair amount of time within this building. One day I wish to be a lawyer and a good proportion of my career will take place within the building."

In December 2016, Alex Murdaugh sold the valuable Moselle property, worth millions, to Maggie for just $5 "and love and affection," read the property record. It was a sleight-of-hand property deal for the vast 1,772-acre tract straddling Hampton and Colleton Counties, which would later raise legal eyebrows. Palmetto State Bank, run by his friend Russell Laffitte, held a $2 million mortgage lien on Moselle.

In early 2017, eighteen-year-old Paul Murdaugh started dating Morgan Doughty, an attractive blonde who also attended the Thomas Heyward Academy. She would be a frequent visitor to Moselle for hunting weekends, where alcohol was freely served. And she soon became a regular at the University of South Carolina Gamecock games, sitting with the Murdaughs and cheering on their favorite team.

Paul was now drinking every day, often using Buster's ID to buy alcohol. With his drunken alter ego Timmy appearing more and more often, he became increasingly violent with Morgan.

In March, she flew to Phoenix, Arizona, with the Murdaugh clan for the

2017 NCAA Men's Basketball Tournament to cheer on the Gamecocks. She was alongside Alex as he was interviewed at Charleston Airport by a local TV news station about the tournament.

"Hampton County representing!" an excited Maggie posted on Facebook. "Live interviews at charleston [sic] airport."

The next day she posted a photograph of the Murdaughs wearing VIP laminates at the semifinals, where the Gamecocks were soundly beaten by Gonzaga.

A couple of weeks later Paul and Morgan Doughty went on a trip to the Bahamas with Alex and Maggie. Paul could legally drink there and became so drunk that he vomited in the hotel gift shop, while his parents looked on. Later, Morgan staged an intervention.

"We discussed that Paul got drunk and vomited in the gift shop," said Morgan, "in front of and with [his] parents."

In late May, Paul graduated from the Thomas Heyward Academy. To celebrate, Maggie posted a Kodak-moment photograph of her posing with her smiling son, complete with black robe, mortar board, and shades. Soon afterward, she posted another from Paul's prom. In it, he looks slightly drunk in a crumpled tuxedo, with his arm around Morgan, who's wearing a figure-hugging, floor-length evening dress.

There were also less formal Murdaugh family celebrations for Paul. At one graduation party, Morgan filmed Paul playing beer pong, a drinking game in which players throw a Ping-Pong ball across a table into a cup full of beer. Once a ball lands in a cup the opposing team has to drink the alcohol.

In the video, Paul appears to be partnered by his father, who also supplied all the party alcohol.

"Happy Graduation Day to Paul Murdaugh," wrote his cousin Mills Goettee, "and the best of luck to his new empty-nester parents, Alex and Maggie! So excited to watch another of this crazy brood go places!"

After graduating, Paul spent the summer working for his Uncle John Marvin's rental company. But his arrogant, often drunken behavior was getting him into trouble, and over the next year he would be cited for half a dozen minor offenses.

He was now drinking heavily on top of his ADHD medication, once crashing his truck late at night. He immediately called his father for help, who paid off locals to tow it away before police arrived.

"Paul consumed alcohol on an almost daily basis," said Morgan, "and regularly to the point of becoming grossly intoxicated. [Alex, Maggie, and Buster] were often present when Paul would drink to the point of becoming grossly intoxicated."

According to Morgan, Alex and Maggie allowed him to drive his truck or their boats when he was drunk.

On Memorial Day, Paul was charged with possession of alcohol as a minor by the South Carolina Department of Natural Resources (SCDNR), who police the waterways. Although driving his father's boat at the time, he was not charged with the far more serious Boating Under the Influence (BUI).

His father and godfather Cory Fleming would defend him in court on the charges, filed the same day he paid a $510 littering fine after an incident at McCalleys Creek sandbar in Beaufort County.

Soon afterward, Paul brought Morgan on a family trip to Arizona, where there was more heavy drinking. According to Morgan, Alex and Fleming, now defending him against the minor drinking charge, gave Paul alcohol and he became "extremely intoxicated."

On June 19, 2017, Paul's two defense attorneys requested a jury trial, which would be rescheduled five times over the next year. He was finally sentenced to attend an alcohol diversion program. The charges were eventually dismissed after he completed it, and the incident report was later expunged.

A couple of months later, Morgan accompanied the Murdaughs to a wedding, where Paul got extremely drunk.

"Paul's parents actually provided me with a sleeve of Fireball Cinnamon Whisky mini bottles that night," recalled Morgan. "[They] witnessed Paul's consumption of alcohol and ultimate state of intoxication. His father drove us home after the wedding."

In December, Paul used Buster's ID to buy alcohol for a party at Moselle. He then got so drunk that his belligerent alter ego Timmy came out, and Maggie had to come and collect him and Morgan.

"[She] picked us up that night," said Morgan, "because Paul was so drunk and acting crazy. Afterward, his father was made aware of what happened as it was discussed with him."

That Christmas, Alex and Maggie threw a party for their sons at Moselle, supplying all the alcohol. Once again, according to Morgan, Paul drank too much and became "grossly intoxicated."

From then on, things would only go downhill as a medicated Paul drank to excess at every opportunity, aided and abetted by his parents, who seemed blind to what everyone else could see: Paul was an accident waiting to happen.

18

GLORIA SATTERFIELD

On January 4, 2018, Winter Storm Grayson dumped eighteen inches of snow, paralyzing South Carolina. It was the first blizzard the Palmetto State had seen in almost a decade and locals nicknamed it Snowmageddon. It wreaked havoc, with hundreds of car accidents in the deadly black ice and all hands on deck for South Carolina state troopers, whatever their rank.

Lieutenant Thomas Moore was on duty in Orangeburg County at the height of the storm when he was sent out to help an overturned Chevrolet Trailblazer that had landed in a ditch.

"The road was iced in most places," he said, "and we had wrecks galore."

He was sitting in his patrol car on the shoulder of the road writing down the driver's information when another car skidded off the road onto the shoulder, plowing into the back of his cruiser at high speed.

"I just felt a big jolt and my seat broke and threw me backwards," he told WCIV-TV. "It felt like I was being . . . shocked with electricity."

A doctor later diagnosed him with a strained neck and treated it as such. But the crippling pain continued for the next few months.

"Things were not getting better," he said. "They were getting worse."

He saw another doctor who diagnosed multiple vertebrae fractures, requiring immediate surgery. Three levels of his neck needed to be repaired and there was permanent nerve damage. But his workers' compensation plan did not cover it, and Lieutenant Moore was desperate.

In May, four months after his accident, a friend recommended hiring Alex Murdaugh, who he'd heard had a great reputation for winning personal claims. When they met at the PMPED office, the state trooper was impressed.

"He was a good attorney," said Moore. "A very nice man. Very cordial. He was confident I had a case [and] everything would be okay in the end."

On May 14, Alex Murdaugh filed a civil negligence suit on behalf of Trooper Moore in the South Carolina Court of Common Pleas. It alleged that his client's injuries were the direct result of "negligent and reckless conduct."

"The plaintiff . . . was forced to suffer personal injuries," read the suit. "He has been forced to incur doctor and medical bills [and] suffer great mental anguish and physical pain."

Soon after the suit was filed, Trooper Moore felt confident enough to undergo $250,000 worth of surgery, paying for it himself. He then waited for his attorney's call about his settlement.

Just one month after Trooper Moore's crippling accident, Murdaugh family housekeeper Gloria Satterfield had an accident of her own, but this one had fatal consequences. At around 9:00 A.M. on Friday, February 2, she arrived at Moselle and was walking up the eight brick steps to the main entrance when she tripped and fell backward headfirst onto the concrete below.

Later there would be many questions about whether she had been deliberately pushed, or had been thrown off balance by one of the four family hunting dogs—Bubba, Bourbon, Blue, and Sassy—who were all roaming freely around the grounds.

Maggie Murdaugh was inside the house when she heard the commotion, rushing out to find Gloria lying semi-conscious in a pool of blood. She then called Alex at his PMPED Hampton office for help before dialing 911 at 9:24 A.M.

"My housekeeper has fallen and her head is bleeding. I cannot get her up," she told the dispatcher.

"Ok," replied the 911 operator, "You said she's fallen and she's bleeding from the head."

"Yes."

"How old is she?"

"I'm not sure," replied Maggie. "Like fifty-eight, maybe."

"Where did she fall from?" asked the operator. "Do you know if she fell from standing or not?"

"No, she fell going up the steps," said Maggie. "That's the brick steps."

"Ok, and is she on the ground or is she up."

"She's on the ground."

"Is she conscious?"

"No, not really."

Maggie said Gloria was awake but not responding, but when the operator asked for further details, Maggie became impatient, demanding to know when the ambulance would arrive.

"I already have them on the way," the operator reassured her. "And me asking questions does not slow them down, ma'am. The medic needs to know if she's responding at all to you?"

"Not really. No."

"Ok, so she's not responsive at all?"

"Well, I mean she's mumbling."

After Maggie said Satterfield was bleeding heavily from her head, the operator asked if she had put a compress on to control the bleeding.

"No, I haven't even tried," replied Maggie, agreeing to put a "clean rag" on the top of her head.

"How about an ambulance coming?" she asked.

Then there was a long silence followed by the sound of a commotion. Then an anguished Maggie sighed, "Ah, I've got you."

"What happened?" asked the operator.

"She just fell back down," said Maggie, sounding irritated. "Can I get off this phone so I can go down there?"

The operator asked Maggie to bring her cell phone down to Gloria, so they could ask her about her pain. Instead, Maggie handed the phone to Paul.

"Hello," he said.

"Yeah, can you ask the patient what kind of pain she's having?"

"Ma'am, she can't talk," Paul replied. "She's cracked her head. There's blood on the concrete and she's bleeding out of her left ear."

"Okay, she's bleeding out of her ear?"

"And out of her head, she's cracked her skull."

The operator asked what happened when they'd tried to stand Gloria up and she'd fallen again.

"No," replied Paul. "I was holding her up and she told me to turn her loose. She was trying to use her arm and then she fell back over."

"Do you guys know who she is?"

"Yes, she works for us," said Paul.

"Ok, do you know if she's ever had a stroke or anything before?"

"Ma'am," replied Paul, testily. "Can you stop asking a lot of questions and pick up the ambulance?"

"I already have them on the way," the operator replied. "These are relevant questions that I have to ask for the ambulance. One of my questions is, has she ever had a stroke?"

Paul calmed down slightly, saying he didn't think she'd ever had a stroke. Then the operator asked if the patient was able to talk or was unconscious.

"She's not unconscious. She's just mumbling," said Paul. "I believe she maybe hit her head and maybe has a concussion."

"How long is this going to take?" he asked, ending the six-minute call.

While Maggie and Paul were waiting for EMS to arrive, Alex pulled up in his SUV. He would later claim to have found Gloria lying at the bottom of the steps semi-conscious, her head and face covered in blood. According to him, she had briefly regained consciousness to tell him that the dogs had caused her to fall, although no one else heard it.

Finally an ambulance arrived and took Satterfield to a hospital in Savannah, Georgia, where she was helicoptered to the Trident Medical Center in North Charleston, South Carolina, and put in intensive care. She was diagnosed with a subdural hematoma, wherein blood collects between the skull and the surface of the brain, and several broken ribs. Gloria was initially able to give her name and address, saying she did not know what had caused her fall and never mentioning the Murdaugh dogs.

She then underwent surgery to repair her broken ribs and reconstruct her chest wall, as well as to remove large amounts of blood from her chest cavity. The subdural hematoma was found to be inoperable but she was made as comfortable as possible and moved out of the ICU when her condition slightly improved.

Then she suffered a brain bleed and was put back in the ICU, where her condition deteriorated fast. She developed pneumonia and had to be placed on a ventilator.

For three agonizing weeks, Gloria was near comatose and unable to communicate. Her family was constantly at her bedside, but Maggie Murdaugh only visited once and Alex and his sons never came at all.

"I took her hand and I asked her, 'Mom, what happened?'" said her son Brian Harriott. "And she couldn't tell me nothing."

Gloria's brother Eric Harriott Jr. visited almost every day and would desperately try to communicate with her.

"I tried to get her to smile, laugh, and stuff like that," he later told NBC's *Dateline*, "and she would just look at me like, 'Who are you?'"

Gloria Satterfield died on Monday, February 26, of an acute subdural hemorrhage due to a stroke. Her death certificate listed the cause of death as natural, with no coroner ever being notified or an autopsy performed. The actual cause of her injury was marked "not available."

Her obituary described her love of kids and tennis and how she would be remembered for her laughter and outgoing personality. It also made special mention of Alec [sic] and Maggie Murdaugh and their sons, whom "she loved as her family."

Gloria's funeral service was held at the Sandy Run Baptist Church at 3:00 P.M. on Wednesday afternoon, just six miles down Sandy Run Road where Stephen Smith's body had been found two and a half years earlier.

She was buried at the Johnson-St. Paul Cemetery in Hampton. Alex and Maggie Murdaugh attended the funeral, and he was already planning to cash in on the tragedy. At what exact point Alex came up with the idea to sue himself for Gloria's death, by claiming his hunting dogs had caused it, is unknown. But after the service he offered his condolences to Gloria's two sons, saying how badly he felt. He then told them that he was responsible for their mother's death because his dogs had made her fall on his property. He then promised to make it right, suggesting they file a wrongful death lawsuit against him to pay for funeral expenses, as well as financial compensation for the loss of their mother.

The Satterfield boys totally trusted Alex, whom they viewed as family, having known him all their lives. Over the years, he had represented them in several family probate cases, as well as an auto accident in which he'd recovered personal injury damages for them.

"He would take care of us," said Tony Satterfield, "and kind of look out for us."

Alex recommended they use a personal injury lawyer named Cory Fleming of the Moss, Kuhn & Fleming law firm, neglecting to mention how they were best friends and former college roommates.

Soon afterward, Alex invited Tony Satterfield to his PMPED office and introduced him to Fleming, who he said would be handling the personal injury case. It was agreed that Tony would be named as the personal representative of his mother's estate.

After the meeting, Fleming wrote out a list of demands for Alex to send to his insurance company. There was never a formal lawsuit. Alex now claimed that Gloria was only at Moselle to collect a check for someone else, so the insurance company couldn't use a workers' compensation defense and refuse any future payouts. He also admitted full liability for the accident, claiming his dogs had caused her to fall.

Over the next few months, it was rumored that Paul Murdaugh had lost his temper and pushed the Murdaughs' beloved housekeeper down the steps. Some said that she had found his drugs and then confronted him about them, while others maintained she had taken him to task and he'd exploded. It was said that Paul had proudly boasted about killing her to friends.

"Did Paul really push her down the steps and kill her?" asked Hampton historian Sam Crews III. "I don't think they'll ever prove that. Did

Paul perhaps say that to some people? He may have, but it was to make him look important, cool, or something stupid."

In May, Buster Murdaugh graduated from Wofford College and his parents attended a graduation party, where Alex proposed the official toast: "You are known by the company you keep." Buster spent the summer clerking for PMPED, before becoming the fifth Murdaugh son to study at the University of South Carolina School of Law.

Paul, now nineteen and due to start at the University of South Carolina to major in criminology that fall, spent another summer working at his Uncle John Marvin's equipment rental store. He was partying harder than ever, snorting cocaine and smoking marijuana on top of the alcohol and ADHD medication.

"I saw Paul do coke," said his girlfriend Morgan Doughty. "He was friends with a lot of potheads [and] they just smoke and [he'd] go up and hit it. But I don't think he ever brought anything himself."

Paul was also increasingly violent with Morgan when he'd had too much to drink and Timmy came out. He'd swear and spit at her, even hitting her on occasion.

One drunken night on the way back to Moselle, he crashed his truck. Later, Morgan would tell friends that Paul had been out of control and had almost killed them both.

On July 4, Alex took Paul and Morgan out on his boat to celebrate. During the day the underage Morgan shot a selfie video of her giving the visibly inebriated fifty-year-old Alex a shot of liquor.

"All minors . . . were provided the alcohol by Paul's parents," Morgan later explained.

Still underage, Paul often borrowed Buster's driver's license to buy alcohol, although he looked nothing like his elder brother, who was more than seventy pounds heavier. Buster, who now had to use his passport for ID, found it "annoying," although he still let Paul use it.

The brothers often went out drinking together, craftily using the same ID. But on one occasion, they were caught and thrown out of the Dockside Bar & Grill in Edisto.

"Buster went in first," said Morgan, "and had someone bring the ID out to Paul, so [he] could go in with Buster's ID. Then the bouncer realized and he kicked them both out."

Morgan Doughty was now working for the chic boutique It's Retail Therapy in Bay Street, Beaufort. Her best friends, Mallory Beach and Miley Altman, also worked there and were dating cousins, Anthony and Connor Cooke. They had all known each other from childhood, and often socialized together.

Paul's family river house on Chechessee, known as Murdaugh Island, was a popular party place, and Paul often took them in one of his father's boats for a night out at one of the rowdy Beaufort bars.

There were also hunting weekends at Moselle that were often attended by Alex and Maggie, who would post photos of Paul and Morgan smiling in camouflage outfits, holding armfuls of dead ducks.

"They had parties," said Connor Cooke, "all kind of stuff out there. [Alcohol] was provided, but I normally drank my own."

On July 13, everybody went to the Annual Beaufort Water Festival, one of the Lowcountry's most popular events. As Alex, Maggie, and Buster looked on, Paul and several friends staged a shotgun beer competition, captured by Morgan on video. First, a hole was punched in the side of the can, then the tab was pulled, sending the beer gushing into the drinker's mouth. The first one to down the can was declared the winner and Paul was known for his shotgunning prowess.

A few days later at a wedding, Paul got very drunk, and on the way home Alex got into a heated argument with Maggie, scaring Morgan, who witnessed it.

"Alex took a painkiller and became very aggressive," she remembered. "We dropped Alex off at his parents' house because of his aggressive behavior."

On September 12, 2018, Alex Murdaugh's lifelong friend Barrett Thomas Boulware Jr. died of cancer at the age of sixty-one. Two months earlier Boulware, whose family had been close to three generations of Murdaughs, had granted Alex full power of attorney to take complete charge of all his business dealings.

Boulware, who had been arrested along with his father in the 1980s as a suspected drug smuggler before the case was dropped after a key witness died, had sold Moselle to Alex for just five dollars five years earlier.

Fast approaching death, Boulware had granted Alex the power to make all decisions regarding his health care. He also gave him the power to change the beneficiaries on his insurance policies, as well as deposit "any monies from any source whatsoever for me . . . with any bank and to draw and deliver checks in my name."

Curiously, he made it clear that Alex could not enter into any agreement or contract that would impugn his rights to "a jury trial for any matter."

Four years later, federal investigators would begin trying to unravel the complex web of financial dealings between the Murdaughs and the Boulwares going back over half a century.

19

"WE HAVE SO MUCH TO BE THANKFUL FOR!!!"

On September 20, 2018, South Carolina governor Henry McMaster awarded Alex's father Randolph (Randy) Murdaugh III the Order of the Palmetto, the state's highest civilian honor. It marked the pinnacle of success for the Murdaugh family, who had now dominated the Lowcountry's judicial system for almost one hundred and ten years.

At a special ceremony on the Hampton County Courthouse lawn, the seventy-eight-year-old Murdaugh family patriarch joined the ranks of other state icons such as novelist Pat Conroy, soul singer James Brown, and former US Ambassador to the United Nations Nikki Haley.

The historic event was witnessed by his wife, Libby, sons Randolph IV, Alex, and John Marvin, and the entire Murdaugh family.

"I want to thank you all for coming here," said Randy, to thunderous applause. "I am a fortunate man, there's no question about that."

Then he joked about the vital role that trains and combatting the railroad had played in the Murdaugh success story.

"A train killed my grandfather in 1940," he told the crowd, "and they have been killing our people ever since."

After the official presentation came speeches lauding Randy Murdaugh, his father, and his grandfather's eighty-six years of service as 14th Judicial Circuit solicitors. They failed to mention Buster having to resign in 1956 after a federal indictment for violating state liquor laws.

"This is for your lifetime of service," intoned Randy's PMPED partner,

Johnny E. Parker. "I'm sure that Buster is looking down now, so proud of Randolph."

After the ceremony, the Murdaugh-founded law firm PMPED threw a big reception in their new headquarters across the road.

"The police blocked off the street in front of the firm," said Sam Crews III, who was one of Randy's personal guests. "So you just walked over and it was a beautiful affair."

Less than one month after his father was awarded the Order of the Palmetto, Alex allegedly stole more than $120,000 from his own brother, taking advantage of a mistake made by their law firm. At the beginning of each year, PMPED partners customarily loaned money to PMPED to cover operating expenses. It would then be repaid a few months later with interest.

In early 2018, Alex's brother Randy, also a PMPED partner, had lent the firm $121,358, and in the spring a repayment check was erroneously written out to Alex, who had not made a loan. Alex covered up the mistake and had the accounting office write another check for the same amount in his name, and void his brother's in the firm's internal system.

Then on October 12, he deposited the check covering his brother's loan into his own account for his personal use.

Two weeks later, on October 31, Cory Fleming summoned Gloria Satterfield's son Tony to his office. He then persuaded him to resign as personal representative of his mother's estate, saying the "business issues" involved were beyond his experience.

Fully trusting the experienced attorney, Tony agreed to step away in favor of Chad Westendorf, a friend of Alex and Cory Fleming and vice president of Palmetto State Bank. Alex himself prepared the transfer documents, surreptitiously acting as a lawyer in the wrongful death case against himself.

From then on, Westendorf completely controlled the Satterfield lawsuit, leaving Tony totally unaware of any future settlements.

The very next day Fleming filed a wrongful death lawsuit against Lloyd's of London, Murdaugh's insurance provider. Alex admitted to causing Gloria Satterfield's death through negligence, saying he had no defense. He urged them to pay out to save his professional reputation and standing in the Hampton community.

Lloyd's then hired attorney Scott Wallinger to investigate the claim on behalf of Alex Murdaugh. In his subsequent report, Wallinger advised against fighting the suit, as Murdaugh was "a third-generation lawyer practicing with his family's law firm in Hampton."

The report noted that if contested, the wrongful death action would be held in front of a jury in the 14th Judicial Circuit, where the Murdaugh law firm PMPED was highly respected.

"Hampton County," wrote Wallinger, "is among the most pro-plaintiff trial venues in South Carolina, largely because of the influence of Mr. Murdaugh's law firm in pursuing cases there. I tend to think Mr. Murdaugh would be very favorably viewed by a jury in Hampton County or in Colleton County."

After reading the report, Lloyd's decided to settle. On December 4, the insurance company sent a check for $505,000 to Chad Westendorf, although the documents to appoint him as personal representative were still unsigned.

Two weeks later on December 18, Westendorf officially became the personal representative of the Satterfield estate. The very next day, Westendorf petitioned the Hampton Court of Common Pleas to approve a "partial settlement" of $505,000, listing $166,000 for attorney's fees and $11,500 for expenses.

"The petitioner verily believes," read the petition, "that it is in the best interest of the Estate of Gloria Satterfield, deceased, and her heirs, survivors, and beneficiaries that the said proposed partial settlement be consummated."

According to the court docket, longtime Murdaugh family friend Judge Perry Buckner approved the settlement.

In early January 2019, at Murdaugh's direction, Cory Fleming sent a check from his Moss, Kuhn & Fleming law firm for more than $403,000 to Alex Murdaugh's phony Forge account, which he then cashed and quickly spent.

Over the next few months, Cory Fleming filed more wrongful death claims on behalf of the Satterfield estate against Murdaugh's other home insurance providers.

The Satterfield family was never told and it would be years before they discovered Alex Murdaugh's cruel betrayal.

That Thanksgiving, as Alex was preparing to spend Gloria Satterfield's wrongful death money, Maggie posted a Murdaugh family photo on Facebook. It showed their long dining room table at Moselle all laid out for a Thanksgiving feast.

"We have so much to be thankful for 🦃!!!" she wrote.

The following day, Paul and Morgan went to see the South Carolina Gamecocks and Clemson Tigers NCAA football game in Clemson, South Carolina. During the game, which the Gamecocks lost thirty-five to fifty-six, Paul snorted cocaine in public.

"I saw Paul do coke at the . . . game," Morgan admitted later.

On December 31, 2018, Alex hosted a family quail hunt at Moselle before a party to ring in the new year. Maggie posted a photograph of underage Morgan mixing cocktails and another showing two empty bottles of Tito's vodka.

"Christmas Cheer ☺" she quipped.

Paul got so drunk that night that he borrowed his father's truck and crashed it into a friend's BMW.

"Alex paid cash to fix the car after the collision," said Morgan Doughty.

PART III

20

THE BOAT CRASH

In early February 2019, Paul and Morgan drove to the University of South Carolina Law School, where Buster was studying for his law degree. The sole reason for the trip was for Paul to get his older brother's license, so he could buy alcohol at an upcoming party. They met at the Thomas Cooper Library, where Buster handed over his ID.

Morgan and her best friends Miley Altman and Mallory Beach had all been invited to an oyster roast by Madison Wood, who also worked at the It's Retail Therapy boutique. They decided to make it a romantic Saturday date night, so Morgan invited Paul, and Miley and Mallory asked their boyfriends, Connor and Anthony Cook.

Paul suggested they stay over at his grandfather's river house on Murdaugh Island and take his father's fishing boat, since the Beaufort police DUI task force would be out in force.

At 5:30 P.M. on Saturday, February 23, Paul Murdaugh arrived at Parker's 55 gas station and convenience store in Ridgeland, just across the road from his family's river house. His white truck was towing his father's seventeen-foot Sea Hunt fishing boat.

Paul went inside and picked up a six-pack of Michelob Ultra Beers, a fifteen-pack of Natural Light beers, and a twelve-pack of White Claw seltzers for Morgan. At the counter, he asked the cashier for a packet of Marlboro cigarettes and some mint gum, showing his brother's ID and using his mother's credit card for the $48.61 bill. Then he walked out to his truck, triumphantly hoisting the two bags of booze over his head for Miley and Connor, who were waiting outside in a Jeep.

They followed Paul to the Lemon Island Marina Landing, where Connor helped him put the boat into the water. Paul sailed down the Chechessee River to the river house, while Connor drove his truck to meet him.

Around six o'clock, Morgan Doughty arrived to find the party well underway. Paul, Connor, and Miley were already into their second beers, so Morgan cracked open a White Claw Mango and joined them.

Soon afterward, Anthony Cook and Mallory Beach arrived with overnight bags, and Mallory went upstairs to change. Then Paul and the others went out to the boat moored outside and began loading up the two coolers with alcohol.

At 7:07 P.M., they boarded the small boat and set off for the oyster roast, which was eighteen miles north on Paukie Island. Paul was driving and everyone was drinking beer and sending Snapchat videos to their friends. Paul was also shotgunning cans of beer and an old bottle of Crown Royal whisky was being passed around.

It was getting dark with temperatures in the upper fifties as Paul drove through Archers Creek and downtown Beaufort on the way to Paukie Island. Everyone was in good spirits and ready for a big night out.

At around 8:00 P.M., they arrived at the oyster roast, which was being hosted by Brunson Elementary School principal Kristy Wood and her husband, James. Paul's Uncle Randy and his wife, Christy, were already there, as were Miley Altman's parents.

It was a BYOB event for those of legal age, and there were oysters, appetizers, and a Lowcountry boil, composed of shrimps, sausages, and potatoes. Paul had moored the boat in a neighbor's dock, and for the rest of the night everyone went back and forth to collect beers from the coolers.

For the next few hours, the twenty guests ate and drank and played cornhole. Some sat around a roaring fire while the younger ones played H-O-R-S-E basketball.

"Morgan made a beautiful shot," Kristy Wood later remembered.

By the time they left the roast after midnight, everyone was drunk. Paul refused Kristy's offer to stay the night, as she was concerned it was getting cold and foggy. Anthony, who saw signs of Paul turning into his drunken alter ego Timmy, offered to call an Uber, but no one else wanted to.

"They were stubborn," said Anthony. "They were going to ride on that boat no matter what."

The three couples left the dock at 12:11 A.M., according to the boat's Garmin GPS system. Paul then announced he wanted to go to a bar in Beaufort "to get shots," but no one except Connor wanted to.

It was foggy over the saltwater creeks and none of the navigation lights worked, so Connor held a little flashlight as Paul drove. Paul had to use the boat's Garmin navigation system because the visibility was almost zero. There were life jackets on board, but no one bothered to put them on. Everyone was still drinking beers, and Mallory was sitting on Anthony's lap at the back of the boat.

At 12:35 A.M., the tiny boat almost collided with the Woods Memorial Bridge and Connor had to grab the wheel to avoid it. Paul was insisting they go to Luther's Rare & Well Done bar in Beaufort, saying he knew the barmaid and could get everyone in with his brother's ID. Connor also wanted to go.

When the others protested, saying they just wanted to go back to the river house, Paul yelled that it was his boat and he would do what he wanted. Morgan was furious and said she wanted to go home, but Paul ignored her.

Four minutes after almost hitting the bridge, they drew into the day dock in downtown Beaufort and tied up the boat. A cruise ship was coming through the swing bridge, and they took Snapchat videos.

"It was clear that Paul was just drunk," said Morgan, "because no one wanted to go. I know if Paul kept drinking his behavior would [get even worse]. He was so belligerent."

Suddenly, Paul angrily pushed off from the dock and sped away. Then he changed his mind and returned to the dock, tying up outside It's Retail Therapy.

"Morgan was yelling at [Paul] not to go," said Miley. "He was going to get a shot no matter what."

Anthony almost came to blows with Paul, he was so desperate to go home with Mallory.

Paul and Connor then walked over to Luther's bar across from the dock, while the others sat on the wooden swings in Waterfront Park.

At 12:55 A.M. the boys entered Luther's through the rear entrance and bouncer Jake Price asked for their IDs. They showed him their illicit driver's licenses and he stamped their hands with the letters "PX." Then they sat at the end of the bar to order drinks.

Paul ordered shots of Jägermeister and paid the $16.50 bill with his mother's Discover card. He asked Luther's manager Kayla Canavan, whom he knew from high school, if she could get their underage outside friends in. She said no.

Then as they downed the Jägermeister bomb shots, Paul and Connor both posted videos of them doing so on Snapchat. Connor then ordered two lemon drop shots, a mixture of vodka and lemon, and they downed them in one gulp.

On the way out of the bar, Paul almost got into a fight after drunkenly knocking over a chair. When someone joked, "What did that chair ever do to you?" Paul took offense, asking Connor, "What did he say to me?"

Paul then demanded to know if the man had a problem with him. Connor had to physically hold Paul back to diffuse the situation.

Just nine minutes after arriving, Paul and Connor left Luther's and joined the rest of the group by the swings outside. Then they walked along the seawall toward the boat. CCTV video taken at 1:13 A.M. shows Paul unsteady on his feet as he appears to argue with Morgan, who distances herself from him. Bringing up the rear are Anthony and Mallory, looking affectionately at each other and laughing.

Mallory then posted a photo on Snapchat with the words "Date Night" on it.

At 1:13 A.M., Sunday morning, they pushed off from the dock. Everyone wanted Anthony to drive because Paul was so drunk, but Paul refused, screaming that it was his "fucking boat" and he knew the river better than anyone else.

Morgan and Miley were at the front, Paul and Connor were in the middle behind the center console, and Anthony and Mallory were at the back. No one wore life jackets although there were plenty on board.

At first, Paul steered the small boat in the wrong direction, motoring back under the swing bridge, which they would have hit if Connor hadn't grabbed the wheel. Then Paul turned around and headed south toward Port Royal Sound and Murdaugh Island.

The conditions were deplorable. It was only about fifty degrees and there was a thick sea fog hovering over the water. Their only light was from the handheld flashlight, which was almost useless.

Then Paul started "driving crazy" and "horsing around." He hit the throttle and sped up before slowing down and going in donut circles. He had become Timmy, with his telltale stretched-out arms and hands and fingers spread wide apart.

"Paul hit that stage of being drunk," recalled Anthony, who knew the signs well. "Timmy is out!"

When he almost hit a sailboat, Morgan begged him to let Connor drive, saying he needed to stop and that he had their lives in his hands.

"This is my boat!" Paul screamed at her, taking a hit of beer. "I'll be damned if someone else drives."

At 2:13 A.M., an hour after leaving Paukie Island, they entered Archers Creek, an extremely narrow, winding waterway.

Mallory said she was scared and Anthony demanded he take them to the nearest dock. Paul turned and pointed at Mallory, ordering her to "shut up."

"I stood up and said, 'Paul, don't make that mistake,'" said Anthony. "He knew better to say anything else. So he fell across the seat and started taking his clothes off . . . like he was on drugs. And it's forty degrees outside."

An irate Paul stripped down to his boxer shorts, throwing his clothes on the floor. He staggered back to the steering wheel, grabbing it from Connor and slamming down the throttle.

"I fell back into the bottom of the boat and grabbed Mallory and told her to hold on," said Anthony. "She sat on my lap . . . and I put my head on her chest trying to block the wind and closed my eyes."

Then Paul took his foot off the throttle and went to the front of the boat to confront Morgan, accusing her of being disloyal and not taking his side. Connor took the wheel to keep the boat on course.

"He just started calling her a bitch," recalled Miley, "and was like, 'You're such a whore.' And [he] was really yelling at her and Morgan was yelling at him, too."

Morgan pushed him away and asked, "Are you going to hit [me] like you have all those times before?" He viciously replied by spitting on her and slapping her in the face. Morgan burst into tears and hid under a blanket on a cooler with Miley, who comforted her.

Paul strutted back to the steering wheel and grabbed it from Connor, who backed off to let him drive. Over the next few minutes, Paul repeatedly left the wheel to scream at Morgan, leaving Connor to drive.

"Paul would argue with me and Connor would take over," said Morgan. "It was like a switch. Paul would get in my face and we would fight and [then he'd] go back and [drive] and Connor would go back to his spot. But my body could tell when Paul was driving and Connor was driving. [Connor's driving] wasn't erratic and felt better."

Around 2:20 A.M., after berating Morgan one more time, Paul stormed back to the helm of the boat, pushing Connor out of the way and flooring the throttle. The Garmin GPS device recorded the boat abruptly going from idling speed to around thirty-five miles per hour.

As the boat sped up, Morgan heard Miley screaming Connor's name and looked up to see Archers Creek Bridge hurtling towards them.

"I saw the bridge coming and I was just in shock," Miley later remembered. "I braced myself [and] at the last second I screamed."

The boat slammed into the bridge's dolphin head of three wooden pilings lashed together, before making a sharp right into two other pilings. It then took off into the air, slamming into the bank and coming to a halt on top of some rocks.

Paul, Anthony, and Mallory were thrown into the freezing water, while the other three were knocked to the floor. Connor hit the console and lost consciousness, suffering multiple jaw fractures and a deep laceration to his face. Miley woke him up, asking if he was all right, and they went to check on Morgan, who had sustained a serious hand injury and was screaming hysterically.

Anthony woke up in the fifty-five-degree water under the bridge on the opposite bank, about forty yards away from the others. The current was so strong that he had to cling to a piling to stop himself from being swept away.

Although it was pitch-black, he managed to swim to the other bank, going from piling to piling. He passed Paul, who was holding onto a piling and lying in the deep mud under the bridge, screaming for Morgan.

As soon as Anthony reached the shore, he asked where Mallory was.

"Miley came running up to me, and said, 'What do you mean where's Mallory?'" Anthony later testified. "And I said, 'She's not up here?'"

"And she said, 'No!'"

Everybody started screaming for Mallory, and Anthony jumped back in the water to look for her.

"That's when I realized something bad had happened," said Miley. "Mallory is missing and [Anthony] was screaming. Paul was still in the water . . . hanging onto the [piling]. I mean he wasn't even yelling like he was scared or anything. He was just yelling for Morgan."

Finally Paul came out of the water only wearing his boxers and socks and went over to Morgan, who told him Mallory was missing and to get away from her.

"She didn't want to talk to him at all," said Miley. "He didn't care that Mallory was missing. It just didn't register with him that she was missing."

21

"Do Y'all Know Alex Murdaugh?"

At 2:26 A.M., while Paul Murdaugh assured everyone it would all be okay, Connor Cook called 911 on his cell phone. Despite his broken jaw he calmly described where they were, although a lot of valuable time would be lost due to confusion.

"911, what's your emergency," asked the female dispatcher.

"We're in a boat crash on Archers Creek," said Connor. In the background, Morgan screamed in pain from her bleeding hand.

"Whereabout on Archer Street?" asked the dispatcher.

"In Archers Creek," replied Connor. "The only bridge in Archers Creek."

"Archer Street?"

It took several more attempts before she understood they were at the Archers Creek Bridge, outside the main entrance of the Parris Island Marine barracks.

"OK, what's going on?" asked the dispatcher.

"We're in a boat crash."

"You're in what kind of boat?"

"A boat crash," said Connor. "We have someone missing."

The operator told him to hang on for a second, while Morgan could be heard screaming, "Mallory!!! Oh my fucking God!!!"

"Who's that in the background?" asked the dispatcher when she returned.

"There's six of us," answered Connor, "and one is missing."

For the next few chaotic minutes, the operator tried to pin down their location, which could have been found with a simple Google search.

"We're under the only bridge in Archers Creek," Connor told her, as Morgan shouted, "I'm losing so much fucking blood! I'm soaked in blood."

"Okay, we're on the way," said the dispatcher. "You need to give me as much information as you can. Is anybody injured?"

"There's one that's injured," replied Connor, "and there's one that's missing."

Eight minutes into the call, Morgan hysterically screamed, "Where are they? They've got to hurry. I got wood all up in my arm. Please hurry."

Connor remained on the phone, patiently giving further directions, as Miley and Anthony walked up to the road leading up to the bridge and flashed a light for EMS to see. But it would seem like an eternity before help arrived.

Three minutes after Connor Cook dialed 911, the Beaufort County dispatcher began alerting EMS, the fire services, and military police to the unfolding emergency. But unfortunately, she sent them to the Russell Bell Bridge—a mile and a half away from the crash site. Over the next hour, dispatchers gave out the wrong location fourteen times to various emergency services, wasting valuable time to save Mallory Beach.

"We've got a water emergency under that Bell Bridge," the Beaufort County dispatcher told the military police at 2:29 A.M. "A boat hit the bridge. We have one person missing."

"What bridge?"

"The bridge leading onto Parris Island is what I've been told."

When the first responders reached the Bell Bridge and saw no signs of an emergency, they radioed back to the dispatcher.

"No, no, no," she told them. "It wasn't the Russell Bell Bridge."

At 2:40 A.M., Corporal John Keener and Sergeant Troy Krapf of the Beaufort County Sheriff's Office were the first to arrive on the boat crash scene, after first going to the Bell Bridge. Fire and EMS were still trying to find their way there.

"I was met by Connor Cook, Miley Altman, and Paul Murdaugh at the base of the bridge," remembered Corporal Keener. "Paul appeared to be highly intoxicated . . . and only had on a pair of boxers, soaking wet. And there was another girl in the boat that had her hand cut up pretty good that was kind of sitting there in shock. Everybody was upset."

After getting a brief physical description of Mallory Beach—that she had blond hair and was wearing a pink shirt—Keener radioed it to the dispatcher.

The two officers searched the shoreline on either side of the bridge down current, but there was no trace of Mallory in the dense fog and the soft pluff mud was too thick to venture any farther.

"I was able to follow a blood trail and footprints," said Keener. "It led from the boat, under the bridge, and out into the marsh . . . one of them had already been out there looking for Mallory Beach."

The boat was beached at the base of the Archers Creek Bridge, with its hull split down the middle. There was a huge six-foot gash and severe damage to the port side. It was lying on the rocks at a forty-five-degree angle, with the bottom of the 115-horsepower motor a foot above the water.

It was impossible to gauge the damage to the bridge in the heavy fog.

Officer Keener tried to round everybody up so he could get their names and ages and find out what had caused the crash. They were all underage and he could smell alcohol on their breath, but the half-naked red-haired boy was by far the drunkest.

When Keener asked who was driving when the boat crashed, everyone was evasive.

"They didn't want to say who was driving the boat," he said, "because they were all drinking and they didn't want to get in trouble, and their friend's missing."

Anthony was still desperately looking for Mallory and screaming her name, while Paul wandered around aimlessly in the marsh in his sodden boxer shorts and nothing else.

He tried to use his soaking wet cell phone to call his grandfather for help, throwing it on the ground in frustration when it didn't work.

"Can I use your phone?" he asked Corporal Keener.

"I ain't got my phone on me, brother," replied the officer. "You dropped yours on the grass right back there. What's your last name, buddy?"

"Murdaugh," answered Paul, then spelling out each letter.

Finally, Miley Altman handed Paul her phone, and he called his grand-father, Randolph Murdaugh III. He said that Connor Cook had been driving the boat when it crashed and he needed to come immediately. Paul had no idea where they were and gave the name of the wrong bridge.

"We were running hard and hit the Lemon Island/Callawassie Bridge," Paul drunkenly sobbed. "Mallory is gone and we can't find her."

Connor and Miley both overheard the conversation, in total disbelief that he was already trying to blame it all on Connor.

At 2:55 A.M., more than half an hour after Connor's initial 911 call, fire and water rescue services began arriving. Behind them were officers from the Port Royal Police Department, the South Carolina Highway Patrol, the Coast Guard, and the Department of Natural Resources, who offi-cially police the Lowcountry waterways.

By the time Beaufort County deputy sheriff Stephen Domino arrived at the scene, it was mayhem.

"Everybody was crying, scared, shocked," he later told CBS's *48 Hours*. "Just worried about their friend."

As they waited and waited for EMS to arrive, Deputy Domino calmed Anthony Cook down enough to interview him in the back seat of his pa-trol car. Anthony said his mother worked for SLED (South Carolina Law Enforcement Division) and he needed to call her.

"Y'all need to come to Beaufort quick," he told his mother, sobbing. "We hit a bridge in the boat. Connor's messed up bad, we can't find Mal-lory. Morgan's messed up bad . . . we can't find Mallory."

He asked his mother to call Mallory's parents and tell them what had happened.

Just then Paul Murdaugh walked toward them with a big grin on his face.

"Get that motherfucker there away from me!" yelled Cook. He tried to get out of the car to attack Paul and had to be restrained.

"Calm down," Deputy Domino told him. "I'm hanging with you, okay?"

"That motherfucker needs to rot in fucking prison," Anthony screamed back. "He ain't gonna get in no fucking trouble."

Then Paul drunkenly smiled at Anthony, who completely lost it.

"Bo, you fucking smiling like it's fucking funny!" he screamed. "My fucking girlfriend's gone, Bo! I hope you rot in fucking hell!"

Domino asked if the half-naked drunken guy he was shouting at had been driving the boat when it crashed.

"He was the last one driving whenever I got down on the floor and held onto my girlfriend," Anthony replied. "Yes, sir. I begged to drive the fucking boat."

Breaking down, he asked how he could live with himself now that his girlfriend was gone.

"Is anybody in the water looking for her?" he asked. Deputy Domino assured him that the Coast Guard already had their boats in the water and a helicopter was on the way.

"Do y'all know Alex Murdaugh?" he asked.

"Yeah, I know that name," replied Domino.

"That's his son."

"His son [was] driving the boat?"

"Good luck!" Anthony told him, sarcastically.

The first two ambulances finally arrived at 3:04 A.M., thirty-eight minutes after the 911 call. Paul was being totally uncooperative and police were keeping him away from Anthony, who remained in the police cruiser.

EMS paramedic Shayna Orsen wrapped Paul in a blanket to keep him warm, but he kept insisting he was fine and didn't need any medical attention. He was still very drunk and getting confrontational with the deputies, who were trying to help him.

"Paul was just going on and on and on," said Miley. "He got into . . . the officer's face and was like, 'You think that you're a bigger man than I am?'"

The police put Miley and Connor in one ambulance while Morgan was taken off the boat on a stretcher. When an EMS worker removed the bloody towel from her injured hand, she had a panic attack. She was carried to an ambulance and taken to Beaufort Memorial Hospital.

Anthony refused to go to a hospital, even though he had a shoulder injury, insisting on staying at the scene and searching for Mallory.

Paul almost had to be handcuffed in order to get him into the ambulance with Miley and Connor. Then he tried to get out to find Morgan and had to be restrained.

"The Murdaugh boy was just being belligerent," said Corporal Keener. "He was being so stupid and drunk [and] wouldn't listen to anyone. He couldn't comprehend anything and [was] falling all over the place."

Finally EMS requested that a deputy ride in the ambulance with Paul for everyone's safety. Then Paul started cursing at a female EMS worker who tried to calm him down. He became so aggressive that the deputy had to strap him down so they could take his blood pressure and run other tests.

"He was being rude," said Miley, "to the point of almost [being] taken to jail, because he wouldn't cooperate."

On the short trip to the hospital, Connor and Miley kept asking if Mallory had been found. But Paul's only concern was to call his dad.

"I need to call Big Red!" he kept saying, using Alex's nickname. "I need to call Big Red!"

At 3:30 A.M., well after the ambulances left, the South Carolina Department of Natural Resources (SCDNR) finally arrived at the scene of the boat crash. The agency would oversee the investigation, and many of its officers knew the Murdaugh family personally, from attending their barbecues and parties over the years.

Conservation officer Austin Pritcher was the first SCDNR officer on the scene. He found around fifty officers from multiple agencies milling around in the heavy fog. Some said that Paul had been driving the boat while others said it was Connor.

Pritcher was informed that one of the boaters was sitting in a patrol car, so he went over to interview a distraught Anthony Cook, who kept asking where Mallory was.

"Who was driving the boat?" asked Pritcher, with his dashcam video recording.

"[When] I grabbed my girlfriend and got down to the bottom of the boat," Anthony said, "Paul was driving."

"Paul was driving?" asked Pritcher.

"Yes, sir," replied Anthony.

Later, in his official SCDNR report, Pritcher wrote that Anthony did not know who was driving the boat when it crashed, contradicting the dashcam video.

22

"HE'S AS DRUNK AS COOTER BROWN!"

At around 3:00 A.M., Morgan Doughty arrived at Beaufort Memorial Hospital and was put in ER Room 16. While she was waiting to be seen by a doctor, she told male nurse Lupe Moreno she was very worried about her missing friend, Mallory Beach. She blamed the crash on her boyfriend Paul's alcohol abuse, saying she was going to break up with him. Morgan then had the nurse call her mother and tell her to come to the hospital.

Soon afterward, Connor Cook was carried into the ER on a stretcher; Miley was walking alongside him. They insisted on being put in the same room. When Miley was told that only one patient could be seen in an ER room at a time, she walked out to the lobby to get a visitor's pass and went back to Connor's room.

Paul Murdaugh was brought in and strapped down on a stretcher, swearing at staff. Photos taken by Pritcher inside ER Room 10 show Paul visibly drunk and still only wearing his wet boxer shorts. Covered in scratches, he's hooked up to a cardiac machine, which he would disconnect three times over the next hour.

When nurse Karen Taylor asked how much alcohol he had consumed that night, he angrily lashed out at her.

"Y'all should be doing your jobs and looking for my friend," he yelled.

Then he was asked what exactly he had been drinking.

"Yes, all kinds of alcohol," was his reply, "[and] all kinds of drugs."

Then he demanded his clothes back, saying he was leaving the ER, and had to be physically restrained.

A few minutes later, Paul's father and grandfather arrived at the ER to do damage control. After checking into the front desk, the two attorneys went straight into Paul's room and ordered him to calm down and start cooperating.

Paul was overheard asking if he was going to be okay, and his grandfather told him to "shut the fuck up!"

His drunken behavior toward the hospital staff bordered on obscene. When ER technician Laura Kent handed Paul a portable urinal, he asked if she was going to hold his penis for him. When she returned to the room to collect his specimen, he lecherously pointed to her buttocks, saying, "That's nice."

Physician assistant Kristin Strickland ran a trauma test on Paul, classifying him as having "Altered Mental Status," because of the severity of the crash and his subsequent irrational actions.

"Paul was clearly intoxicated," said Dr. Mark Mercier, who had been called in because of Paul's unruliness. "[He] was slurring his speech and . . . would fall over anytime he tried to stand."

The nursing staff also noticed how passive Alex seemed toward his unruly son, while his grandfather Randy was visibly angry.

At one point, the former 14th Judicial Circuit solicitor stormed out of his grandson's room, declaring, "He's drunk as Cooter Brown!" a Southern reference to the town drunk that dated back to the Civil War.

For the next hour, Paul's grandfather remained by his bedside while Alex paced up and down the hallways and into the lobby, introducing himself to ER staff. He smelled of alcohol and seemed "on edge." The charge nurse asked a security guard to keep an eye on Alex, as he was "trying to enter other patients' rooms."

Alex made all the medical staff uncomfortable, wandering around and making phone calls. He called Maggie several times, assuring her that Paul was fine but Mallory was still missing.

"She's gone, baby," he was overheard saying. "She's gone, don't worry about her. Love you, bye."

The experienced personal injury lawyer especially wanted to talk to

Paul's longtime girlfriend, Morgan Doughty, presumably so they were on the same page that Connor was driving the boat when it crashed. After he went into her room, Morgan told her nurse not to let Alex back in on any account.

"I was in surgery for two hours," Morgan later told police. "When I got out, Alex Murdaugh kept trying to enter my room multiple times, but my nurse would not allow him to. He kept saying I was with him and that he needed to tell me what to say."

Connor Cook had suffered a fractured jaw and a deep gaping cut under his mouth. He was in terrible pain. ER nurse Elizabeth McAlhaney was assigned to his room and smelled alcohol on his breath as soon as she walked in.

At first, he was very cooperative, but became defensive and vague when the nurse asked what had happened. Miley, who was with him in the room, told another ER worker, Kristin Strickland, that Paul Murdaugh had been driving when the boat crashed. Connor nodded in agreement.

A CAT scan was ordered, and as Connor, under strong pain medication, was being pushed along the hallway in a wheelchair, Alex Murdaugh intercepted them. He asked the CT tech to give them a minute alone.

"Mr. Alex stopped me in the hallway," Connor later remembered. "[He told me] that everything was going to be all right. I just needed to keep my mouth shut and tell them I didn't know who was driving and that he's got me."

Meanwhile, at Archers Creek, the search for Mallory was well underway. There were multiple vessels in the water, including the Parris Island Fire Rescue and the Beaufort Marine Rescue Squadron. There were also scores of people looking from the bridge and along the banks using handheld lights.

The conditions were deplorable, with heavy fog and less than ten feet visibility. It would be hours until the fog cleared and divers and the Coast Guard could join in the search.

At 3:40 A.M., SCDNR Sergeant Adam Henderson arrived at Archers Creek, photographing the wrecked boat from the shore and observing blood on its deck. He introduced himself to Anthony Cook, who was sitting on the ground with his mother, wrapped in a blanket.

Henderson asked if Paul had been driving the boat when it hit the bridge. Still in a state of shock, Anthony replied that all he could say for certain was that Paul had been driving when they'd left the dock at downtown Beaufort.

"He couldn't be sure," remembered Henderson.

At 4:00 A.M., one hour and forty minutes after the crash and three hours after he'd downed the shots at Luther's, Paul was given a blood test for medical purposes. It revealed he had a blood alcohol level of .286, three-and-a-half times the legal limit to operate a boat. It would have been far higher at the time of the boat crash.

But SC Department of Natural Resources, who were in charge of the investigation, never gave him or Connor a standard field sobriety test after they refused to take one at the hospital.

They also failed to seize critical evidence at the crash scene, such as Paul's cell phone, wallet, and clothes. And much of the biological evidence, which was being collected from the boat itself, would mysteriously disappear.

After undergoing the CT scan, Connor Cook was taken back to his room, where his concerned parents were waiting. Alex had previously cornered them in the hallway, suggesting it would be in their interests to hire an attorney named Cory Fleming to represent them in any resulting criminal investigation as to who was driving the boat. He was also seen speaking to Morgan's mother.

At around 4:35 A.M., SCDNR conservation officer Austin Pritcher arrived at Beaufort Memorial Hospital and went straight to Paul's room, where he was still strapped to a gurney with a security guard camped outside. His first question was about who was driving the boat when it crashed.

"Why do you need to know who was driving?" screamed Paul. "That isn't going to help find Mallory. What if it was me who was driving the boat?"

The Hampton County sign welcoming visitors. *(Courtesy of John Glatt)*

In 1920 Randolph Murdaugh Sr. was elected as South Carolina's first 14th Judicial Circuit solicitor, launching a legal dynasty that would rule the Lowcountry for the next eighty-six years. His portrait, along with those of his son Buster and grandson Randy, still hang in the General Sessions courtroom in Hampton County Courthouse. *(Courtesy of John Glatt)*

Randolph "Buster" Murdaugh Jr. served as solicitor from 1940 to 1987 and became legendary for his overly dramatic courtroom antics. *(Courtesy of John Glatt)*

Randolph (Randy) Murdaugh III became the third generation of his family to hold the post of solicitor, from 1987 until his retirement in 2006. *(Courtesy of John Glatt)*

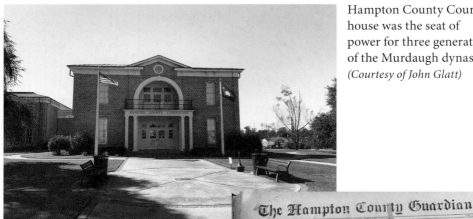

Hampton County Courthouse was the seat of power for three generations of the Murdaugh dynasty. *(Courtesy of John Glatt)*

The shocking July 1940 front page of *The Hampton County Guardian* announcing Solicitor Murdaugh's tragic death after being hit by a train. It remains a mystery as to whether it was an accident or suicide. *(Courtesy of John Glatt)*

Randolph Murdaugh Sr. founded the PMPED law firm in 1910, which went on to became one of South Carolina's biggest, raking in many millions of dollars in personal injury suits. Alex Murdaugh now stands accused of plundering the firm where he was a partner. *(Courtesy of John Glatt)*

LIBBY ALEXANDER and RANDOLPH MURDAUGH
Most Athletic

Alex's parents, Randy and Libby, were high school sweethearts and appeared together in the 1956 Wade Hampton High School Yearbook.

Maggie posted this picture of the happy family dressed to the nines for a December 2015 black-tie event at the Carolina Yacht Club on Facebook.

The entrance to the Murdaughs' hunting lodge home at 4147 Moselle Road, Islandton, where Maggie and Paul were shot dead close to the dog kennels. *(Courtesy of John Glatt)*

Alex, captured in a video by his son Paul's then-girlfriend, Morgan Doughty, taking a shot of booze onboard one of his boats.

Paul Murdaugh shotgunning beer in a competition with friends in another video taken by Morgan Doughty and used in her lawsuit.

Stephen Smith was in young Buster Murdaugh's class at Wade Hampton High School. After his mysterious death in July 2015, Buster became a person of interest for investigators. *(Courtesy of Wade Hampton High School)*

Stephen's yellow Aveo Car, as it was found after his death, with the gas cap still hanging out. *(Courtesy of the South Carolina Highway Patrol Multi-Disciplinary Accident Investigation Team)*

Stephen's twin sister, Stephanie, is convinced he was murdered and there was a cover-up. *(Courtesy of John Glatt)*

Stephen's memorial on Sandy Run Road near the spot where his body was found. *(Courtesy of John Glatt)*

One of the images of Mallory Beach, the drowning victim of Paul Murdaugh's drunken boat crash, which appeared atop the Facebook Memories of Mallory Beach page.

Paul buying alcohol just hours before the boat crash at Parker's 55 Convenience Store in Ridgeland. *(Courtesy of the South Carolina Department of Natural Resources)*

Luther's Rare & Well Done Bar, where Paul and Connor Cook downed a couple of shots each just before the boat crash. *(Courtesy of John Glatt)*

An inebriated Paul plowed his father's boat straight into a pylon at Archers Creek with tragic results. *(Courtesy of John Glatt)*

The badly damaged Sea Hunt boat the morning after the crash. *(Courtesy of the South Carolina Attorney General's Office)*

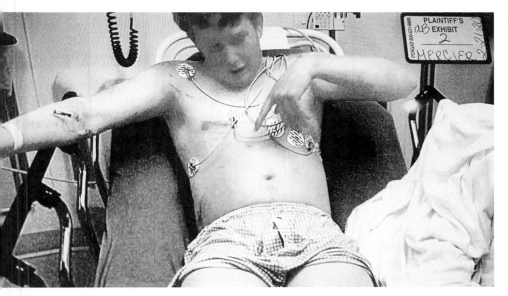

Paul Murdaugh photographed in the emergency room after the crash. "He's as drunk as Cooter Brown," said his angry grandfather Randy Murdaugh when he saw the state he was in.

Paul's mug shot after receiving VIP treatment at his arraignment. *(Courtesy of the SC Attorney General's Office)*

Alex was arrested again in October on charges related to stealing millions in personal-injury payouts from Gloria Satterfield's two sons. *(Courtesy of the Orange County Sheriff's Office)*

Maggie's grave in Hampton Cemetery. Her husband, Alex, stands accused of killing her and their son Paul. *(Courtesy of John Glatt)*

Paul's meager grave in Hampton Cemetery next to his mother's. *(Courtesy of John Glatt)*

Just hours after a judge denied Alex bond, his brother John Marvin and son Buster were spotted and photographed gambling on the Las Vegas strip with the photographs promptly made available to and published by the South Carolina news website FITSnews. When his father asked how he was recognized, Buster responded: "I'm a national figure, I think."

Alex ordered his distant cousin and alleged drug dealer Curtis "Fast Eddie" Smith to shoot him point-blank in the head in a botched suicide attempt. *(Courtesy of the Colleton County Sheriff's Office)*

Alex was arraigned in July 2022 for the murders of his wife, Maggie, and son, Paul. After spending nine months behind bars he was hardly recognizable and had adapted well to prison life. *(Courtesy of the Colleton County Sheriff's Office)*

Stephen Smith's mother, Sandy, was the guest of honor at a Columbia fundraiser in late 2021. *(Courtesy of John Glatt)*

When Pritcher repeated the question, Paul said he was definitely not driving and that these were all his best friends.

"[He] was acting pretty out of control," Pritcher later testified in a sworn deposition. "Bloodshot eyes, slurred speech."

Pritcher then went to interview Connor, who was in his ER room with Miley, waiting to go to a Charleston hospital for surgery on his broken jaw. Connor's father was present, and was observed giving his son "a signal across his neck," telling him not to say anything to the investigator.

"I don't remember hitting anything but the bridge," Connor said, and Miley backed him up, saying she didn't know who was driving either.

The SCDNR investigator went back to Paul's room, asking if he could give an official statement.

"He responded, 'Yes I can,'" stated Pritcher in his official report. "I began to get my forms out when Mr. Randolph Murdaugh and Mr. Alex Murdaugh walked into the room and began to tell Paul that he doesn't need to give a statement to me. I told [them] that I was talking to Paul. Mr. Randolph then said, 'Well, I'm his lawyer starting now, and he isn't giving any statements.'

"That's kind of when everything clicked in who the Murdaughs were."

He then went to interview Morgan Doughty, who was in her room with her mother. When Alex suddenly appeared at the door during the interview, Morgan told the nurse not to let him in. She wanted all the doors and curtains closed, so no one could hear what she was going to say.

Morgan now claimed that Connor had been driving at the time of the crash, because Paul was too drunk.

"She was a little skittish," said Pritcher, "freaked out [and] something was bothering her."

At around 6:30 A.M. Sunday morning, Paul Murdaugh was officially discharged from Beaufort Memorial Hospital. He was given paper scrubs to wear and escorted out by his grandfather. A few minutes later, Paul returned to the ER nursing station demanding to see Morgan, who had just undergone hand surgery and was filling out paperwork.

"It was obvious that [she] did not want to have a conversation with him," said Nurse McAlhaney.

As soon as she saw him, Morgan fled back into her treatment room. Paul tried to hug her, but she pushed him away. His father then arrived to take him home.

23

THE SEARCH

As Paul Murdaugh was leaving Beaufort Memorial Hospital, Renee Beach was learning that there had been a serious boating incident and her daughter Mallory was missing. She immediately got in her car and headed out to Archers Creek, where she met Mallory's father, Phillip.

An area at the foot of the bridge had been set aside for friends and family members of the missing girl, and a chaplain had been summoned. Mallory's parents, who were separated, were told it was too dangerous for them to go down to the water where the wrecked boat lay.

"[They were] obviously upset and wanted information," said Officer Christopher Williams, of the Parris Island Marine Corps Recruit Depot, who was in charge of the entry control point. "I told them there was an active investigation and we were currently searching for their daughter. I had a case of water delivered to the family."

Over the next few hours, more than twenty family members and friends gathered by the bridge, anxiously awaiting word from the various search and rescue teams.

"We are still hoping and praying that we find her alive," said Mallory's sister, Savannah Tuten. "Everybody loves her."

Anthony Cook remained at the scene all day with his parents, refusing to go to the hospital for treatment. He was interviewed by Officer Williams as he waited for news of his missing girlfriend.

"Paul killed my girlfriend," he told the officer, "and Murdaugh was driving at the time of the crash."

By 7:00 A.M., the fog began lifting and the sun broke through, allowing the full-scale search to begin. A US Coast Guard rescue helicopter hovered above, searching the soggy marshes around the accident scene. A twenty-nine-foot response boat was also on its way. And SCDNR divers were preparing to search under the bridge, as sonar had shown blurred images that could have been the missing girl.

"I just kept praying that they would see her on a sandbar or somewhere," remembered Renee Beach. "That she just couldn't get to us, but she was safe."

SCDNR officers examining the fiberglass boat could still smell the alcohol. They found several cans of beer scattered around and large blood stains on the floor where Morgan had been sitting. There were also mud stains from where the ejected boaters had climbed back in the boat to retrieve their belongings.

That Sunday morning, the tragic boat crash was the talk of Hampton Episcopal Church. Sam Crews III, who used to teach Mallory at Wade Hampton, was there with LaClaire Laffitte, whose son Russell was a close friend of Alex Murdaugh, when the subject came up.

All through the morning, curious onlookers began showing up at the Archers Creek Bridge. SDNR officers taped off the whole area, to stop them from taking photographs and disturbing the crime scene.

At 12:40 P.M., the damaged boat was removed from under the bridge and towed to the Battery Creek landing on Parris Island for a forensic examination. Earlier, Alex's younger brother had called SCDNR Captain Pritcher to volunteer his services in moving the boat.

"He just called me," said Pritcher, "and said, 'Hi, this is John Marvin Murdaugh, and I'm bringing the trailer.' He had to go pick it up over at their house over by Chechessee."

John Marvin, who knew many of the SCDNR officers from Murdaugh barbecues and hunting weekends, was waved through to the crime scene with his pickup truck and trailer, though his nephew was being investigated for causing the boat crash.

After John Marvin left, another boat pulled the Sea Hunt off the rocks and towed it to Parris Island. But the Murdaughs had demanded SCDNR get a search warrant for the boat, so investigators had to wait several hours for a judge to sign one.

At 5:05 P.M., after getting the search warrant to look for any evidence of "negligent or reckless operation of the boat," the boat was photographed from all angles, before being processed forensically to try and determine who had been driving when it crashed. It had rained overnight, so most of the fingerprints had been destroyed.

"I did not locate any fingerprints," said Sergeant Brandon Disbrow of the Beaufort County Sheriff's Office. "There were two White Claw alcohol cans in the back of the boat, which were open and mostly empty."

Investigators also found twenty-two unopened bottles or cans of beer, and twenty-seven empty ones.

After being swabbed for DNA, the boat was hooked up to John Marvin's trailer and taken to the SCDNR laboratory in Charleston. Much of the forensic evidence that was collected would later go missing.

On Monday morning, more than twenty-four hours after Mallory Beach went missing, *The Beaufort Gazette* reported that her family was asking for prayers. As the search entered its second day, they still remained hopeful for her "safe return."

Anthony Cook was back at the bridge, his arm in a white sling, as he anxiously waited with Mallory's family for any news. He gave a dramatic interview to *The Beaufort Gazette* reporter Stephen Fastenau, saying he had clung to a bridge piling after being ejected from the boat, screaming for Mallory.

"I knew that if I didn't turn back then," he said, "I wouldn't make it."

The search was now systematically expanding out from Archers Creek Bridge, with the chances of Mallory being found alive fast diminishing.

"The problem is we don't have an exact location," explained SCDNR captain Robert McCullough. "It doesn't look like a big area until you start searching the bottom, and it's a huge area. The other problem is with the fast-moving water . . . you could get pulled out a long way if you're struggling or fighting or have a life jacket on."

Later that morning, Morgan Doughty texted Captain Pritcher, asking to change her statement. She met him at the Port Royal Police Department for a second interview.

"Last night it all started coming back to me," she said. "I have the strongest feeling Paul was driving."

A couple of hours later, while Connor Cook underwent surgery on his fractured jaw, his parents met Cory Fleming in his office. They hired him to represent their son in any resulting criminal investigation, completely unaware that he was Paul's godfather and Alex's best friend.

After hearing that Paul was driving the boat when it crashed, Fleming instructed Connor not to cooperate with law enforcement and direct them to him instead.

Later that day, the 14th Judicial Circuit solicitor, Duffie Stone, recused himself from the criminal investigation because of his close ties to the Murdaugh family. In a letter to South Carolina attorney general Alan Wilson, he asked him to take over the case.

"SCDNR is currently investigating a boating incident," read Stone's letter. "One of the occupants of the boat is still missing. As there is a possibility that charges may be brought and [SCDNR] may need legal assistance with their investigation, I am asking that you either assign someone from your office or another Solicitor's Office to this case."

Meanwhile, said a 14th Judicial Circuit spokesman, the former solicitor Randy Murdaugh and his son Alex would continue to work for the office on other criminal cases.

On Tuesday morning, *The Beaufort Gazette* reported that alcohol may have been a factor in the crash, with some of the underage boaters lawyering up and refusing to be interviewed by SCDNR investigators. Asked if anyone on the boat had been tested for blood alcohol content, SCDNR spokesman Captain McCullough replied, "Not that I'm aware of."

The search for Mallory Beach had become a recovery effort, and for the next four days, her family and friends waited by the bridge for any news. They would be joined by scores of other boaters who answered the

Beach family's plea to join in the search. SCDNR even set up a special hotline for anyone in the boating community who had seen anything "abnormal."

"We are asking crabbers and fishermen to keep their eyes open," said Mallory's uncle Randy Beach.

On Friday, March 1, six days after Mallory Beach went overboard, the Port Royal Police Department reported that the underage boaters had all been "grossly intoxicated" when law enforcement had first arrived. Investigators had narrowed down the driver at the time of the crash to two of the six passengers. Although none of the boaters were named, the report revealed that the boat was owned by Alex Murdaugh.

Around 1:30 P.M. on Sunday, March 3, local fisherman Kenneth Campbell and his brother Keith went out on their boat to look for Mallory. It was their day off, so they decided to join in the weeklong search.

"That accident was front page of the paper," said Kenneth. "Everybody seemed to know somebody involved in it [and] the whole community was out there looking."

Soon after setting off from the Broad River boat landing, they spotted someone lying in the grassy marshes about five miles downriver from the crash site. As they approached, they saw that it was a white female with blond hair lying facedown in the muddy bank of a small creek, fully clothed with boots on. They immediately called 911.

"We're on the search team rescue," Kenneth told the operator. "We think we've found her."

Within minutes of their arrival, the Beaufort County Sheriff's Office identified the body as Mallory Beach. It was then photographed before being put in a yellow body bag and transported to Beaufort County deputy coroner David Ott's office for autopsy.

That morning, Phillip and Renee Beach had gone to church to pray for their daughter. They were driving toward the boat landing after the service when they spotted a lot of activity.

"We'd seen these cars pull up," Phillip later told ABC's *20/20*, "and I looked at this one gentleman with a shirt and it said 'Coroner' on it. I just knew."

On Monday morning, the coroner performed an autopsy, finding the cause of death to be drowning and secondary blunt force trauma to the head. Later that day, the boutique where Mallory had worked posted a moving tribute on the front window.

"Our sweet Mallory was found on Sunday," it began. "Unfortunately, it was not the outcome we were praying for. Our Retail Therapy family is absolutely heartbroken. ☹ . . . Rest in Peace sweet baby girl! We love you Mallory!!❤❤"

On Thursday morning, more than five hundred mourners attended Mallory's funeral at the Open Arms Fellowship Church in Hampton. Almost a quarter of the small town turned up to honor the tragic nineteen-year-old, who was remembered for her love of animals, family, and strong faith in God.

Paul Murdaugh attended with his parents and later went to the cemetery for Mallory's burial.

"Many of us on the outside would say, 'What a disaster,'" Pastor James Porter told the mourners. "But God said, 'No, no. I got a plan for peace.'"

24

"THE MURDAUGHS ARE OUT TO PIN IT ON HIM"

Over the next week, Alex Murdaugh used all his power and influence to blame Connor Cook for Mallory Beach's death. Well aware that a murder charge was possible, he was trying to shield Paul from any criminal responsibility that could blacken the Murdaugh name.

Scheduled SCDNR interviews with Connor Cook, Miley Altman, and Morgan Doughty were abruptly canceled. Only Anthony Cook would cooperate with law enforcement, giving a written statement that Connor now denied driving the boat when it crashed.

"Anthony said that he spoke with his cousin Connor Cook," wrote SCDNR inspector Yongue in a report. "He was scared because 'The Murdaughs' are out to pin it on him."

Under the Fifth Amendment, there was nothing that could be done to compel the suspects to talk, and if they lied, they risked being prosecuted for perjury.

SCDNR spokesman Captain McCullough told *The Beaufort Gazette* that criminal charges were "very possible," including reckless homicide, which carries a fine of up to ten years' imprisonment.

"Worst-case scenario would be murder," he said. "That would be the max charge that would be available, but I don't know if the evidence would show that."

* * *

While the SCDNR officers investigated Paul Murdaugh, his father was busy working on a second settlement of up to $5 million for Gloria Satterfield's wrongful death. This was on top of the $505,000 he and Cory Fleming had already received. With Chad Westendorf of Palmetto State Bank acting as the Satterfield estate's personal representative, her two sons still had no idea what was going on.

Fleming held mediation talks with the Nautilus Insurance Company, where Alex had a $5 million umbrella policy. He pressured them to settle quietly before the case reached a Hampton County courtroom, telling the adjuster how jurors would always favor a Murdaugh. According to later depositions, Alex was threatening to admit full liability for Gloria's death in front of a jury, leaving the insurance company wide open to a massive payout.

A few days later, on March 20, Renee Beach filed a wrongful death lawsuit in Beaufort County against Parker's 55 convenience store and Luther's Bar, which had sold alcohol to an underage Paul Murdaugh before the boat crash, as well as the hosts of the oyster roast. With the surviving boaters refusing to cooperate with the SCDNR investigation, Mallory's parents worried about a cover-up. They filed the lawsuit hoping to force the survivors to be deposed under oath about what had led up to the crash.

"[Mallory's] parents hope that this lawsuit shines a light on the significant dangers posed by the sale or service of alcohol to minors," said the Beaches' attorney, Mark Tinsley, "as well as the dangers of providing children with a place to illegally consume alcohol to the point of intoxication and then let them drive."

The next day, Anthony Cook posted a photograph of himself and Mallory on Facebook, alongside a harrowing personal account of the boat crash and the pain he was in.

"I have to live the rest of my life," he wrote, "with the memory of getting thrown into the freezing pitch-black water with the love of my life in my arms. I had to swim against that current for fifteen minutes in a panic screaming her name, begging her to answer me."

He wrote that he now lay in bed every night "crying myself to sleep," and was fed up with the social media obsession about it.

"It may just be some '19 year old girl' to some of you," he wrote, "but that was MY HEART!"

That very night, R. Alexander Murdaugh was being feted at the 2019 Frampton Court of Honor Induction Dinner at the Columbia Metropolitan Convention Center. More than a hundred alumni from University of South Carolina Law School's Kappa Alpha Order fraternity honored him for his outstanding service and accomplishments.

"Alexander," read the official citation, "is a Hampton, SC attorney and serves as the Assistant Solicitor for the 14th Judicial Circuit. He completed his term as President of the South Carolina Association for Justice in 2016. Brother Murdaugh is now on the Board of the Arnold Fields Community Endowment and was Chairman of the Hampton County Democratic Party from 1996–2006."

On Friday, March 29, attorney Mark Tinsley, representing the Beach family, filed a new wrongful death lawsuit in Hampton County, after dismissing the first in Beaufort County. This time it included Randolph III, Alex, and his son Buster.

It accused Paul's grandfather of allowing minors to consume alcohol at his river house and leave in an "intoxicated state." It also alleged that Alex allowed his minor son to purchase and drink alcohol on a regular basis, and claimed Buster gave his underage brother his license in order to buy alcohol.

"[Randolph Murdaugh] undertook a duty to supervise minors' consumption of alcohol," read the lawsuit, "so as not to allow them to unnecessarily endanger themselves or others, including Mallory Beach."

Under South Carolina law, a lawsuit can be filed in whatever county a defendant resides, explained Tinsley, adding that the Murdaughs were judicially "sophisticated" and the mounting evidence against them was indisputable.

"What motivated me was getting evidence of everything," Renee Beach later told *20/20*. "I knew who we were up against and how things would probably disappear if we didn't act quickly."

In the wake of the new lawsuit, Connor Cook fired Cory Fleming and hired attorney Joe McCulloch instead. The Murdaughs in turn hired noted Columbia attorneys Jim Griffin, known as a "white-collar crime specialist," and prominent multimillionaire Democratic State Senator Dick Harpootlian to represent Paul.

Five weeks after Mallory Beach's tragic death, there was growing outrage as people questioned why no legal action had yet been taken, with the finger pointing straight at Paul Murdaugh.

"It has been 38 days since the fatal boat crash and no charges have been filed," stated a front-page story in that week's *Hampton County Guardian*. "No one has stepped forward to claim responsibility as the driver of the boat."

The Murdaughs refused to comment on the Beach lawsuit, only issuing a media statement through their family law firm, PMPED.

"Our thoughts and prayers have and will continue to go out to the Beach family," it read, "and all families and friends affected by this tragedy."

Under increasing pressure to take action, SCDNR spokesman McCullough defended the investigation, saying it was not on the "public's timeframe" and progressing well, and adding that the South Carolina Law Enforcement Division, SLED, had been called in.

"The case will come to fruition," he promised. "And it will work out."

On April 5, 2019, *The Beaufort Gazette* printed a damning indictment of four generations of the Murdaugh dynasty. It was a thoroughly researched, no-holds-barred history that would prove to be a game changer.

"Powerful SC family faces scrutiny following boat crash that killed 19-year-old woman," ran the headline alongside portraits of Randolph Sr., Buster, and Randy Murdaugh, all still hanging in the Hampton County's General Sessions Courtroom A.

"For nearly a century, the Murdaugh name has stood for power, justice, and big money," it began. "But in an odd twist of fate, four members of the Murdaugh dynasty are now implicated in the fatal boat crash, exposing the youngest to possible criminal charges, and two older generations to civil liability."

It outlined how after the boat crash, which had involved heavy drinking, Paul's father and grandfather had arrived at Beaufort Memorial Hospital, stopping all interviews and preventing the "grossly intoxicated" minors from being Breathalyzed.

"Some kind of action should have been taken," said SC Crime Victims' Council executive director, Laura Hudson. "I'm surprised that nothing has taken place."

The article also mentioned the July 2015 death of Stephen Smith, long rumored to have involved young Buster Murdaugh.

"Investigators reported he was the victim of a hit-and-run accident," read the article, "despite police reports showing no evidence that ever took place."

Stephen's mother, Sandy Smith, was quoted, saying that her son would never get justice in Hampton County.

As the pressure mounted to indict Paul Murdaugh, 14th Circuit judge Perry Buckner, who had been a key speaker at Randy Murdaugh's Order of the Palmetto Award Ceremony, recused himself from the case because of his close ties to the family. So did Judge Carmen Mullen, who had attended law school with Alex.

That same day, it would later be alleged, Alex stole a six-figure sum from a landmark personal injury case, where Judge Buckner had awarded a PMPED client $2.25 million. It had all hinged on whether a bigamous marriage should be recognized under South Carolina law.

Charles and Blondell Gary of Yemassee were married with two children when they divorced sometime in the 1970s. Then in 1982, Charles married again and after that marriage broke up, he remarried Blondell in November 1999—two years before his divorce was finalized.

The couple lived together as husband and wife until February 2012, when fifty-seven-year-old Blondell was killed after an ambulance they were traveling in crashed into a tree.

As personal representative to her parents' estate, Angel Gary then hired Alex Murdaugh and PMPED to file a wrongful death lawsuit against Lowcountry Medical Transport for reckless negligence causing Blondell's death. PMPED reached a settlement in 2015 for $2.25 million.

A few months later, Angel filed a petition in Hampton County Court, accusing her father of bigamy when he had remarried her mother, rendering the marriage void. Charles denied it, asserting that as Blondell's surviving spouse he was the sole beneficiary of her estate.

On November 13, 2015, Judge Buckner ruled in favor of Alex Murdaugh's client Angel Gary, stating her father's "purported marriage to Blondell Gary was void from its inception."

Charles subsequently appealed Judge Buckner's decision in the South Carolina Court of Appeals and lost.

Then on April 11, 2019, Alex Murdaugh allegedly diverted a $112,500 wrongful death settlement check, meant for the Estate of Blondell Gary, into his bogus Forge bank account for his own personal use.

A few days later, the newly formed Malz Palz, a nonprofit set up in honor of Mallory Beach to raise money for the Hampton County Animal Shelter, staged a special event to thank the first responders who had taken part in the search. The Beach family had decided that all memorial donations should go to the shelter to celebrate Mallory's love of animals.

Within the first three months, it raised almost $50,000 to build a new animal shelter in Hampton.

25

THE ARREST

On Thursday, April 18—which would have been Mallory Beach's twentieth birthday—Paul Murdaugh was indicted on one count of causing her death while boating under the influence of alcohol or drugs. He was also charged with two counts of causing great bodily harm to her and Connor Cook.

Paul now faced a maximum of fifty-five years in prison, if found guilty of all three felony counts. The case would be prosecuted by South Carolina Attorney General Alan Wilson's Office, after the current 14th Circuit solicitor, Duffie Stone, had recused himself.

Paul's attorney, Jim Griffin, refused to comment on the indictments, saying he had not seen them yet.

The Beach family said they were relieved Paul had finally been charged, as they had expected the Murdaughs to dodge another bullet.

"Everyone was thinking it wouldn't get resolved," Phillip Beach told *The Beaufort Gazette*. "My faith has been strong . . . prayers answered."

Later, on Facebook, Renee Beach poignantly wished her daughter a "Happy Birthday in heaven."

"I never imagined I wouldn't be able to celebrate your 20th birthday with you," she wrote.

From the beginning, Paul Murdaugh was treated very differently from any other defendants. He was never ordered to turn himself in for arrest and processing before his first court appearance to set bond. He also waived his right to a preliminary hearing, where all the evidence against him would have been aired in open court.

At 11:20 A.M. on Monday, May 6, Paul Murdaugh walked into Beaufort County Court with his parents for his arraignment. His grandfather did not attend. The fifteen-minute hearing was in front of South Carolina's 15th Circuit judge Steven H. John, as 14th Circuit judges Buckner and Mullen had both recused themselves from the case.

Paul entered the courtroom wearing a dark suit and blue checked shirt, taking his seat at the defense bench as his father went over to shake Phillip Beach's hand. The courtroom was packed with reporters, local attorneys, and members of the public.

"He is presumed innocent," his lawyer Dick Harpootlian told Judge John, after waiving the reading of the three indictments. "He's pleading not guilty, and as a result, he should be afforded a release on his own reconnaissance. His parents and grandparents have lived in this community for literally a hundred years."

Prosecutor Megan Burchstead of the SC Attorney General's Office described Paul Murdaugh's alcohol consumption as worrying.

"We would have some concern as to the danger to the community, given that this case involves the use of alcohol," she said. "It would be a concern of the state pending stress at trial that we would not have a misuse of alcohol."

In a defense memorandum previously filed into court, Murdaugh's attorneys wrote that Paul was not a flight risk and would surrender his passport.

"Paul has very strong family ties to the community," it read, "so much that his family ties have led to an increase in media coverage of this tragic accident."

Judge John released Murdaugh on a $50,000 personal recognizance bond, on the condition that he surrender his passport and not leave the five counties comprising the 14th Judicial Circuit.

"No evidence [has been] presented to this court," said the judge, "that the defendant will not appear when he is called to court. In fact, all the evidence points otherwise."

At the end of the hearing, Paul Murdaugh was given the VIP treatment as he was escorted out of the back of the courtroom to have his mug shot and fingerprints taken. When a bailiff came forward to cuff him, the prosecutor told him it was unnecessary. As Paul left the courtroom he was followed by a SLED agent carrying an ancient wooden fingerprint machine, so he would not have to be processed in jail like anybody else.

"I recognized it from forty years ago," said defense attorney Jared "Buzzard" Newman, who happened to be in court for another case. "That was all prearranged."

The onetime 14th Circuit assistant solicitor under Paul's great-grandfather Buster was disgusted by the deferential treatment Paul was receiving.

"The optics on that were horrible," said Newman. "I mean [Alex's] son walking in and out of the courthouse getting charged with a couple of counts of felony DUI with death and great bodily injury. If he'd been my son, and I had the power, I'd say, 'You're going to walk into that jail like everybody else.'"

Twenty minutes later, Paul returned to the courtroom with his attorneys, before leaving with his parents and refusing to answer reporters' questions.

When Paul Murdaugh's mug shot, taken with an iPhone 7 in a courthouse hallway, was later released by the attorney general's office, he was not wearing the orange scrubs usually worn by defendants facing criminal charges. Instead the defendant, now in his sophomore year at the University of South Carolina studying criminology, was dressed in his preppy checked shirt, a smirk on his face.

Two months earlier, Nautilus Insurance Company had caved on Alex Murdaugh's threats to tell a Hampton County jury he was responsible for Gloria Satterfield's death. The company agreed to pay out $3.8 million, on top of the $505,000 wrongful death settlement from Lloyd's of London.

On April 11, the Satterfield estate's representative, Chad Westendorf, signed a release, with Nautilus agreeing to the settlement.

But under South Carolina law, it then had to be officially ratified by 14th

Circuit judge Carmen Mullen, who had graduated in the same law class as Alex Murdaugh and Cory Fleming.

The May 13 settlement hearing came just three days after Paul Murdaugh's bond hearing, which Judge Mullen had recused herself from. It took place behind closed doors in the judge's chambers in Hampton County Courthouse. Only Westendorf, Fleming, and Judge Mullen were present, and there was no court stenographer or law clerk.

Fleming asked the judge, as a favor, not to name Alex Murdaugh in the official settlement papers, citing his being sued in the boat crash civil action. He explained that Alex wanted to avoid unwanted scrutiny of his assets by the Beach family attorney, especially the recent multimillion-dollar Satterfield wrongful death payout.

"I understand," Westendorf would later testify under oath that Judge Mullen had replied. Fleming then told her, "We're not going to file it because of publicity over the boating accident, and she said, 'Okay.'"

Judge Mullen then signed the order approving settlement, which was never given a case number or officially filed into the court records. But it did give the court's stamp of approval to release a total of $4,305,000—comprising the initial $505,000 payout and the new $3.8 million one.

Nearly all of it was soon siphoned into Alex's Forge bank account, with Fleming and his law firm receiving $166,000 and Westendorf getting $30,000. Within a few months, the rest of the Satterfield payout was in Alex's personal account, used to pay off a $100,000 credit card debt and write a $300,000 check to his father.

Gloria Satterfield's two needy sons, Tony and Brian, were blissfully unaware of any of the payouts for their mother's death and that they should have been millionaires.

That spring, young Buster Murdaugh was kicked out of the University of South Carolina School of Law in his second semester for low grades and plagiarism. It was a huge embarrassment for the Murdaughs, after four generations of the family studying for the bar there.

Alex immediately started calling in favors to reinstate his eldest son, who was supposed to continue the family's legal dynasty, finally paying a top Columbia attorney and fixer $60,000 to make it happen.

"There was an alleged cheating scandal," said Murdaugh family friend Kim Brant, "in which he reportedly submitted work that was not his but a close friend's."

In the meantime, Buster had started dating another USC School of Law student named Brooklynn White. Over the next several years, the relationship blossomed, and Brooklynn was accepted into the Murdaugh family after getting her law degree in 2021.

At the end of June, Randolph Murdaugh III was appointed Grand Marshall of that year's weeklong Watermelon Festival. After all the negative publicity of his grandson's drunken boat crash, it was a welcome opportunity for the former solicitor to take center stage once again for one of South Carolina's biggest outdoor events.

John Marvin drove a red tractor down Hampton's main street, towing a colorful float with Randy Murdaugh and two of his granddaughters under a large umbrella.

"Mr. Randolph Murdaugh the Third," intoned the commentator on WTOC-TV, which was broadcasting the entire parade live. "He received the Order of the Palmetto—that's the highest civilian honor you can receive for South Carolina. He was the 14th Circuit solicitor from 1986 to 2006."

Five months after the boat crash, Paul Murdaugh's attorneys, Jim Griffin and Dick Harpootlian, filed a motion to relax Paul's bond conditions.

On July 29, his father brought him to the Beaufort County Courthouse so his lawyers could plead his case in front of 12th Judicial Circuit judge Michael G. Nettles. Mallory Beach's parents were in the public gallery but did not speak during the ten-minute hearing.

Griffin told the court that Paul needed his $50,000 bond restrictions amended, so he could continue his criminology studies at USC in Columbia. The current bond only allowed him to move within the five counties under the 14th Circuit.

Prosecutor Megan Burchstead voiced the state's "real concerns" about the defendant's drinking in a college situation. She argued for a higher bond and an ankle monitoring bracelet.

"Most of us who have been to college," she told the judge, "understand the potential peer pressure for alcohol."

Griffin countered that Paul had not violated his bond agreement, and there was no indication that he had drunk any alcohol in the three months since his bond had been set.

"It is illegal for him to drink," said Griffin. "This case has gotten a lot of media attention and scrutiny. [If] he was drinking alcohol underage, I'm confident the attorney general's office would learn about that."

Judge Nettles agreed to allow the defendant to travel anywhere within South Carolina, refusing the prosecution's request for GPS monitoring and a higher bond.

But despite the conditions of his $50,000 bail, Paul continued drinking heavily and had several more run-ins with the law. A few months later, he received a speeding ticket after police clocked him in his truck towing a boat at seventy-eight miles per hour in a fifty-five-mile-per-hour zone. In the police dashcam video, it looked like his father's Sea Hunt fishing boat, having been repaired.

Two months later, the Philadelphia Indemnity Insurance company filed a lawsuit in the US District Court, after Alex Murdaugh filed a claim to cover him from the Beach family's wrongful death suit. The insurance company, which could have been liable for up to $6 million, asked the court to shield them, well aware of the family's legal prowess in South Carolina.

The suit maintained that Murdaugh's two commercial policies only covered "private hunting operations," and that Mallory Beach's wrongful death case was not business related. The filing also mentioned alleged wrongdoing, regarding "the monitoring or supervision" of Paul by his father and older brother.

The court ultimately found that Philadelphia Insurance was not liable, leaving Alex Murdaugh without any insurance protection in the Beach civil suit, which could ruin him.

In mid-November—nine months after the boat crash—the Beaufort County Sheriff's Office released its official report on the case. It revealed that an hour after the crash, Anthony Cook had told investigators that Paul had been driving and was very drunk.

But the report's concluding remarks said otherwise.

"It is unclear at this time whether Connor Cook or Paul Murdaugh was driving the boat," it stated. "All occupants of the boat were underage and were intoxicated."

In the wake of the report, there were questions about whether the Murdaugh family had pulled strings to muddy the waters as to who was driving at the time of the fatal crash. It was later revealed that two of the sheriff's deputies at the scene had direct links to the Murdaughs, who had represented them in other cases.

Now facing financial ruin and sinking in debt, Big Red continued to act like everything was business as usual. Still an assistant solicitor with the 14th Judicial Circuit, Alex served as the lead attorney in a drug case that ended in a mistrial, and he was still handling civil cases for PMPED.

Meanwhile, Maggie had gone into overdrive on Facebook, posting happy family pictures from sports games and other social events. At the end of November, Alex, Buster, and Paul were photographed in their tuxedos, with Maggie in a full fur coat, on their way to what she described as the "Kennedy's Deb Ball."

And even after his huge payout from the Satterfield estate, Alex Murdaugh was always on the lookout for more unsuspecting victims.

Elease Mallory of Hampton hired him after her thirty-five-year-old daughter Sandra Taylor died in June 2019 when the car she was in crashed. The driver was later arrested and charged with DUI.

Murdaugh deftly negotiated a $180,000 settlement from the State Farm Insurance company, which was then sealed in an envelope and kept secret.

The respected attorney told Elease, who was her daughter's estate's personal representative, that he could only recover $30,000, offering to waive his typical legal fees because the payout was so low.

Then, it is alleged, Murdaugh charged her legal fees and minor expenses anyway, before transferring the remaining $152,866 into his fraudulent Forge bank account for his own use.

26

THE SMOKING GUN

In early 2020, Mallory Beach's family's civil suit against the Murdaughs ratcheted up. Paul Murdaugh's girlfriend Morgan Doughty was deposed and she held nothing back, describing how Paul often used his older brother's driver's license to buy alcohol.

"Did anyone appear intoxicated when you left the oyster roast?" she was asked during a deposition in January.

"Yes," she replied. "Paul was really drunk."

"What made you think Paul was really drunk at that time?"

"His hands . . . it's just very weird."

"Was he angry at that time?"

"He was really riled up," she replied. "He wanted to still party and we were all pretty much done."

Morgan then described how she'd gotten into a fight with Paul, and he had left the wheel to rage at her while she sat on a cooler.

"Did he slap you?" she was asked.

"Yes, ma'am."

"Did he spit on you?"

"Yes, ma'am."

"Had he ever done that before?"

"Yes."

"Did Paul take his clothes off on the boat?"

"Yes, ma'am."

"Do you know why he took his clothes off?"

"Because he was drunk," Morgan replied. "He's a crazy drunk. He does weird things."

Then she described Paul furiously hitting the throttle, sending the boat hurtling into Archers Creek Bridge.

"Do you know what caused it to speed up?"

"I've gone over it in my head so many times," said Morgan. "Paul is an angry drunk and he thinks he's invincible. . . . I just feel like he put it in full motion."

At boat crash survivor Miley Altman's deposition, she described the minutes leading up to the crash, when a drunken Paul had slapped Morgan and spat on her in front of everyone.

"Everybody started yelling at him," she testified, "about us not getting anywhere. He got super mad and took off his [clothes] and then threw them [on] the floor of the boat and was just like running without them. It was freezing cold. He was obviously very mad about it or very drunk at the time."

Connor Cook was deposed next, admitting to initially lying about who was driving the boat when it crashed.

"Did you ever say you didn't remember who was driving the boat?" he was asked.

"Yes, sir. A bunch of times."

"When did you decide that you remembered when Paul was driving the boat?"

"I knew the whole time that Paul was driving."

"Why were you not up front with the officers?"

"I was told . . . by Alex Murdaugh that I didn't need to tell anyone who was driving."

In February 2020, a Hampton man named Christopher Anderson hired PMPED's personal injury specialist, Alex Murdaugh, after being injured on the job. After negotiating a $750,000 settlement, Murdaugh channeled the check into his fraudulent Forge account, telling Anderson it would be held in an annuity account for a structured settlement.

By this point, investigators believe, Alex was drowning in debt and was juggling huge sums of stolen money to stay afloat. He was secretly writing hundreds of thousands of dollars in checks to his cousin and drug dealer Eddie Smith and several others, who would later be accused of manufacturing and distributing hard drugs. He was also involved in a drug ring that was laundering more than $2 million of stolen money.

For many years, according to state investigators, Alex had been aided and abetted by his childhood friend Russell Laffitte, soon to succeed his father, Charles, as CEO of Palmetto State Bank.

In February 2015, Laffitte had granted him a line of credit, secured by real property with Palmetto State Bank. Three months later, Alex was more than $50,000 overdrawn but the bank still upped his credit line to one million dollars.

Three years later, his account was still overdrawn, owing nearly $34,000. And by the summer of 2020, Alex's Palmetto State Bank checking account constantly had a negative balance, some months owing as much as $53,300.

On May 1, 2020, Alex Murdaugh sold 515 Holly Street for $375,000, moving the family full-time to Moselle, fifteen miles away in Islandton. The fact that he sold the twenty-year-old four-bedroom house was a surprise to many, as it was one of the finest properties in town.

"They built that house when they moved to Hampton," said Kim Brant. "The boys had grown up in it."

With the mounting stress, the Murdaugh marriage was increasingly on the rocks and there were rumors that Alex was having an affair and seeing more prostitutes.

"He may have had some little piece on the side," said Brant, "because it would follow that the apple isn't falling far from the tree, and there were rumors that Murdaughs have always cheated on their wives."

But Maggie still kept up appearances, posting a happy Father's Day family photograph of her, Alex, and the boys posing by a boat, all smiles.

"Happy Happy Father's Day to the best who everybody loves ❤" she wrote. "You work so hard for your family and our kids r so lucky! Dad, Coach, Teacher, and Best friend 😊 "

By mid-July, though, Maggie had moved out of Moselle and into the Edisto Beach house, reportedly telling a friend she could no longer stand to live with Alex.

Later there would be speculation that Maggie had found out about Alex's heavy opiate use, and that they were sinking into an abyss of debt. Maggie had started selling personal possessions on the resale website Poshmark, including a pair of $27 Coach shoes.

"Alex was running through all these millions of dollars that he had stolen from clients," said Brant, "and I have to wonder how much of that was just to try and keep Maggie happy."

That summer, eighteen months after the boat crash, Gregory Parker, the owner of the convenience store that had sold Paul Murdaugh alcohol prior to the accident, hired a crisis management team to dig up dirt on the Murdaughs. The Beach family's attorney, Mark Tinsley, would later accuse Parker of using a private investigator named Sara Capelli to follow Paul and shoot video of him drinking, partying, and talking about killing Mallory Beach. He also wanted evidence that Buster was gay, in order to implicate him in Stephen Smith's murder.

Over the next year, Capelli secretly tailed Paul, even placing a CCTV camera by the driveway to Moselle. She also hung out at some of the Columbia bars Paul frequented, allegedly buying drinks for underage kids in exchange for information to use against the Murdaughs.

"We think that Parker reimbursed her for buying alcohol for minors," Tinsley later told a judge, "to get information about Paul."

In mid-October, Mark Tinsley filed a motion to force Alex Murdaugh to disclose his net worth and provide a detailed breakdown of all his finances. It came two weeks after mediation fell through and the Murdaughs refused to settle with Mallory's family.

The motion demanded a complete list of all his checking and savings accounts, 401(k) accounts, property, life insurance policies, investments, and all financial bank statements. It threatened to expose Alex's bogus

Forge account and all the other financial smoke and mirrors he had employed over the years to rob his personal injury clients of millions.

"Defendant objects to this Interrogatory on the grounds that it is overly broad and unduly burdensome," his attorneys at the Charleston-based law firm of Haynsworth Sinkler Boyd, P.A., fired back, "and seeks material that is irrelevant, immaterial, and not reasonably calculated to lead to the discovery of admissible evidence."

Alex was also asked by Tinsley if he or anyone acting on his behalf had spoken to any of the other boaters about what had led up to the boat crash that killed Mallory Beach.

"The Murdaugh Defendants object to this Interrogatory to the extent that it seeks information or documents protected by attorney-client privilege," his attorney responded. "Further, the Murdaugh Defendants object to the Interrogatory as vague and ambiguous."

Reporter Mandy Matney of the South Carolina online news blog *FITS-News* covered the story, briefly mentioning how Alex Murdaugh had recently settled another $505,000 wrongful death claim. Her story mentioned a fifty-seven-year-old woman who had died after a trip-and-fall incident somewhere in Hampton County.

Although the story did not name Gloria Satterfield or where it had happened, it provided a direct link to the court papers that did.

It was the smoking gun that would trigger Alex Murdaugh's downfall.

Soon after the *FITSNews* story went online, Tony Satterfield read it and learned about the $505,000 settlement in his mother's wrongful death suit. No one had told him or his brother about it. Three years after their mother's death, they were struggling financially and the family home had recently been repossessed, leaving them homeless.

After reading the story, Tony took it to other members of his family, who decided to hire an attorney to find out exactly what was going on.

"At that point, we knew that the boys had got no money," said his uncle, Eric Harriott Jr. "There's something fishy about this thing."

The Satterfield family contacted lawyer after lawyer about taking the case, but as soon as they heard Alex Murdaugh was involved, they wanted nothing to do with it.

"You don't cross the Murdaughs," a local attorney told *People* magazine, "or if you do cross them, you don't let them find out that it was you who crossed them. Because they'll come down on you, hard. And they'll come on you with all that they've got. They have a lot of influence and power, and they'll use it against their enemies."

It would be months before the Satterfield family could find a South Carolina lawyer with enough guts to take it on.

Now eighty-one years old, Randy Murdaugh was very ill with lung cancer and heart disease and spent October in the hospital for treatment. He was released just in time to spend the holidays with his family.

"Prayers have been answered!" wrote John Marvin on Facebook. "Daddy is home and doing well after being in the hospital for a month! Thank you for all the prayers, calls, texts, cards, etc.!"

Randy's wife, Libby, was suffering from severe Alzheimer's, requiring around-the-clock nursing at their home.

"She has good days and bad days," said her daughter, Lynn Goettee. "Some days she doesn't know what's going on."

Maggie returned to Moselle to spend Thanksgiving with her family. She posted a cheerful photograph of them all together on Facebook.

But at that year's PMPED Christmas party, Maggie kept her distance from Alex and seemed cold and distracted.

"She showed up looking like a million bucks," a former PMPED employee told *People*, "but she and Alex didn't talk at all. They didn't walk around as a couple. She did her thing, and he did his."

Three years after State Trooper Tommy Moore's crippling accident, where he had been rear-ended by a car during a massive snowstorm, his attorney, Alex Murdaugh, informed him that they'd finally won an insurance settlement. After paying more than $250,000 for surgery for his broken neck, Tommy received a $125,000 compensation check in the mail from his insurance company. Then he handed it straight over to Alex, after being told it had to be placed in a special PMPED "frozen" bank account until his workers' compensation case was fully resolved.

"The check was put in his hand," Trooper Moore later testified, "and it never went into an account at that law firm. It went into [his] account and then it was cashed . . . the exact same day that I gave it to him."

Murdaugh also allegedly forged the trooper's signature on a disbursement form, acknowledging receipt of the payout, before transferring it into his fake Forge account.

"It wasn't my signature," said Trooper Moore. "I don't know who actually signed it."

PART IV

27

"MY WIFE AND CHILD HAVE BEEN SHOT BADLY!"

Maggie Murdaugh spent the spring of 2021 renovating her Edisto Beach house and preparing to move on with her life. She weighed the pros and cons of divorcing Alex after twenty-seven years of marriage, telling friends that he made her "miserable." Now that Buster and Paul had left home and she was an empty nester, it was time to start anew.

"She was looking forward to a future without Alex," said her friend Amy Perrine.

At the end of April, Maggie reportedly met with a divorce lawyer in Charleston, who advised her to start "gathering numbers." She had never paid much attention to family finances and where all the money came from, but now she started probing.

A few weeks earlier, Maggie had been socially embarrassed after a check to one of her favorite charities bounced. She had felt humiliated and began asking questions about Alex's stake in the family law firm, PMPED. Something seemed very wrong.

Since her move to Edisto Beach, Alex's PMPED colleagues had noticed how cold she had become toward him. She rarely visited the law firm's offices, and when she did, she ignored Alex.

"When Buster was a clerk here," a former PMPED associate told *People*, "Maggie would come by all the time and greet Alex with a kiss. She was a really sweet lady, but she went from coming over a few times a month to never being here. He stopped talking about her entirely [at the office]."

As she took a hard look into Alex's affairs at PMPED, Maggie may have discovered that he'd been borrowing large sums of money from its associates. In early March, Alex's PMPED law partner Johnny Parker loaned him $150,000 as well as a further $327,000 over the next several months. He was also borrowing heavily from his brother Randy.

But even more puzzling was the torrent of checks from his Bank of America Forge account to Alex's distant cousin and reputed drug dealer, "Fast Eddie" Smith, eventually totaling more than $2 million. Later investigators would allege that Smith was only one of the players in a complex money-laundering and drugs operation that Alex was up to his neck in.

After so many years of marriage, Maggie must have suspected her husband was now a hardened drug addict. Whether or not she ever confronted him on that is another matter.

With the next hearing of the Beach family's civil lawsuit scheduled for June 10 in Orangeburg, South Carolina, Alex was under tremendous pressure. A judge looked certain to order him to reveal all his assets and financial information, exposing the millions of dollars he had stolen over the years. In addition, there was another motion due to be heard, adding Paul and Maggie to the lawsuit and opening Alex up to even more wrongful death liabilities, with zero insurance coverage.

With his father in the hospital dying of terminal cancer, Alex was at breaking point.

Prosecutors believe that this was when Alex decided to murder Paul and Maggie, so that the hearing would never take place and expose him for the cheating fraud he was.

On Saturday, June 5, Maggie Murdaugh accompanied Alex and Buster to a South Carolina Gamecock baseball game. Father and son seemed in high spirits, ordering drinks at the bar, while Maggie sat quietly with Buster's girlfriend, Brooklynn, looking "aggravated" and "mad."

At one point, Alex returned from the bar with a bag of peanuts, practically throwing them at her without saying a word.

"It was weird," a witness told *People* magazine. "Something was off."

On Monday, June 7, a PMPED colleague confronted Alex Murdaugh about money missing from one of his client's accounts and financial mismanagement. He was asked to explain where exactly the cash had gone.

The conversation was cut short when Alex received a phone call informing him that his father had entered hospice care and didn't have long to live.

Soon afterward, Alex called Maggie with the news that his father was in the hospital on his deathbed and that she needed to come and say goodbye. He suggested meeting at Moselle first and going on from there. But Maggie demanded they meet at the hospital instead, as she did not want to be alone with him.

When Alex refused to tell her which hospital her father-in-law was in, Maggie reluctantly agreed to come to Moselle and follow him to the hospital.

During the hour-long drive in her Mercedes from Edisto Beach, Maggie texted a close friend that she was suspicious of her estranged husband.

"It's fishy," she wrote. "He's up to something, but I don't know what."

Maggie arrived at Moselle at around 9:30 P.M., leaving her car running for a quick getaway. Investigators believe that Alex was already waiting by the kennels with an AR-15 rifle at the ready. A bitter argument ensued, during which Alex grabbed the semi-automatic rifle containing 300 Blackout ammo. As she tried to run away, Alex shot her in the back and she fell to the ground facedown. Then her husband and the father of her children stood over her, firing again and again.

Unknown to Alex, Paul was inside the dog kennels, using his smartphone to film an ailing dog he was looking after for a friend. The video audio track captured his parents' "tense" and "strenuous" argument, followed by a series of loud shots.

When Paul rushed out of the kennels to see what was going on, investigators believe his father was waiting with a shotgun. The last thing he must have seen was his dead mother lying facedown in a pool of blood, and his father approaching, brandishing the shotgun.

At close range, Alex fired point-blank into his son's head and then into his chest.

Paul's body was later found "half in and half out" of the kennels, just forty feet away from his mother's body. His cell phone, containing the incriminating audio, would later be discovered under his body.

At precisely 10:07 P.M., after walking to the other side of his property and composing himself, Alex Murdaugh called 911.

"Hampton County 911, where's your emergency?" asked the dispatcher. Alex could be heard weeping in the background.

"This is Alex Murdaugh at 4147 Moselle Road," he gasped breathlessly in an eerie, high-pitched voice. "I need the police and an ambulance immediately! My wife and child have been shot badly!"

He was told to stay on the line, while the Colleton County dispatcher, Angel Fraser, was patched in.

"I have an Alex Murdaugh on the line calling from 4147 Moselle," the first dispatcher told her. "He's advising that his wife and child were shot."

"Okay, and try to give me the address again," Fraser told Alex.

"It's 4147 Moselle Road. I've been up to it now. It's bad," he wailed.

"Okay, and are they breathing?"

"No, ma'am."

"Okay, and you said it's your wife and your son?"

"My wife and my son."

She asked if they were in a vehicle.

"No, ma'am," he replied. "They're on the ground out at my kennels."

"Did you see anyone? Is he breathing at all?"

"No, nobody's breathing," he sobbed.

"Do you see anyone in the area?"

"No, ma'am. No, ma'am."

"And what is your name?"

"My name is Alex Murdaugh."

"Okay," said Fraser, "and did you hear anything, or did you come home and find them?"

"No, ma'am. I've been gone. I just came back. Please hurry," he pleaded.

"We're getting somebody out there to you," said the dispatcher, over the sound of the hunting dogs barking in the background. "What is her name?"

"Maggie and Paul. And please hurry."

After reassuring him that help was on the way, Fraser asked if he was certain they were both dead.

"Is he moving at all, your son?" she asked. "I know you said that she was shot, but what about your son?"

"Nobody," he sobbed. "Neither one of them is moving. All right, I'm going back down there. Are they close, ma'am?"

"I have multiple people coming out there to you, okay," she told him. "I don't want you to touch them just in case they can get any kind of evidence, okay?"

"I already touched them, trying to see if they were breathing," said Alex. "Ma'am, I need to call some of my family."

Before hanging up, the dispatcher asked him to turn on his hazard lights, so he could be seen by the emergency services when they arrived.

Alex then called his brothers John Marvin and Randy to tell them that Maggie and Paul had been murdered. Later, they would recall hearing the harrowing news that would change their lives forever.

"His voice . . . the fear . . . he was just distraught," remembered Randy. "I didn't know if something was still happening. He was only able to tell me it was very, very bad [and] he thought they were dead. And of course, I rushed over."

As soon as John Marvin heard his elder brother's trembling voice that Monday night, he knew that something was terribly wrong.

"He just kept repeating, 'It's not good! It's not good!'" said John Marvin. "'Come as fast as you can! Paul and Maggie have been hurt!' I dropped the phone, got dressed, and started driving."

Twenty minutes after Alex's initial 911 call, Colleton County sheriff's deputies arrived to find the bullet-riddled bodies of Maggie and Paul by the dog kennels. Alex immediately told the officers the killings were probably in revenge for the 2019 boat crash that killed Mallory Beach.

At 10:20 P.M., they called in SLED to help investigate the scene, realizing they had a conflict of interest with a gruesome double murder involving the powerful Murdaugh family.

Under questioning, Alex Murdaugh claimed to have a "cast-iron alibi." At the time of the murders, he had been taking his father to the hospital, before stopping off at Moselle for a nap. When he woke up there were no signs of Paul or Maggie, so he went to check on his mother, who suffered from dementia and lived twenty minutes away in Varnville. He watched a game show with her and a caregiver before heading back to Moselle.

He claimed to have entered through the back entrance to discover Maggie and Paul lying dead by the dog kennels and immediately called 911.

Randy Murdaugh arrived at Moselle to find the first responders sealing off the murder scene as they waited for SLED CSI officers to arrive. Using yellow crime scene tape, they blocked off a perimeter of around fifty yards around Maggie and Paul's bodies, now covered with sheets.

"I could see the white sheets," said Randy. "I still couldn't believe it could be them."

He then was allowed onto the active crime scene to comfort Alex.

"He was standing at a distance looking on in disbelief, crying," said Randy. "He would try to talk and he would break down."

Alex attempted to call his oldest son, Buster, who was 160 miles away in Rock Hill, South Carolina, with the horrible news. But cell reception was so bad that Randy finally had to call him.

At one point, Alex Murdaugh, still a 14th Judicial Circuit assistant solicitor, told law enforcement that he and his brothers would wait inside the house, not wanting to leave. Despite the house being a vital part of the crime scene, they were waved through without any further questions.

Later that night, Alex and his brothers left Moselle to spend the night at their father's house on Yemassee Highway in Varnville.

At 11:05 P.M., twenty-two-year-old Paul Murdaugh was officially pronounced dead with shotgun wounds to the chest and head. His fifty-two-year-old mother was certified dead shortly afterward.

Forty minutes later, SLED Lowcountry regional agents arrived to work with Colleton County deputies on evaluating the crime scene and took over the investigation. They soon found Paul's phone, which had captured his parents' bitter argument just prior to the killings.

Just after midnight, SLED's crime scene investigators arrived and worked through the night, collecting evidence to be submitted to the agency's forensic lab for testing.

They found bullet casings from a shotgun and a semi-automatic rifle by the kennels, revealing that Maggie and Paul had been shot by two different weapons. The assault rifle used to kill Maggie belonged to the Murdaugh family and has never been recovered, though SLED did seize a number of weapons from Moselle for forensic analysis.

At 12:29 A.M. on Tuesday morning, SLED phoned 14th Circuit solicitor Duffie Stone's office to officially inform him about the murders. Stone, who was very close to the Murdaughs, would now play a major role in investigating the double homicide.

Early the next morning, the three Murdaugh brothers returned to Moselle with Alex's son, Buster. Although still an active crime scene, they were allowed to freely roam around the property without any supervision.

Maggie's cell phone was missing, and Buster told investigators he had a special app on his phone that could ping hers. John Marvin agreed to use it to track down Maggie's phone, and was photographed walking towards Moselle's front gate with three 14th Circuit solicitor's office investigators. It would later raise many questions about the Murdaughs' strong ties to Solicitor Stone, and why he hadn't immediately recused himself from the investigation, as he'd done in the Mallory Beach case.

John Marvin later insisted that he was only helping investigators locate Maggie's phone, but upon reaching the gate had realized it was farther away. He had then gotten in a car with Solicitor Duffie Stone's investigators, finally locating the cell phone on a side road just off the property.

SLED investigators secured the scene around Maggie's phone and photographed it, examining it for DNA. Alex helpfully provided the passcode to unlock it.

Later that morning, a black SUV registered to PMPED, which had been parked near the dog kennels, was towed away for forensic examination. A 2019 Chevrolet Silverado, also owned by the law firm, was parked nearby but was not taken away.

Meanwhile, Colleton County Sheriff's deputies had begun canvassing neighboring homes for surveillance cameras. However, it would be months before they discovered private eye Sara Capelli's video camera hidden in the trees outside Moselle's main gate.

28

"There Is No Danger to the Public"

Shock and horror reverberated through the Lowcountry at the news that two members of the powerful Murdaugh family had been brutally murdered. Nonstop police and ambulance sirens all through the night had woken many people up, and word soon spread that Maggie and Paul Murdaugh had been gunned down execution-style.

"The sirens started around ten thirty," remembered Tangie Peeples Ohmer, a longtime friend of the Murdaughs. "Siren after siren after siren. Our families knew one another so it's just been disbelief . . . just shock."

As soon as it was light out, locals started gathering on Moselle Road outside the Murdaugh hunting lodge to see what was going on. But they were kept well back by deputies, now guarding the immense property. There was little to see as the main house and kennels were set so far back from the street.

When approached by reporters, many locals feared talking openly about the Murdaughs because of the consequences.

"We are a close community," a Hampton woman told *The Post and Courier*, refusing to give her name. "Our families have been here for generations. There are all kinds of connections, whether it be friendship or marriage."

It was initially thought that the homicides must be connected to the fatal boat crash that had killed Mallory Beach. Through their attorney, Mark Tinsley, the Beach family immediately issued a statement of condolence to the Murdaughs, volunteering to undergo DNA tests.

"The Beach Family extends its deepest and warmest sympathies to the Murdaugh family during this terrible time," it read. "Having suffered the devastating loss of their own daughter, the family prays the Murdaughs can find some level of peace from this tragic loss."

Others wondered if there was a heavily armed crazed gunman, or gunmen, on the loose in Hampton County.

To put everyone at ease, Colleton County Sheriff's Office spokeswoman Shalane Lowes issued a statement, saying there was nothing to worry about. SLED set up a tip line for any information about the murders.

"At this time," Lowes said, "there is no danger to the public. If information is received that dictates otherwise, we will immediately notify the public."

That confusing statement coming so early on in the investigation gave the impression that law enforcement already knew who was responsible, and it was only a matter of time until an arrest would be made.

Later that morning, the Murdaugh family hired attorneys Dick Harpootlian and Jim Griffin—who had been representing Paul in the criminal proceedings from the boat crash—for a reported up-front payment of $500,000.

"This is a tragic situation, and our prayers are with the Murdaugh family," Harpootlian told a reporter.

All through the morning, tributes and condolences to Alex Murdaugh poured in.

"This is a heinous crime," said Michael Gunn, Murdaugh family friend and the executive director of the SC Association of Justice. "On behalf of the association . . . we extend our deepest sympathies . . . this is an extremely difficult time they're going through."

At noon, the Murdaugh law firm PMPED issued a statement to confirm the deaths.

"The Murdaugh family and PMPED wish to thank everyone for the many calls and condolences in the aftermath of the deaths of Maggie and Paul Murdaugh. We ask for your continued patience and prayers through this tragic time."

Soon afterward, Alex Murdaugh's niece Mary Elizabeth Murdaugh issued a tweet on behalf of the family. "If you are going to report this case please only speak of those who have been killed. It is not respectful to discuss the family or any reputation. They have passed away. [D]o not bring up any piece of negativity [from] the past. Give us a moment please."

The State newspaper posted one of the first stories online about the murders. It would be the beginning of an avalanche of intense press coverage that would bury the Murdaughs over the next few months.

"Tragedy for SC Powerhouse Legal Family: Paul Murdaugh, Mother Found Shot to Death," screamed the headline. "The bodies were found by Alex Murdaugh, husband of Maggie Murdaugh and father of Paul. Alex Murdaugh told authorities he had been out at the time of the shooting and found them when he arrived home."

The *FITSNews* blog reported that Maggie and Paul had been "killed execution-style," according to its police sources.

"The only information sources familiar with the crime scene were willing to share with me," wrote editor Will Folks, "was that it was 'very ugly.'"

But there was an immediate backlash against all the negative publicity the Murdaughs were now getting, as story after story recounted Paul's part in Mallory Beach's tragic death as well as previous family scandals going back generations.

"They are not the monsters the other media outlets are portraying them to be," Tangie Peeples Ohmer told *The Hampton County Guardian*. "My problem with all of this is that, regardless of how anyone feels about Paul's past, a family lost a son, a grandson, a brother, nephew, and cousin! And Maggie paid the ultimate price as well."

Another family friend, Katelyn Ginn, accused the community of not supporting Alex Murdaugh and his family enough in their time of need.

"A husband and father now have to live this life without his life partner and child," she said. "We should not focus on the past or mistakes made, but the fact that there is a family that just had their world turned upside down. They have a very tough journey ahead."

That Tuesday, the SC Attorney General's Office announced it would officially dismiss all criminal charges against Paul resulting from Mallory

Beach's death, as they could no longer proceed. Thursday's scheduled civil hearing was also postponed letting Alex off the hook with having to reveal all his finances.

On Wednesday, *FITSNews* reported that Alex Murdaugh was now a "person of interest" in the double homicide investigation, although it stopped short of naming him as a suspect. A SLED spokesman refused to comment.

Maggie's and Paul's obituaries, prepared by the family, had now been posted online by the Peeples-Rhoden Funeral Home, who were handling funeral arrangements. They made no mention of the horrible way they had died.

"Margaret 'Maggie' Kennedy Branstetter Murdaugh, 52, entered into eternal rest with her son Paul Terry Murdaugh the evening of Monday, June 7, 2021," it began.

It outlined how she had met her husband Alex thirty years earlier at the University of South Carolina, and later raised their two sons in Hampton.

"Maggie had a heart of pure generosity," it read, "and loved welcoming friends and family into her home on any given occasion. Maggie is survived by her loving husband Richard Alexander Murdaugh (Alex) [and] her older son Richard Alexander Murdaugh Jr. (Buster)."

Paul's obituary focused on his love of the outdoors and hunting with his father at Moselle.

"Paul never met a stranger," it read. "He was always eager to lend a helping hand to anyone in need. His personality was one-of-a-kind."

The next morning, Paul's and Maggie's autopsies were performed at the Medical University of South Carolina in Charleston. Colleton County Coroner Richard Harvey refused to release any details about the cause of death, except that they had both suffered multiple gunshot wounds and died on Monday night between 9:00 P.M. and 9:30 P.M.

"SLED is handling all other information," he told reporters.

On Thursday afternoon, Randolph Murdaugh III died at his Varnville home at the age of eighty-one. The former 14th Judicial Circuit solicitor and lead prosecutor in more than two hundred murder cases finally succumbed to lung cancer and heart disease.

His son Alex was reported to have visited him a couple of hours before his passing. His half brother Roberts Vaux, now seventy-five, had also secretly gone to say goodbye and spent an hour with him.

"That was at their house," said Sam Crews III. "It was very low-key and all the family was there waiting on him to die."

Elsewhere in the house was Libby, who was suffering from advanced dementia and knew nothing of her husband of sixty years' death or the murders of her grandson and daughter-in-law.

At 5:20 P.M., PMPED, the law firm founded by Randy's grandfather more than a century earlier, posted the tragic news on its website.

"We are sad to announce the passing of Randolph Murdaugh, III," it read. "Please continue to keep the Murdaugh family in your thoughts and prayers."

LaClaire Laffitte, whose family owns Palmetto State Bank and had always been very close to the Murdaughs, called it a tragedy beyond words.

"Randolph had been sick a while," she said, "and it was really a sad thing to have this much happen to one family in one week."

LaClaire, who runs the Hampton County Museum, feared everyone was losing sight of who had killed Maggie and Paul, and were focusing on the boat crash instead.

"We need to find out who did it," she said. "Everybody really wants to know, what? Why? You just don't know how to comprehend what happened."

At 11:55 A.M. on Friday, June 11, hundreds of mourners gathered at Hampton Cemetery on Holly Street for Maggie and Paul Murdaugh's funeral services. They had been cremated and the double funeral was being billed as a "celebration of their lives."

Law enforcement from a slew of different agencies directed traffic around Hampton. It was a public funeral, although the media were asked to keep a respectful distance. A ring of uniformed officers surrounded the ceremony area by two freshly dug graves, across from where Paul's great-great-grandfather Randolph Sr. was buried.

A couple of hours earlier, high-profile attorney and former member of the SC House of Representatives Bakari Sellers tweeted condolences for his longtime friend Alex Murdaugh.

"'Big Red' is a kind gentle soul," it read. "Keep him in your prayers as this week he's lost his wife, son, and father."

Alex, his surviving son, Buster, and Maggie's parents sat in the front row, hugging anyone who came up to offer sympathy. Throughout the funeral, the new widower wiped away tears with a handkerchief. It was already a sweltering ninety-three degrees with heavy rain forecast.

The outdoor ceremony started with an opening prayer by Pastor Ross Chellis, who told the mourners that Randolph III's death a day earlier only "compounds the grief" for the family.

Among the speakers eulogizing Maggie was her sister-in-law Liz Murdaugh, who said she was a great mother who lived for her two sons. She described Maggie and Paul as "well lived and well loved," saying one of the family highlights was Alex's annual reunion at the river.

"Sports was a theme in Maggie's life," she told the crowd, "because that's how she met the love of her life, Alex. [She was] happiest with her toes in the sand at Edisto."

PMPED attorney Ronnie Crosby, also a close family friend, spoke about Paul's love of the outdoors and hunting, saying he "always knew how to brighten up everyone's day with his jokes and laughs."

He also spoke of how close the Murdaugh family were, speculating that Paul's grandfather "chose to go with them" by dying so soon afterward.

During the ceremony, four elderly mourners had to be treated by EMS for the intense heat, before a heavy downpour abruptly ended the service after just an hour, sending everyone rushing to their cars.

But a distraught Buster Murdaugh remained by his brother's grave in the pouring rain, sharing a hug with a family member.

"The rain has me smiling from ear to ear!!!" John Marvin later tweeted. "That was Paul T Murdaugh through and through!! I love you little rooster!!!"

The next morning *The Beaufort Gazette* printed an editorial demanding the authorities be more transparent and release more information about the Murdaugh murders.

"Another Murder Tragedy. Another Reason to Lose Faith in the Criminal System" was the headline.

Written by David Lauderdale, the editorial questioned why law enforcement had only released "sketchy, confusing tads of information" to the public, doing more to "confuse than clarify."

"Why would law enforcement say the community at large had nothing to fear after two people were gunned down on their private property?" it asked. "But one thing we do know about the Murdaugh case is that it has eroded public trust in the criminal justice system."

It then cited all the "special treatment" Paul Murdaugh had received after causing the boat crash that killed Mallory Beach.

"The lawyers immediately injecting themselves in the case at the hospital," it stated, "were Paul Murdaugh's father, Richard Alexander 'Alex' Murdaugh, a part-time prosecutor with the 14th Circuit Solicitor's Office, and his grandfather, Randy Murdaugh, who was the solicitor for two decades.

"In a just world, Paul Murdaugh would already have faced trial and been judged by a jury."

At 1:00 P.M. on Sunday afternoon, a private service for Randolph (Randy) Murdaugh III was held at the Varnville United Methodist Church for family members. It was followed by a long, solemn funeral procession with vehicles from every law enforcement agency, who accompanied the hearse to Hampton Cemetery.

"For 87 consecutive years," stated the funeral program, "three generations of the Murdaugh family served as Solicitor of the 14th Circuit. This 87 years of service in one office, by the same family, is the longest in the history of the United States."

More than two hundred people attended the funeral, with many of the late solicitor's friends and colleagues eulogizing the Lowcountry legal legend.

Former 11th Judicial Circuit prosecutor Donnie Myers eulogized Murdaugh, saying his family was his greatest achievement. Myers explained that although Randy didn't have a favorite child, he would privately tell each that it was them. And he asked his first grandchild, who was female, to call him "Handsome," as no woman had ever called him that before.

"Goodbye, my loyal friend," said Myers, close to tears. "Goodbye, my brother."

Now retired, 14th Circuit judge Perry Buckner, who had adjudicated many Murdaugh cases over the years, told the crowd how Randy had "cherished" his family and friendships.

"I do not know anyone in my life," he told the crowd, "who loved their family more than Randolph Murdaugh."

29

"WE'RE JUST REGULAR PEOPLE"

One week after the savage murders of Maggie and Paul Murdaugh, the story was still making lurid headlines around the world. The mysterious deaths had also reignited interest in the 2019 boat crash, with the *New York Post* obtaining a recent deposition from the civil case that revealed Paul Murdaugh's drunken antics.

"SC Man Murdered with Mom had Drunken Alter Ego," announced the *New York Post* headline, adding that the dead man's friends had nicknamed his drunken alter ego "Timmy."

Other media outlets like *NBC News* focused on the apparent fall of the Murdaugh dynasty, which had ruled the Lowcountry's opaque legal system for four generations.

"For nearly a century," it began, "fathers of three generations of the Murdaugh family wielded power as South Carolina's top prosecutor for a cluster of counties in a swampy coastal region known as the Lowcountry."

It went on to describe how South Carolina's most prominent family first came under "scrutiny" after the boat crash, leading to Paul Murdaugh's arrest.

On Tuesday morning, as SLED investigators refused to divulge any more details on the double homicide investigation, South Carolina governor Henry McMaster, who had awarded Randolph III the Order of the Palmetto, was interviewed by *Fox News*. He said he was being updated on the investigation by law enforcement, who were working around the clock to track down every lead.

"It's just tragedy after tragedy," he said, "and we hope to get to the bottom of it and find those responsible for these two slayings."

Later that day, SLED released a status update on what it called the "Ongoing Murdaugh Double Murder Investigation." It was thin on details, merely giving the times of Alex's 911 call and the arrivals of the various law enforcement agencies at Moselle.

"SLED is committed to conducting a professional and thorough criminal investigation to bring justice in the deaths of Paul and Maggie," it read. "SLED is further committed to transparency and will release any additional information . . . at the appropriate time."

Behind the scenes, SLED investigators had been busy. SLED divers in scuba gear had scoured the swampy Salkehatchie River by the Moselle estate, interviewed Stephen Smith's family, and searched Paul's USC apartment in Columbia.

There were also questions as to why 14th Circuit solicitor Duffie Stone, a close Murdaugh family friend who still employed Alex as an assistant solicitor, still had not recused himself from the murder investigation.

"Duffie Stone . . . is now refusing to say what role his office is playing in the investigation," stated *The Beaufort Gazette*, "into who killed Murdaugh and his mother after they were found shot to death last week."

On Thursday, June 17, as workmen installed a metal gate and "Keep Out" signs outside Moselle, the Murdaugh family finally broke its silence.

Randy and John Marvin gave an exclusive interview to ABC's *Good Morning America* in support of their brother, Alex. In their first and only television interview, the two Murdaugh brothers welled up with emotion as they revealed that the family had received threats before the two murders.

"The person that did this is out there," Randy told reporter Eva Pilgrim, "and there's information, however big and however small it is."

"Did they have any enemies?" asked Pilgrim.

"I really don't know of any enemies," replied Randy. "You hear all this talk on the social media with regard to Paul, but I don't know of anybody that would . . . truly want to harm them."

John Marvin said that Paul had recently received anonymous threats, but they weren't thought to be credible.

"I guess maybe I made a mistake," he said.

Then Pilgrim asked if the perception that the Murdaugh family was above the law was wrong.

"Yes," replied Randy. "You see words like 'dynasty' used, and 'power.' But we're just regular people and we're hurting, just like they would be hurting if this happened to them."

Asked how Alex was doing, Randy put a comforting arm around his youngest brother.

"He's upright and looks strong and making his way," replied John Marvin. "And then he just breaks down . . . it's tough for us."

"It changes you as a family," explained Randy. "And I can't imagine the horror that my brother's feeling."

On Monday, June 21, after several media organizations sued law enforcement agencies for withholding public records, SLED released a highly redacted incident report. The eighteen pages of supplemental reports from the Colleton County Sheriff's Office included eight entirely blacked-out ones.

"I urge the public to be patient and let the investigation take its course," wrote SLED Chief Mark Keel in an accompanying press release.

That same day, Duffie Stone issued his first statement on the murders, as pressure grew for him to recuse himself because of his close ties with the Murdaughs.

"The 14th Circuit Solicitor's Office recognizes the high degree of public interest regarding the recent deaths of Maggie Murdaugh and her son Paul," he wrote. "To my knowledge, there is no clear suspect in this case at this time. As such, speculation about the propriety of my office's involvement is precisely that—speculation."

The next day SLED suddenly reopened the Stephen Smith murder investigation, citing new evidence gathered while investigating the double homicides. Six years after the blond teenager had been found dead in the middle of Sandy Run Road, a SLED investigator visited his mother Sandy's home to deliver the startling news.

"I've been waiting on this day for 2,174 days," Sandy told *FITSNews*. "Thank you, God!"

SLED spokesman Tommy Crosby refused to disclose the new information, vowing that the agency would bring "a fresh set of eyes" to discover how the openly gay nursing student had really died.

"Everybody wants to know what they found to link to Stephen," said his twin sister, Stephanie. "This is a 2021 murder and you're bringing up evidence from a 2015 murder—How? What? Why? Who?"

In July 2015, Smith's death had been officially written off as a hit-and-run accident, although many investigators at the time had believed it was a murder. Former State Trooper Todd Proctor, who had led the investigation, had resigned in frustration after being ordered not to pursue the investigation when the name Buster Murdaugh had come up again and again.

"Nothing about that case looked like a hit-and-run to me," said Proctor. "We kind of hit a brick wall."

On Friday, June 25, Alex Murdaugh offered a $100,000 reward for information leading to the conviction of Maggie and Paul's killer or killers. Inexplicably it expired on September 30, 2021, running in tandem with SLED's new twenty-four-hour tip line, devoted solely to the investigation.

Alex, through his attorney Jim Griffin, had recently hired the Columbia-based NP Strategy PR firm for crisis management and press releases.

The first one, drafted by NP Strategy CEO Amanda Loveday and released online, was Alex Murdaugh's first public statement since the double homicide.

Alex and Buster Murdaugh announced today a reward of
$100,000 for information leading to the arrest and conviction of

the person or persons who brutally murdered Paul and Maggie on June 7, 2021.

"I want to thank everyone for the incredible love and support that we have received over the last few weeks. Now is the time to bring justice for Maggie and Paul. Buster and I, along with Maggie's mother, father, and our entire family, ask that anyone with helpful information immediately call the SLED tip line or Crime Stoppers."

Over the next few weeks, a slew of investigations involving the Murdaughs gathered momentum in the wake of the double murder. SLED investigators secretly investigated Alex's alibi for the night of the murders, refusing to divulge any evidence they found. It would take more than a year for sketchy details to slowly leak out.

Meanwhile, the avalanche of publicity and the dredging up of the dark history of four generations of the Murdaugh dynasty ignited a spate of fresh civil and criminal actions against Alex Murdaugh.

On July 7, Connor Cook accused Alex of conspiring to blame the boat crash on him instead of Paul Murdaugh. A civil suit filed by attorney Joe McCulloch claimed that five key officers involved in the initial investigation had close ties to the Murdaughs and sought to depose them under oath. The suit alleged that it had been a shoddy investigation in which key evidence disappeared.

"[Connor] was not responsible for this accident," said McCulloch. "Alex Murdaugh [is] accountable."

A month later, 14th Judicial Circuit solicitor Duffie Stone quietly recused himself from Maggie and Paul Murdaugh's murder investigation. In an enigmatic letter to SC Attorney General Alan Wilson, he cited certain new developments in the case as the reason.

"Considering the events of today in SLED's investigation of Paul and Maggie Murdaugh," he explained, "I am asking that you assume all prosecutorial functions in this matter effective immediately."

It would be months until it was revealed that investigators already had key evidence linking Alex to his wife and son's murder, including blood spatter evidence, cell phone tracking information, and the kennel video from Paul's phone.

If Alex was feeling under pressure, he certainly did not show it. In late July, Alex and his son Buster were photographed drinking at the prestigious SC Governor's Cup Edisto Invitational Billfishing Tournament.

And then in August, Big Red attended the annual SC Association for Justice meeting at the Marriott Resort and Spa on Hilton Head Island. The former SCAJ president was his usual gregarious self, drinking with friends at multiple bars over the weekend event.

Up until the end of August, according to a later indictment, Alex Murdaugh was still brazenly stealing money from unsuspecting clients. In 2019, a Beaufort woman named Sandra Taylor had been killed by a drunk driver and Murdaugh was handling her wrongful death case. On August 19, he informed Taylor's mother that he had negotiated an insurance payout of $30,000, when in fact he had received over $180,000, which had gone straight into his bogus Forge account.

On Thursday, September 2, one of Alex Murdaugh's PMPED colleagues found a check on his desk made payable to Alex, instead of the law firm, as it should have been. He immediately reported it. PMPED then began investigating every past settlement Murdaugh had resolved, discovering "numerous checks" over the years made out to a Bank of America account in the name of Forge, without any filing documents to back them up.

PMPED immediately contacted the real Forge Consulting company, who were unaware of Murdaugh's Forge checks and had never dealt with any clients named in them.

"[Forge Consulting, LLC] had no knowledge of the improper use of its name or his conduct," PMPED later stated.

The next day, Alex's PMPED partners summoned him into the Hampton office to explain himself. After being confronted with all the evidence, Alex broke down and admitted to stealing millions of dollars for his own use.

The company then demanded his immediate resignation from the law firm his great-grandfather had founded in 1910, and Alex agreed to do so. After the meeting, he asked his brother Randy if he could borrow some cash "to cover an overdrawn bank account."

On the Saturday morning of Labor Day weekend, PMPED officially notified SLED and the Hampton County Sheriff's Office of what Alex Murdaugh had done. A criminal investigation was launched immediately.

It was then that Alex Murdaugh made that fateful call ordering Curtis "Fast Eddie" Smith to kill him, so that his surviving son, Buster, could receive a $10 million life insurance payout.

30

"You Can't Make This Stuff Up"

At 1:30 P.M. on Saturday afternoon, Alex Murdaugh's frenzied 911 call to the Hampton County dispatcher came in.

"Where's your emergency?" asked the emergency dispatcher.

"I'm on Salkehatchie Road . . . by the church," wailed Alex.

"Okay, what's going on?"

"I got a flat tire and I stopped," he explained, "and somebody stopped to help me. And when I turned my back, they tried to shoot me."

"Oh, okay, were you shot?" asked the dispatcher.

"Yes, but I mean, I'm okay."

"Okay, do you need EMS?"

"Yes, I can't drive. I'm having trouble seeing and I'm bleeding a lot."

"What's your name?" asked the dispatcher.

"Alex Murdaugh."

As they were talking, a female driver passed by on Old Salkehatchie Road and also called 911.

"There is a man by the side of the road with blood all over him," she told another operator, "and he's waving his hands. He looks fine but it looks like a setup, so we didn't stop."

Then an anonymous good Samaritan, rumored to be a friend of Alex's, arrived to drive him to the hospital in a white Nissan. On the way, Alex redialed 911, arranging to meet an ambulance on a landing strip in a field off the Charleston Highway in Varnville, seven miles away from where the shooting had taken place.

Upon his arrival, Alex was interviewed by Corporal Kendrell Henderson of the Hampton County Sheriff's Office, before being helicoptered to the Memorial Health University Medical Center in Savannah. The sheriff's incident report, released a few days later, classified it as an attempted murder with no visible injuries.

Deputies blocked off a three-mile stretch of Old Salkehatchie Road until Sunday morning, while forensic evidence was collected and witnesses were interviewed. Several bullet casings were found near the black Mercedes, previously owned by Maggie, before it was towed away for forensic processing.

However, many inconsistencies would spring up in Alex's assassination claims after SLED issued a press release saying he had only suffered "a superficial head wound."

Attorney Jim Griffin tried to clarify the situation by telling *The New York Times* that his client was now conscious and taking phone calls from his hospital bed. In his narrative, Alex had been changing a tire on his Mercedes when someone in a blue truck drove past, before circling back and shooting him in the head. Alex was lucky to be alive so soon after the murder of his wife and son, said his attorney, and had been interviewed at the hospital by SLED investigators.

"It's shocking and very disturbing," said Griffin. "It makes us all wonder what the hell's going on."

A Memorial Health University Medical Center report later stated that Murdaugh had undergone a CT head scan, showing he had sustained a parietal skull fracture and a brain bleed. A urine test had revealed high levels of barbiturates and opiates in his system.

"Of note," it concluded, "patient's wife and son were recently murdered in June of this year."

Late Saturday afternoon, the NP Strategy public relations company released a statement to the press.

"The Murdaugh family has suffered through more than any one family can ever imagine," it read. "We expect Alex to recover and ask for your privacy while he recovers."

On Sunday, Alex Murdaugh remained in intensive care and was

becoming increasingly "irritable." He complained that the three pain-killers he had been given were not working and he wanted to go home.

He was also pacing around the unit, repeatedly pulling IV tubes out of his arm, and unsuccessfully trying to bribe an employee with $20 to use a cell phone.

On Monday, Labor Day, Alex Murdaugh was discharged from Memorial Health University Medical Center and driven by his brothers to a drug rehabilitation center in Marietta, Georgia. Randy paid the $15,000 to cover his treatment. His concerned brothers suspected that the incident had not been a random shooting but a suicide attempt.

"I had real doubts that he was telling the truth," John Marvin later told *The Beaufort Gazette*. "And Randy, in particular, had doubts because he saw him talking to SLED . . . and he just knew how inconsistent he was."

That afternoon, the Murdaughs' public relations company issued another press release from Alex, announcing that he had resigned from PMPED and checked into drug rehab. Although vague, leaving far more questions than answers, it captured national media attention like a bolt of lightning.

"The murders of my wife and son have caused an incredibly difficult time in my life," read his statement. "I have made a lot of decisions that I truly regret. I'm resigning from my law firm and entering rehab after a long battle that has been exacerbated by these murders.

"I am immensely sorry to everyone I've hurt, including my family, friends, and colleagues. I ask for prayers as I rehabilitate myself and my relationships."

At the exact same time, PMPED took their website offline and released a statement of their own, announcing they would be hiring a forensic accounting firm to conduct a complete investigation.

"Alex Murdaugh . . . is no longer associated with PMPED in any manner," it read. "His resignation came after the discovery by PMPED that Alex misappropriated funds in violation of PMPED standards and policies. This is disappointing news for all of us [and] there's no place in our firm for such behavior."

After months of searching for a lawyer to look into Alex Murdaugh's handling of their mother's reported $505,000 wrongful death settlement, Gloria Satterfield's two sons had finally enlisted the help of the Columbia-based law firm of Bland Richter, LLP.

Founded by Eric Bland and Ronnie Richter, the self-described "boutique litigation firm" specialized in legal malpractice involving "unethical" and "self-serving" conduct by attorneys. The Gloria Satterfield suit seemed tailor-made for them, coming on the heels of PMPED allegations that Murdaugh had robbed his clients of millions.

The first week of September, Bland Richter sent a politely worded "notice of representation" to Cory Fleming, who was handling the civil lawsuit on behalf of the Satterfield estate. They wrote that there must have been "a misunderstanding," asking to see the $505,000 settlement agreement, the court order approving it, and the insurance company check.

"When you send a letter like that to lawyers, we expect a response," Bland later explained. "But we got nothing."

On Wednesday morning, *The Washington Post* published an op-ed entitled "The Shocking Saga of South Carolina's Murdaugh Family." It was a damning indictment of the Murdaugh dynasty and the precipitous fall of "Big Red."

"You can't make this stuff up, people say, when a tale seems too crazy—or awful—to be true," began Kathleen Parker's opinion piece. "Here in South Carolina, where storytelling is a time-honored ritual bound to front porches and swampy nights, it's a common refrain, even if everybody knows that stories of local origin rarely need embellishment.

"But few can rival the shocking events of summer 2021 and the unfolding saga of the Hampton, SC, Murdaugh family, a powerful legal dynasty featuring generations of prosecutors who've tried seemingly every case in a five-county area for nearly a century."

It went on to describe how the colorful family was now "embroiled" in two strange murders and accusations of the theft of millions of dollars, which has captured national attention.

"The story has assumed a life of its own," she wrote. "One can hardly wait for the next turn of the screw."

A few hours later, Randy Murdaugh, still an active PMPED partner, issued his own statement to clarify his difficult position.

"I was shocked, just as the rest of the PMPED family," it read, "to learn of my brother Alex's drug addiction and stealing of money. I love my law firm and I also love Alex as my brother. While I support him in his recovery, I do not support, condone, or excuse his conduct in stealing by manipulating his most trusted relationships."

A few hours later, the SC Supreme Court indefinitely suspended Alex Murdaugh's law license. Alex did not oppose the move.

Soon afterward, the 14th Judicial Circuit Solicitor's Office officially ended its relationship with the longtime assistant solicitor.

"We can't have him prosecuting cases for the circuit," explained spokesman Jeff Kidd.

Hampton residents were shell-shocked, as an army of reporters and TV news crews descended on the town. They were all looking for a fresh angle on the fast-breaking story. Many went to Coconuts restaurant, where they found the regulars to be tight-lipped.

"The Murdaughs basically used to run the whole town because of the law firm, and now it's all tumbling down," explained local businessman Charles Hendricks. "The town is very hush-hush and people are reluctant to talk about it. They feel lost in some way because, 'Hey, if we get into a legal issue, we can't go through the Murdaughs anymore.'"

On Thursday morning, the Hampton County Sheriff's Office released its official report on Alex Murdaugh's alleged attempted murder to the media. Initially it stated that he had no visible injuries, but within hours it had been "corrected," with a cross inside the "visible injury" box and the words "other major injury" added.

Sheriff Thomas Smalls explained that there had been a mistake by a deputy accidentally checking off "no" in the wrong box.

Attorney Jim Griffin immediately went into full crisis mode, explaining how his client was lucky to be alive after sustaining an entry and exit wound, a skull fracture, and minor brain bleeding in several places.

"He had significant head trauma," the attorney emailed *People* magazine, "and there was blood at the scene, which is indicated by the evidence cones placed in the roadway. I understand that most of the cones mark blood."

Griffin maintained that his client had already departed by helicopter by the time deputies arrived, even though the amended report stated that "Corporal Henderson met with the victim before he was flown out."

By Friday morning, the string of inconstancies in Alex Murdaugh's alleged attempted murder had become a major news story in itself. Amidst all the media speculation, the NP Strategy public relations company issued a press release to clarify things.

"There has been some misreporting regarding Alex Murdaugh and his shooting on September 4," it read, "so we wanted to clear up a number of facts from that day. After the shooting, Alex had an entry and exit wound; his skull was fractured and it was not a self-inflicted bullet wound. Alex pulled over after seeing a low tire indicator light. A male driver in a blue pickup asked him if he had car troubles. As soon as Alex replied, he was shot.

"We know that SLED is continuing to work diligently to find this person and the person or people that murdered Maggie and Paul Murdaugh."

A few hours later, Buster Murdaugh was photographed at the family's Edisto Beach house with his girlfriend, Brooklynn White, packing up his belongings and loading them into the trunk of a Cadillac. It would be one of his final visits to the house where his mother had been living before her murder.

31

"This Is a Pretty Unbelievable Story"

On Monday, September 13, SLED Chief Mark Keel announced that he had opened an investigation into Alex Murdaugh's misappropriation of funds from his family law firm, PMPED. This marked the fifth state criminal investigation involving the Murdaugh family since the 2019 boat crash. It would also be a major turning point in the Murdaugh saga as the family's century-long hold on South Carolina's legal system began to slip away.

"As Chief of SLED, I continue to urge the public to be patient and let this investigation take its course," said Chief Keel. "Investigative decisions we make throughout this case and any potentially related case must ultimately withstand the scrutiny of the criminal justice process. SLED is committed to conducting a professional, thorough, and impartial criminal investigation, no matter where the facts lead us."

Defense attorneys Jim Griffin and Dick Harpootlian met Alex Murdaugh in a small room at the Marietta, Georgia, detox center, where he finally came clean about the Labor Day weekend shooting. According to Harpootlian, Alex now admitted to hiring his distant cousin and drug dealer Curtis Smith to kill him, so Buster could get his $10 million life insurance policy. After meeting up at a remote location on Old Salkehatchie Road, Alex had handed him a gun and told him to shoot him in the head, which Curtis had done.

After hearing the story, the lawyers immediately telephoned SLED so that Alex Murdaugh could confess and negotiate his surrender.

"He was a hundred percent truthful," Harpootlian later told Cody Alcorn of *Fox Carolina News*. "And he said specifically, 'I need to stop them from wasting their time so they can put resources on solving the murders of Maggie and Paul.'"

That evening his attorneys fired off a one-line statement, reading: "Alex Murdaugh regrets the actions that have taken the focus away from solving the murder of Maggie and Paul."

On Tuesday morning, less than twenty-four hours after SLED announced that Alex Murdaugh was under investigation, his late housekeeper Gloria Satterfield's sons went public about their own investigation. Their new attorney Eric Bland told *FITSNews* reporter Mandy Matney that Tony Satterfield and Brian Harriott needed answers about their mother's wrongful death settlement. They demanded an explanation as to why they hadn't received a cent of the reported $505,000 payout, after not receiving any response from Cory Fleming, who had filed the civil action three years earlier.

"We're not saying anything has been done wrong," Bland explained. "I will not stop until these kids get every answer that they're entitled to and every dollar that they should have gotten . . . as a result of their mother's death."

The story also quoted unnamed sources saying the true insurance payouts for Satterfield's "trip-and-fall" death could run into the millions.

A few hours later, SLED agents arrested Curtis Smith at his Walterboro home. He admitted to being present when Alex Murdaugh was shot on Old Salkehatchie Road and then disposing of the firearm. The sixty-one-year-old was charged with assisted suicide, assault and battery, possessing a firearm, and insurance fraud. He was also charged with distribution of methamphetamine and possession of marijuana, relating to a police raid on his house a week earlier.

Fast Eddie was booked into Colleton County Detention Center, with a bond hearing set for the next morning in Hampton.

On Wednesday morning, when Maggie Murdaugh should have celebrated her fifty-third birthday, Dick Harpootlian appeared on NBC's

Today show to defend Maggie's husband. Just hours before Alex Murdaugh was due to turn himself in, his attorney attempted to put the best spin on the increasingly bizarre situation.

"Dick, you have to admit this is a pretty unbelievable story," began *Today* host Craig Melvin, "your client claiming that he paid someone to shoot him to collect ten million dollars in insurance."

The seasoned SC state senator and attorney, whose wife, Jamie, is the US Ambassador to Slovenia, explained how Alex Murdaugh had been addicted to opiates for more than twenty years and had been taken advantage of.

"The murder of his son and wife ninety days ago," said Harpootlian, "took a tremendous toll on him. His father died of cancer that same week. Most people couldn't get through that. He got through it with the use of opioids."

According to Harpootlian, Alex had been in "a dark, dark place" and decided to end his life. He also wanted to help his surviving son, Buster, benefit from his $10 million life insurance policy, not realizing its suicide exclusion clause had actually run out.

"Let's talk about Maggie and Paul," asked Melvin. "Because your client lied about the circumstances under which he was shot, it wouldn't be a stretch for folks to think he probably also lied about the circumstances under which his wife and son were shot."

In response, Harpootlian cited the eighteen months he'd spent with Alex and Maggie while he'd defended Paul on the boat crash felony charges.

"They were very affectionate," said Harpootlian. "I mean, Maggie and Alex holding hands. Clearly he is distraught about their deaths. He did not murder them!"

Immediately after the *Today* show segment on Alex Murdaugh aired, his two attorneys released an official statement in an apparent bid for public sympathy.

> On September 4, it became clear Alex believed that ending his life was his only option. Today, he knows that's not true. For the last twenty years, there have been many people feeding

his addiction to opioids. During that time, these individuals took advantage of his addiction and his ability to pay substantial funds for illegal drugs. One of those individuals took advantage of his mental illness and agreed to take Alex's life, by shooting him in the head.

Fortunately, Alex was not killed by the gunshot wound. Alex is fully cooperating with SLED in their investigations into his shooting, opioid use, and the search to find the person or people responsible for the murder of his wife and son. Alex is not without fault but he is just one of many whose life has been devastated by opioid addiction.

That afternoon, SLED announced that they were launching a criminal investigation into Gloria Satterfield's untimely death and the handling of her estate, requested by Hampton County coroner Angela Topper. After learning of newly reported information in the wrongful death case, Topper wrote a letter to SLED saying that she felt it "prudent" to investigate further.

She cited Cory Fleming's "Petition for Approval of a Wrongful Death Settlement," lodged in the Court of Common Pleas in Hampton County, which claimed Satterfield had died after a trip-and-fall accident.

"The defendant in this action was Richard A. Murdaugh," she wrote. "The decedent's death was not reported to the Coroner at the time, nor was an autopsy performed. On the death certificate, the manner of death was ruled 'Natural,' which is inconsistent with the injuries sustained in a trip-and-fall accident."

At the exact same time that the SLED press release went out, Bland Richter filed a civil suit on behalf of Gloria Satterfield's sons against Alex Murdaugh, Cory Fleming and his law firm of Moss, Kuhn & Fleming, and Chad Westendorf of Palmetto State Bank. It demanded answers as to what had happened to all the settlement money, which the Satterfield family had only learned about in the press.

"Alex Murdaugh stipulated that he was at fault for the death of Gloria

Satterfield," read the lawsuit, "and his insurance company paid $505,000 of the claims. To date, the children of Gloria Satterfield have not received the first dollar."

It went on to describe Gloria's devotion to the Murdaugh family and how proud she had been to work for them.

"Gloria was told she was part of the Murdaugh family," it read, "and she believed it to be true."

At her funeral, Alex had promised to look after her sons, by suing himself so they could be compensated. Then he had steered them to Cory Fleming, failing to mention that he was Paul's godfather and his own best friend.

"THE PLAINTIFFS ARE VICTIMS," read the civil action. "THE PLAINTIFFS ARE VULNERABLE. THE PLAINTIFFS ARE SCARED. BY THIS ACTION THE PLAINTIFFS SEEK REAL ANSWERS TO THEIR QUESTIONS SURROUNDING THE DEATH OF THEIR MOTHER AND THE DISPOSITION OF THE MONIES SUPPOSEDLY PAID FOR THEIR BENEFIT."

Several hours later, Dick Harpootlian was interviewed by Fox Carolina's Cody Alcorn, who began by asking about the just-announced SLED investigation into Gloria Satterfield's death, and the allegations of financial impropriety with her insurance settlement.

"Well, first of all, [Alex] has no involvement in Gloria Satterfield's death," replied Harpootlian. "These are rumors and innuendoes and maybe SLED feels like they've got to chase every rabbit that's out there. But I think this is going to be a huge dead end."

Harpootlian described any allegations that Gloria's death was unnatural as distractions.

"What Alex would like investigated is who murdered his wife and son," said the attorney, "and that case is now ninety days old and no closer to closure now than it was ninety days ago."

"Look," said Alcorn, "you have five, possibly six, deaths surrounding your client as of this afternoon?"

"I don't know what those six deaths would be," snapped Harpootlian.

"I mean this is just smoke and mirrors . . . and I think SLED feels compelled to . . . look under every bush, scrub any prior allegations so there's no question unanswered."

He claimed that Alex Murdaugh had now hired a private investigator to probe the murders of Maggie and Paul.

"We're conducting an independent investigation," he announced. "We think there's one or two people that could be involved . . . and we're working on that."

"It's bizarre to have one person tied to all these deaths," countered Alcorn. "You have to admit if there's not something behind it, it's a crazy coincidence?"

"I'm a lawyer . . . I don't have to admit anything," said Harpootlian and he laughed.

Late Wednesday night, Alex Murdaugh's other attorney, Jim Griffin, issued one final media statement.

"We have been informed that there is a warrant for his arrest for conspiracy to commit insurance fraud," it read. "He plans to voluntarily surrender tomorrow, and the arraignment and bond hearing will be held at 4 P.M. at the Hampton County Magistrates Court in Varnville."

32

A Tremendous Fall from Grace

At 9:05 A.M. on Thursday, September 16, Curtis "Fast Eddie" Smith was brought into the Hampton County Magistrates Court in shackles, wearing a beige jail jumpsuit and a white face mask, for COVID-19 precautions. He looked disorientated and disheveled, his long, greasy blond hair uncombed. A few hours earlier a Colleton County judge had set a $5,000 bond on unrelated drug charges.

Throughout the thirteen-minute bond hearing, he sat alone, hunched at the defense table, rocking back and forth as two guards stood over him.

Presiding judge Tonja Alexander first read out all the charges he faced relating to Alex Murdaugh's suicide attempt. These included assisted suicide, assault and battery, pointing and presenting a firearm, insurance fraud, and conspiracy to commit insurance fraud.

She then set his bond for $55,000 and ordered him to appear for roll call at Hampton County Courthouse on October 25.

"Mr. Smith, are you interested in a public defender?" asked the judge.

"I'm probably going to look for one, yes," he replied. "Tomorrow or the next day."

As he was led out of the hearing he muttered, "This is bogus . . . all crap."

Soon afterward, Smith posted bail and was driven out of Hampton Jail by a friend.

*   *   *

Just before noon, a beige SUV with a police escort pulled up outside the Hampton County Law Enforcement Center, where a bank of local and national TV trucks had assembled.

There was a loud clicking of cameras as a haunted-looking Alex Murdaugh emerged from the passenger side. He was wearing bright pink Nike sneakers, a light-colored shirt, and gray pants as he was escorted into the jail to officially surrender to SLED agents and be processed.

After being fingerprinted and having his mug shot taken, Murdaugh was charged with insurance fraud, conspiracy to commit insurance fraud, and filing a false police report.

"Nothing like this ever happened in Hampton County before," the Rev. Willie Rakes of the St. James Baptist Church and a former Murdaugh client told a reporter. "Why would he do something like that?"

An hour after Alex's arrest, PMPED issued a statement, further distancing itself from its former partner and founder's great-grandson.

"PMPED is focused on representing our valued clients," it read. "Questions related to Alex's arrest should be directed to the appropriate law enforcement authorities."

Murdaugh's legal team had negotiated his bail bonds well before the hearing even began. Later, a reporter filed a Freedom of Information request and discovered that the exact $20,000 bond amount Judge Alexander had announced in court had been posted on the court's website hours earlier. It clearly demonstrated how much power Alex Murdaugh still had on the 14th Judicial Circuit.

On his way into the bond hearing, attorney Harpootlian was asked about his client's state of mind.

"He's in jail," Harpootlian replied. "That's his state of mind."

At 4:00 P.M., Richard Alexander Murdaugh was led into the Hampton courtroom in handcuffs and heavy ankle restraints connected by a chain. His face was largely hidden behind a large white face mask, with his glasses perched over the top of his head.

He was now wearing a beige Hampton County Department of Corrections jumpsuit, with the letters "3X" stenciled on the back. His reddish-blond hair was immaculately groomed with no visible signs of any head injury, not even a Band-Aid.

He took his place at the defense table next to Dick Harpootlian, with Jim Griffin sitting behind them. Seventeen reporters lined the public gallery, many with cameras, and the hearing was being streamed live by all local media outlets.

Prosecutor Creighton Waters, of the State Attorney General's Office, told the judge that he wanted the defendant to surrender his passport and sign a waiver of extradition, as he planned to continue his out-of-state drug rehabilitation treatment. He also demanded Murdaugh post a $100,000 surety and wear a GPS ankle bracelet.

Although Murdaugh did not have a criminal record, pointed out the prosecutor, the underlying facts of the case were violent.

"An intent to harm oneself," said Waters, "makes that person not only a danger to themselves but that enhances the danger to the community.

"I've seen these types of cases before. Sometimes those who had everything and who are suffering a possible fall from grace, are actually more of a concern than a hardened criminal who's been in this situation before."

Then Dick Harpootlian stood up, asking permission to remove his COVID mask, to make himself better understood.

"Your Honor," he began. "Alex Murdaugh spent his entire life in this county. No prior record. Actually involved in all aspects of this community. Up until this charge, had no blemish on his character whatsoever."

Harpootlian described his client's "significant opioid addiction," which had led him to "financial issues" and being in court today.

"First of all, this crime involved his attempt to have himself shot so his son could collect insurance money," he told the judge. "The only violence he's ever been involved in is . . . to have himself executed. So he's not a danger to the community. The only person he's a danger to is himself."

He said his client was not a flight risk, as he faced financial ruin and had nowhere to go.

"Alex has fallen from grace [and] it has been tremendous," said Harpootlian, as Murdaugh began weeping, his chained legs jiggling under the table. "His wife and son were brutally murdered and that has had an extraordinary effect on him.

"But this is a twenty-year addiction. This is something he's struggling with every day and if anyone wants to see the face of what opioid addiction does, you're looking at it. This is a horrible, horrible disease. We ask you to let him go heal."

Judge Alexander had no further questions and said she was ready to set bond.

"After hearing both sides," she said, "I don't feel that Mr. Murdaugh is going to be a risk to the community. I do however want him to surrender his passport and have a waiver of extradition in place."

She set a total bond of $20,000 in his own reconnaissance, with a breakdown of $10,000 for the false insurance representation, and $5,000 each for the conspiracy and filing a false police report charges—the exact bond breakdown that had been posted on the court's website before Alex had even surrendered.

As the eyes of the world focused on tiny Hampton County, bewildered residents who had known Alex Murdaugh and his family all their lives tried to make sense of what was happening.

"No one likes bad publicity," said LaClaire Laffitte, the president of the Hampton Historical Society. "No one suspected. It's like they say, you don't know what goes on behind somebody else's doors. I guess this is really finding that out."

"It's bizarre," said attorney Jared Newman. "I don't know any other way to describe it. I mean, this is hubris and right out of a Greek tragedy. The dust ain't settled yet, that's for sure."

Others were trying to keep an open mind, with a fondness for the gregarious Big Red they had known and not the monster being portrayed in the media.

"We're all just scratching our heads," said Hampton Library branch manager Chrissy Cook. "They were good to my family."

Local historian and Murdaugh friend Sam Crews III said local feelings on Alex Murdaugh were running so high that for many it was becoming personal.

"It has split some families," he explained. "It's just like politics."

Some questioned how such a rabid opioid addict could have been such a successful lawyer at the same time.

"I've known Alex since he was seventeen," said Newman. "I don't buy the drug story. I'm sorry. There's no way. I've dealt with a number of clients that have opiate addictions and you just can't function."

Physically, Alex just did not look like the typical emaciated junkie.

"He was too fat to have used that many drugs," said Crews. "Druggies get real skinny, but he still had good teeth so he didn't look the part."

LaClaire Laffitte, whose son Russell would soon be indicted for allegedly helping Alex steal millions in various ways as COO of Palmetto State Bank, unwittingly forecast that others would be drawn into the Murdaugh swamp.

"As more and more comes out," she said in November 2021, "it's going to touch more and more people that have no idea they're being touched."

While out on bail, Curtis Smith gave an interview to *New York Post* reporter Dana Kennedy from his Walterboro porch, insisting he was innocent. He claimed to have been set up by his cousin and good friend Alex Murdaugh and that he had never tried to kill him.

"I know what they're trying to say about me and it ain't true," he told Kennedy. "I get a call from Alex that Saturday afternoon to come to where he was. I thought it was maybe to fix something. I just went over there."

Smith claimed that when he had met Murdaugh on Old Salkehatchie Road, his cousin was waving a gun around like he was going to shoot himself. He had then wrestled Alex to the ground to take the gun away so he couldn't hurt himself.

"Then the gun kind of went off above his head," said Smith, "and I got scared to death and ran to my truck and took off."

He admitted being "just plain stupid" to take the gun and then throw it away.

Asked if he was Alex's personal drug dealer, as his attorneys claimed, "Fast Eddie" shook his head and had a message for his distant cousin.

"I wouldn't advise him to try and set me up," he said. "I'd strongly advise him against that."

33

"THE MURDAUGH CITADEL IS GOING TO FALL!"

Before entering an Orlando, Florida, rehab center on September 16, Alex Murdaugh granted his son Buster full power of attorney and ordered him to start liquidating his assets. Buster was now living in an apartment in Columbia, spending weekends at his girlfriend Brooklynn's Hilton Head condo. He was also working in the accounting department of the Wild Wing Cafe corporate office and had just been promoted.

The last week of September, Buster satisfied a nearly one-million-dollar mortgage on a tract of land in Hampton and Colleton Counties, sold his father's stake in the seven-thousand-acre Green Swamp Hunting Club for $250,000, and put a thirty-one-foot, twin outboard boat up for sale for $115,000.

After losing his appeal against the Philadelphia Insurance Company's refusal to cover any damages from the 2019 boat crash, Alex Murdaugh now stood to lose everything.

On September 24, reeling from all the negative publicity, PMPED issued "A Message to Our Community." It further distanced itself from Alex, castigating him for his ultimate betrayal and calling it "a tragic situation."

"We were shocked and dismayed to learn that Alex violated our principles and code of ethics," it read. "He lied and stole from us [and] betrayed our trust."

Soon after SLED launched a criminal investigation into Gloria Satterfield's death, it was discovered that the actual settlement was more than eight times higher than previously thought. In addition to the $505,000 Cory Fleming had wrung from Lloyd's of London, he had also mediated a further $3.8 million settlement from the Nautilus Insurance Company for a total of $4.3 million. Most of it had been laundered through Murdaugh's fake Forge account.

"[Gloria's] sons want justice," attorney Eric Bland defiantly told *FITS-News*. "The Murdaugh Citadel is going to fall!"

On Tuesday, September 28, Alex Murdaugh texted Cory Fleming from rehab, apologizing for getting him involved in his mess.

> Cory—this is Alex. Finally feeling little better each day. Not sick any more just really weak. I know you aren't ready to talk to me yet but wanted you to have my number. The worst part about getting better and thinking clearly is I know how bad I hurt the people I love the most. I cannot rationalize the justifications I used to do the things I did. I know how much trouble I have caused you and I'm willing to do absolutely anything to try and make it right. All my love!

That week's *People* magazine devoted its front-page cover to the Murdaugh saga, revealing that Maggie had seen a divorce lawyer in Charleston prior to her murder.

"A Father's Dark Secrets: New Twists in the Murdaugh Murders," was the lurid headline, with a grinning family photo of Alex in a tuxedo alongside one of him in jail scrubs at his bond hearing.

The story claimed that Maggie had been advised to look more closely at the family finances before her death, hinting at a possible motive for her and Paul's brutal murders.

An unnamed former PMPED colleague told *People* that Alex was finally getting his just deserts for how he'd treated everyone over the years.

"Alex has been going through life f—ing people over," he was quoted as saying. "This is the chickens coming home to roost. He got played and he got burned. Now it's all coming back to haunt him."

An anonymous member of the Murdaugh social circle added: "Behind the black ties and fancy dresses were some pretty miserable people."

Immediately after the *People* story hit the internet, NP Strategy's Amanda Loveday vehemently denied any problems in the Murdaugh marriage.

"The most recent allegations by *People* magazine regarding the state of Maggie and Alex Murdaugh's marriage are totally inconsistent with what we have been told by friends and family members," read her statement. "Also, we have reviewed many years of text messages on Alex's phone, and the conversations between Alex and Maggie portray a very loving relationship.

"It is our hope that the media will continue to focus on covering the investigation of the person or people responsible for the murder of Maggie and Paul and not reporting salacious stories with no credible sources connected to the Murdaugh family."

Murdaugh defense attorney Dick Harpootlian told the *New York Post* that he had witnessed firsthand what a devoted couple they had been.

"I even saw them holding hands," he said. "SLED has Alex's phone and Maggie's phone. Don't you think if they were splitting up and talking divorce there'd be more proof of it by now?"

The next day—September 30—Alex Murdaugh's much-publicized $100,000 reward for information leading to the capture of Maggie and Paul's killers was due to expire. It was now four months after the murders and SLED had been unusually quiet on the murder investigation, without a single press conference to announce any developments.

When local media questioned if the reward would continue, Murdaugh family spokeswoman Amanda Loveday released a statement.

"We are disappointed that no one has stepped forward with any leads to solve the murder and claim the $100,000," it read. "At this time, the family is evaluating what additional steps can be taken to solve the murders of Maggie and Paul."

On Friday, October 1, Cory Fleming and his law firm Moss, Kuhn & Fleming agreed to repay all the legal fees and expenses received from the $4.3 million recovered from the Gloria Satterfield wrongful death suit. A few days earlier, Palmetto State Bank's Chad Westendorf had returned the $30,000 he got as the Satterfield estate's personal representative.

"Mr. Fleming stepped forward and did the right thing by the Estate," said Satterfield estate law firm Bland Richter, in a joint statement with Cory Fleming and his law partners. "Mr. Fleming trusted his close friend and colleague to deal with him truthfully and honorably, only to be misled and deceived in one of the worst possible ways for a lawyer: Alex Murdaugh lied to Mr. Fleming to steal client funds."

The story of the Murdaugh murders had now taken on a life of its own to become an American obsession. HBO Max and Netflix both announced plans to film documentaries and there were half a dozen weekly podcasts, putting every new development under the microscope. A plethora of Facebook groups had thousands of avid subscribers, with names such as "The Murdaugh Murders," "Horror in Hampton," "Murdaugh Mysteries," and "Murdaugh in the Lowcountry."

And all three major TV networks were working on specials, sending production crews to Hampton, seeking fresh angles and locals who would agree to go on camera.

"The Hollywood feeding frenzy has begun," announced *FITSNews*, whose news director Mandy Matney had broken many exclusives since the 2019 boat crash. "The 'Murdaugh Murders' crime saga in South Carolina is all the rage right now—with national networks, Hollywood production companies, and global streaming services battling for exclusive access and insights into this still-unfolding Southern Gothic mystery."

Many lifelong Hampton residents were angry that their beloved town was being caricatured.

"The Murdaughs are part of our community," said LaClaire Laffitte, whose family runs Palmetto State Bank, founded in 1907. "What they represent, we all represent and it's been [all over] the press. It's a baffling story and of course it's going to be a movie . . . I just hope it doesn't come out until after I'm gone."

On Wednesday, October 6, Alex Murdaugh was sued by PMPED, who accused him of embezzling millions of dollars. It was the final humiliation for the disgraced Murdaugh scion, whose great-grandfather had started the storied law firm more than a century earlier.

The lawsuit also revealed how Murdaugh had created a fictitious bank account in the name of "Richard A. Murdaugh d/b/a Forge" to steal PMPED money for his personal use.

"Alex Murdaugh knew that his actions would evade detection based on his experience with PMPED," read the lawsuit, "and its long-standing relations with Forge Consulting, LLC, in Columbia, South Carolina."

PMPED announced the lawsuit in a statement, saying that every single case Alex Murdaugh had ever worked on was now under forensic investigation, to try and recover his "ill-gotten" gains. The firm also wanted to know if Murdaugh had signed any movie or book deals to exploit his story.

Jim Griffin described the lawsuit as "a very sad development," going to Twitter to claim that his client had "pledged" his full cooperation in any investigation.

"Alex holds every member of the [PMPED] firm in very high esteem," he tweeted.

Alex Murdaugh would later take the Fifth Amendment, his sole response to the lawsuit accusing him of stealing as much as $10 million from his family company.

Two days later, Cory Fleming's license to practice law was suspended, amidst allegations that he helped Alex Murdaugh steal $4.3 million from his late housekeeper's two sons. It was the exact same "Interim Suspension" that Murdaugh had received a month earlier, and the SC Bar's website had amended both their statuses to "Not Good Standing."

Immediately after Fleming's suspension, the Beaufort law firm of Moss, Kuhn & Fleming, where he had worked for twenty-five years and made partner, removed his name from the company letterhead and erased all mention of him on its website.

"[It's] a very good day for the South Carolina Bar," said Satterfield attorneys Eric Bland and Ronnie Richter in a statement. "The rule of law and the rules of professional conduct will always prevail over lawyer misconduct."

On October 12, almost three months after Maggie and Paul Murdaugh's murders, Jim Griffin sat down with Fox Carolina's Cody Alcorn for an exclusive one-on-one interview. Although it was meant to bolster public support for his client, about to be arrested on two felony charges related to the Satterfield wrongful death lawsuit, it did the opposite.

"Now we've had a series of bombshell revelations, unsolved crimes, and six active investigations underway," said Alcorn, "all tied to the Murdaugh family that have captured national and international attention. The big question is, who killed Alex's wife and youngest son, Paul? Although no suspect has been named, Alex Murdaugh is a person of interest."

"SLED has said from the get-go that Alex was a person of interest," replied Griffin, "which is still mind-boggling to us. You would think that if Alex was the one who did it, that SLED would have been able to establish that pretty easily that night."

Griffin questioned why, after searching the Moselle house, investigators still hadn't come up with anything to link his client forensically to the murders.

"What we do know as his lawyers," explained Griffin, "is that he had no motive to kill them. He loved his wife. He loved his son. The murders were done in a most brutal fashion."

Then Alcorn asked how Alex's twenty years of opiate addiction had gone unnoticed.

"I didn't know," said Griffin. "It was a surprise to a lot of people in how he was able to mask it."

According to his attorney, Alex had undergone medical detox several times before but never stayed the course, telling colleagues that he was taking golfing vacations.

"It's a Shakespearean tragedy," said Griffin. "A man who is at a high level falls from grace and crashes. He's not trying to justify what he did [but] it doesn't make him a murderer."

As Alex Murdaugh's high-powered attorneys went on a media offensive, Curtis Smith also started speaking out. He gave an impromptu interview to *The New York Times* from his modest Walterboro porch, saying he was the fall guy in his cousin's bungled suicide attempt.

"I don't know if betrayed is even the word for it," Smith explained. "I thought of him as a brother, you know, and loved him like a brother. And I would have done almost anything for him. Almost."

On Thursday, October 14, Curtis Smith and his new Columbia-based attorney Jonny McCoy did a round of interviews with all three TV network morning shows.

"I didn't shoot him. I'm innocent," Smith protested on the *Today* show. "If I'd shot him, he'd be dead. He's lied."

"What percentage are you positive that he didn't get shot?" McCoy asked Smith during the interview with anchor Craig Melvin. "You can put a percentage on it."

"A thousand," replied Fast Eddie, adding that there hadn't been blood on anyone.

McCoy maintained that his client had been deliberately set up by a chronic drug addict, going through "horrific withdrawals" after twenty years of opiate usage.

"Jonny, did your client ever sell drugs to Alex?" asked Melville.

"No, absolutely not," replied the attorney.

"Did he ever provide drugs to Alex?"

"So to my knowledge, absolutely not. You're perpetuating the lie that Alex Murdaugh put out. He's used to people listening to his word . . . and running with it. And that's exactly what happened in this case."

In an interview with *CBS Mornings*, Smith claimed to have taken Murdaugh's gun away and disposed of it, so he couldn't kill himself later. "If

I hadn't took the gun," said Smith, as his attorney looked on approvingly, "I don't know what he would have done."

Responding to Smith's interviews, Jim Griffin accused him of lying and offered to provide hospital reports to prove it.

"Alex was definitely shot in the head," he told reporters. "This is not something that is open to debate."

34

"ALEX MURDAUGH NEEDS TO GET COMFORTABLE GETTING UNCOMFORTABLE"

As millions watched Curtis Smith describe his version of the bungled suicide attempt, SLED agents arrested Alex Murdaugh at his Orlando drug rehabilitation unit. It was his second arrest in a month; this time for allegedly swindling millions from Gloria Satterfield's two sons.

The SLED agents arrived without any warning and took Murdaugh into custody. He was booked into the Orange County Department of Corrections on two felony counts of obtaining property by false pretenses, until an extradition hearing could be arranged. Each charge carried a maximum ten-year prison sentence.

"Today is merely one more step in a long process for justice for the many victims in these investigations," said SLED Chief Mark Keel. "We are committed to following the facts wherever they may lead us . . . until justice is served."

Later that day, Murdaugh waived an extradition hearing but spent two nights behind bars before being escorted back to South Carolina by SLED agents. On Saturday afternoon, he was booked into the Alvin S. Glenn Detention Center in Columbia. His bail hearing was scheduled for Tuesday.

"He surrendered himself to SLED [and] didn't fight extradition and he's coming back," announced Dick Harpootlian. "He wants to face these charges. It's a shame he didn't get to finish his rehabilitation."

On Tuesday morning, Alex Murdaugh was brought into Richland County Courthouse in handcuffs attached to shackles around his waist and leg irons. He wore a loose-fitting navy detention center suit and matching face mask, his glasses resting on his head.

The courthouse was packed with media. In addition to the fifteen television cameras, there were crews from *Dateline*, *48 Hours*, and CNN, as well as several dozen reporters. Also sitting in the public gallery were Gloria Satterfield's sons, Tony and Brian, with their attorneys.

Throughout the forty-two-minute hearing, a downcast Alex Murdaugh sat rocking between his two defenders, Dick Harpootlian and Jim Griffin.

After Judge Clifton Newman brought the court into session, prosecutor Creighton Waters outlined the state's case against the defendant, accused of two charges of obtaining property by false pretenses. He described how Gloria Satterfield had been the Murdaughs' housekeeper and nanny for more than twenty years before falling down the steps of the family house, Moselle. After she died, Murdaugh accepted blame, offering to find her two sons a good lawyer so they could file a claim for compensation.

"He takes the boys to a very close friend of his," Waters told the judge. "A person by the name of Cory Fleming."

Then the prosecutor explained how Murdaugh had set up a fraudulent bank account called Forge in 2015, mimicking the legitimate company Forge Consulting, which handled structured settlements.

"And this led to a chain of events, Your Honor, that I've never seen before," said Waters. "Mr. Fleming talks the boys into appointing as personal representative a person at Palmetto State Bank, where Mr. Murdaugh has a long relationship."

Fleming had then negotiated millions of dollars in wrongful death settlements from two separate insurance companies, which went straight into Murdaugh's fraudulent Forge account.

"[It's all] supposed to go to these boys back here," said Waters, pointing at the Satterfield boys in the public gallery. "But the reality is that [it] went into that Forge account that Mr. Murdaugh controlled, and within a few months he had transferred all that money for personal use.

"He had been carrying a $100,000 credit card balance for months. That gets paid off. He writes a $300,000 check to his father. He writes a check for $604,000 to himself. He writes a check for $125,000 to himself. Not a dime goes to this family back here, Your Honor. He absolutely used his position, his prestige, his reputation to steal from this family. They trusted him."

Waters asked the judge to set a $200,000 surety bond, with conditions of a GPS tracker and the surrender of his firearms. This case was only "the tip of the iceberg," he explained, with more crimes by the defendant soon to be revealed.

"We're all aware of the unspeakable tragedy that his family has suffered," said Waters. "His professional life is coming apart at the seams. He's facing very serious charges with additional ones to come, and that can really make someone very unmoored and very dangerous."

When it was his turn, Dick Harpootlian reminded the judge that his client was presumed innocent, and that he was not there to defend the allegations against him. He complained that SLED had not given "a heads-up" before arresting Murdaugh in rehab, saying he would have willingly surrendered. The defense attorney maintained that after six weeks of drug detox, Alex was no longer a danger to himself.

"In an opioid-addled mental condition," said Harpootlian, "he asked someone to shoot him in the head. But that's not where he is today."

Jim Griffin then took over, asking the judge to grant Murdaugh a personal recognizance bond. That would mean not having to put up any of his own money, just a written promise to return to court at a later date.

"Mr. Murdaugh has family ties in the community," Griffin told Judge Newman. "He had been a longtime practicing lawyer in the State of Carolina . . . until he was confronted by his law firm for financial misconduct, which he readily admitted to and resigned. His license has been suspended and we are cooperating with the Office of the Disciplinary Council."

Then Eric Bland addressed the judge on behalf of the Satterfield estate, calling the defendant a "liar" and a "cheat" who had stained the legal profession.

"Today is the day that Alex Murdaugh needs to get comfortable getting uncomfortable," he declared. "This is a man who used a gun on Labor Day weekend. This is a man who used a pen to steal [millions]. It's no different from someone walking into a bank and using a gun. We've never seen such a breach of trust . . . a man who stole money from the very family of the housekeeper who helped raise his kids."

Bland's partner Ronnie Richter then asked bond to be set "for a serious amount," saying the defendant had the ability to pay.

"What's a serious amount?" asked the judge. "Ten million, twenty, thirty, fifty, one hundred?"

Richter replied that, as there was a $4.3 million figure involved in the charges, $4 million would be appropriate.

"I want it to be clearly stated," said the judge, "that I'm not bound by any suggestion or proposals from either side. I'd like to hear from the law enforcement agency in charge of investigating the matter."

SLED special agent Phillip Turner stood up to address the court, explaining the web of investigations now underway into Alex Murdaugh.

"We are investigating multiple different allegations . . . at this point in time," he told the judge. "These include the Stephen Smith death, the actual cause of Miss Satterfield's death [which] we're looking into. And numerous other financial investigations dealing with fraud or possible other criminal actions."

Dick Harpootlian then blamed Cory Fleming and Chad Westendorf for any alleged financial irregularities that may have taken place involving the Satterfield settlement.

"I think it's important that the court understand," he told the judge, "Mr. Murdaugh was not a lawyer in the Satterfield matter. He was the defendant. He had no authority over any money whatsoever. The lawyer was a friend of his [and] the one that issued those checks. . . . and there's a personal representative who is a banker. They were responsible for making sure that Mr. Murdaugh could not, if in fact he did, purloin that money."

Judge Newman then called a fifteen-minute recess to review documents provided by both sides, before he made his decision.

When the hearing resumed, Judge Newman expressed concern about the "safety issues" involved, not only to the defendant but the entire community.

"There's no amount of bond that the court can set that would safely provide protection to Mr. Murdaugh or to the community," he said. "I am requiring Mr. Murdaugh to undergo a psychiatric evaluation to be submitted to the court for a further consideration at a later date."

Murdaugh was led out of the courtroom by sheriff's deputies, looking dejected and stunned, to a barrage of clicking cameras.

Outside the court, Harpootlian was asked about his comments that Cory Fleming was to blame instead of his client.

"Alex is not the lawyer," said Harpootlian. "Fleming is the lawyer. It's just amazing to us that the focus is just on Alex, there are other people who have participated in this process."

Just hours after Judge Newman denied Alex Murdaugh bond, his son Buster and brother John Marvin were spotted gambling at the Venetian Hotel in Las Vegas. They were photographed at the roulette wheel before moving on to the blackjack table, where they sipped cocktails into the early hours of the morning.

When the photographs hit the media, they caused some unfortunate optics for the beleaguered family. During a phone call to his father, now an inmate at the Alvin S. Glenn Detention Center, Buster complained about being photographed.

"So I did go gambling," he said. "Someone took a picture of me and John Marvin in the casino. The next day, there was an article created about how I'm misusing funds by gambling."

"You're kidding me," replied Alex, sounding shocked. "What a fucking . . . are you kidding me? How they recognize you?"

"I'm a national figure, I think."

"I guess you're going to have to wear a hat . . . when you go places," said his father, and he laughed.

The day after the Las Vegas photographs were published, three plaintiffs involved in separate Murdaugh civil cases filed identical motions to freeze Alex Murdaugh's assets and monitor his spending.

"Upon information and belief," read a motion by attorney Mark Tinsley on behalf of Mallory Beach's family, "Buster Murdaugh was recently at the casino in the Venetian Hotel, Las Vegas, Nevada, as evidenced by the photo . . . attached."

Attorneys for the Beach family, Connor Cook, and Gloria Satterfield's sons all asked a judge to appoint a receiver to investigate, identify, and locate all Alex Murdaugh's assets. They also demanded a temporary injunction to prevent Buster, who now held his father's power of attorney, from disposing of any assets without court approval.

"We hope that this will stop some of the wasting of assets that appears to be occurring," Mark Tinsley told *FITSNews*, "and will begin the process of figuring out what has happened to date."

On Thursday, October 28, the day before a hearing to decide whether to freeze his assets, Alex Murdaugh was sued by his own brother Randy and former law partner Johnny E. Parker for almost half a million dollars. In a complaint filed at the Hampton Court of Common Pleas, Randy Murdaugh alleged that he had lent Alex $75,000 to cover an overdrawn account at Palmetto State Bank, with a promise that it would be paid back within thirty days.

"[The] Defendant did not disclose that he was in poor financial condition," read the lawsuit.

It went on to state that after Randy had driven his brother to a drug rehab center after his alleged suicide attempt, he had written out a $15,000 check for Alex's initial treatment.

"Randolph Murdaugh IV has not been reimbursed for this money," stated the lawsuit.

The complaint added that Alex's total debt of $90,000 had dropped to $46,500 after Buster had sold his uncle a Kubota tractor and a rotary cutter against what his father owed.

In a separate lawsuit, Parker claimed he had lent Alex a total of $477,000 in three installments and had never been repaid.

On Friday morning, just before a hearing on whether a receiver would be appointed to oversee all his assets, Alex Murdaugh signed two confessions of judgment—one for what he owed Randy and the other for his former law partner, Johnny E. Parker. They would both be officially filed the following week, ensuring the debts would be paid, whatever receivership decision would be made.

When attorney Mark Tinsley learned about the two confessions of judgment, he was livid. He described it as "the height of arrogance" for Alex's brother and former law partner to "move to the front of the line" before anybody else could be paid.

The noon hearing to freeze his assets was held in Chesterfield County Courthouse in front of circuit judge Daniel Hall. All three plaintiff attorneys attended, but Harpootlian and Griffin were noticeably absent.

Beach family attorney Mark Tinsley told Judge Hall that Alex Murdaugh, now incarcerated, had attempted to "secret away" millions of dollars of family assets that could possibly be collected in the numerous lawsuits against him.

"It's not like we're taking his property," said Tinsley. "We're preserving his property."

He also disputed Murdaugh's lawyers' assertions that their client was penniless, claiming that Griffin was being paid $750 an hour.

"If they don't have any money," said Tinsley, "what would be the harm of enjoining him from spending it? He's living pretty well for someone with no assets. He has a crisis manager."

Attorney John Tiller, representing Alex and Buster Murdaugh in the civil case, argued that the plaintiffs had no legal right to control the Murdaugh family's money.

"They are long in facts and innuendo," he told Judge Hall, saying that any claims would probably be covered by insurance policies.

At the end of the hearing, Judge Daniel Hall said he would make a decision the next week on whether to appoint a receiver or completely freeze the assets.

The next day, the Capitol Club in Columbia hosted a "Standing for Stephen" fundraiser to get Stephen Smith a proper headstone. It would also raise money for Sandy's legal expenses, as well as a scholarship fund in Stephen's name.

The guests of honor were Stephen's mother, Sandy, and twin sister, Stephanie. The emcee was advertised as Fox Carolina's Cody Alcorn but he pulled out at the last minute.

"Miss Sandy is one of the most amazingly strong women I have ever in my life encountered," said organizer Suzanne Andrews. "She's been through hell . . . and in six years, no one has stood up for this mama to help her get a headstone for her child."

Andrews announced that the "Standing for Stephen" GoFundMe had raised more than $12,000 for a headstone, which would be unveiled at the Gooding Cemetery in Hampton the following July.

The same week, Curtis Smith also started a GoFundMe page to raise $20,000 toward his medical and living expenses. Although having allegedly received more than $2 million in checks from his distant cousin over the last six years, Smith now claimed to be broke.

"Well, let me introduce myself," he wrote. "Most of you know me by now . . . Cousin Eddie, Fast Eddie, Curtis Eddie Smith, and the list goes on."

He explained that he had always considered Alex one of his best friends, but everything had changed in September when he tried to help him out.

"I may not have made the best decisions that day," he wrote, "but I did NOT conspire to help Alex take his life and I NEVER would!"

He apologized that, on the advice of his attorney, he could not go into any more detail.

"If you cannot donate," he said, "say a prayer . . . for me, my family, and anyone else that the Murdaughs are going to try to involve in their web of lies."

Soon after firing Alex Murdaugh, PMPED began calling his unsuspecting clients to inform them that they had been robbed and offer compensation. Highway patrolman Lieutenant Thomas Moore was one of the first to receive a call.

"[They] called me and said, 'Look Tommy, there's been a problem,'" Moore later told WCIV-TV. "'Your money's been taken by Mr. Murdaugh, and we're not going to hang you out to dry.'"

PMPED promised to reimburse his bank account with the $125,000 settlement, after deducting its legal fees.

The law firm also notified Jordan Jinks he was owed hundreds of thousands of dollars that Alex had stolen and repaid him. Johnny Bush, who believed that $100,000 of his settlement money had been used for "accident reconstruction," received $95,000, and PMPED repaid Sandra Taylor's estate the $180,000 that Murdaugh had misappropriated.

35

"A Danger to Himself and the Community"

On Tuesday, November 2, Judge Daniel Hall froze all of Alex Murdaugh's assets, appointing attorneys Peter McCoy Jr. and John T. Lay Jr. to take over his finances. It was a massive defeat for Alex Murdaugh. Within days, the judge would also invalidate Buster's power of attorney.

The two court-appointed receivers would now examine and catalog all of Murdaugh's assets and control all his future spending.

Beach attorney Mark Tinsley applauded the judge's decision, saying he was hopeful that the receivers could "begin the process of unraveling the mess created by Murdaugh."

Connor Cook's attorney, Joe McCulloch, called it a big leap forward for all Alex Murdaugh plaintiffs, to stop "the wasting-of-asset train."

One of Lay and McCoy's first actions as co-receivers was to issue an emergency order preventing Randy Murdaugh and Johnny E. Parker from receiving anything from Alex's confessions of judgment.

"This is a clear message that the justice system has had enough of Alex Murdaugh," said Eric Bland. "We don't want him to decide who gets paid and who doesn't."

On November 4, Alex Murdaugh and Curtis Smith were both indicted by a Hampton County grand jury on charges resulting from the Labor Day weekend shooting. The grand jury indictment meant there would not be a preliminary hearing where evidence would be heard, and the two cases would now proceed to trial.

Smith's attorney Jonny McCoy expressed disappointment that he would not be able to cross-examine witnesses in open court about what had really happened during the botched suicide.

If found guilty, Smith faced up to sixty-five years in prison, compared to just twenty for Alex.

Two days later, Judge Clifton Newman denied Alex Murdaugh bond after receiving his psychiatric evaluation. Although its findings remained under seal, the judge ruled Murdaugh should remain behind bars indefinitely.

"After considering the arguments of counsel," read Newman's two-page written decision, "the evaluation submitted, pending charges and other investigations, and the apparent character and mental condition of the defendant, the Court finds that the Defendant is a danger to himself and the community."

Within hours of Judge Newman's decision, Alex Murdaugh's attorneys appealed directly to the SC Supreme Court, filing a petition for a writ of habeas corpus.

"The South Carolina Constitution guarantees every person the right to be released on bail, pending trial," read the defense petition, "except persons charged with capital offenses, offenses punishable by life imprisonment, or violent offenses as defined by the General Assembly."

Calling for a "speedy review of the case," the petition argued that Murdaugh's psychiatric evaluation by Dr. Donna Maddox found that he was not a danger to himself or the community, but did suffer from a "severe opioid disorder." She had recommended a further eight to ten weeks' drug treatment at a residential facility, as well as "grief counseling and trauma therapy."

"We appreciate the court's concern about Alex's well-being," explained Jim Griffin, "and whether he is at risk of harming himself. We respectfully disagree with the court's decision to deny bond."

Accompanying the petition was an explanation to the supreme court as to what had caused Murdaugh's ruinous decline. It claimed his opioid addiction had started more than twenty years ago, after being prescribed painkillers after knee surgery.

"Since then, he has spent millions of dollars supporting this insidious addiction," it claimed.

On November 17, Alex Murdaugh's attorneys asked a judge to dismiss the Gloria Satterfield civil suit, claiming her sons had already been well compensated for their loss. A day earlier, Cory Fleming and his former law firm had agreed to repay all the legal fees and expenses they had received. Their malpractice insurance carrier would also repay the full limits of the policy.

"Mr. Fleming acknowledges that material mistakes were made by him," stated an official press release issued by both parties, "and sincerely apologizes to Ms. Satterfield's sons for everything they have been through. Alex Murdaugh lied to Mr. Fleming to steal client funds."

In a three-page response to the civil suit, attorneys Harpootlian and Griffin argued that because the sons had already received far more than the original $4.3 million from other parties, Alex Murdaugh did not owe them anything. They demanded the case either be dismissed or put on hold until the criminal case against Alex was resolved.

Satterfield attorney Eric Bland called the motion "despicable."

"You mean Alex Murdaugh gets to keep stolen money because the heirs were so dogged in making other people pay?" he asked. "Think about how tone-deaf and arrogant that is."

The next day, a South Carolina state grand jury indicted Alex Murdaugh on a further twenty-seven charges in five different counties. These included: four counts of breach of trust with fraudulent intent, seven counts of obtaining signature or property by false pretenses, seven counts of money laundering, eight counts of computer crimes, and one count of forgery.

Only one of the fresh indictments related to Gloria Satterfield; the others involved more alleged Murdaugh victims, Manuel Santis-Cristiani, Deon Martin, and highway patrolman Lieutenant Thomas Moore.

"Altogether," said SC Attorney General Alan Wilson, "Murdaugh is charged with respect to alleged schemes to defraud victims and thereafter launder $4,853,488."

Alex Murdaugh now faced over a hundred years in prison if found guilty.

"This doesn't appear to add anything new to the case," scoffed Jim Griffin, "other than additional charges."

On Monday, November 22, a contrite Alex handwrote a letter of apology to his former best friend, Cory Fleming, from his cell at the Richland County Detention Center.

> *Dear Cory,*
> *Happy Thanksgiving to all of you!*
> *I am so sorry for all the damage I have caused you & your family. You are the last person I would want to hurt & I know I did. I'm still not sure how I let all this happen.*
> *I think about you all the time. I miss you more than you could know. I hope you are doing as good as you can under the circumstances. Let Jim know if I can do anything at all to help in any way.*
> *Just wanted to say hello.*
> *I miss [Maggie] and Paul so bad but I am more proud of [Buster] than ever. He has been so strong. Not sure how he does it given all I've put on him. Check on him if you get time or feel like it.*
> *All my love,*
> *Alex*

Sam Crews III's mother, Betty Ruth, died in late November aged ninety-six, and Alex's sister, Lynn Goettee, attended her visitation. Sam's sister Aline told her that a couple of days before she passed, Betty Ruth had a special message for Alex.

"She said, 'I love all those Murdaughs,'" Lynn later told him in a jailhouse phone call. "She knew you had done some stuff you weren't supposed to, but you were a good person and had a good heart."

"Well, that's nice to say," said Alex.

While he waited for his next bond hearing, Alex Murdaugh spent his time scrubbing his cell with a mop and working out. Housed in the medical wing for his own protection, Alex had limited social interaction with the other inmates. He had trouble sleeping because the inmate next door yelled all night long, while others communicated through the prison vent system.

"I'm trying to make the best of it," he told his sister, Lynn. "You know what? Every day I do is one less day."

But his two defense attorneys feared for their client's safety, because of what the Murdaugh family represented.

"[They] are worried that I'm going to get shivved," he told his brother Randy. "That's what they call it in the pokey when somebody sticks you with a knife."

"Are there people there that have some reason to have animosity towards you?" asked Randy.

"Just because there's been so much publicity and talk about me being a prosecutor," replied Alex. "So they're worried somebody might want to make a statement. But I told Jim and Dick that I used to be a pretty bad dude. I'm kind of soft now, but I think I can take most of the people in this medical ward. I don't know how good I'll do out in the general population."

Another major concern was paying his defense attorneys, who were now demanding $550,000 up front. They were pressuring Alex to cash in his PMPED retirement account, which had $2.2 million in it. He and his family were debating whether to do that or get a loan.

John Marvin had deep reservations about using the retirement fund, which would incur high penalties.

"I trust Jim one hundred percent," he told Alex, "but I just feel they're trying to get the easiest money. Jim said [they] are both charging $250,000 and they want $50,000 of expense money. I feel that's a lot of money for something not going to trial."

"They talked to me about those numbers," said Alex, "and I just said,

'That's too much for a civil case.' We already had that conversation . . . if they charged me with Maggie and Paul['s murder]. But . . . that's so crazy."

John Marvin said Harpootlian had told him it was a possibility, although he didn't believe it would come to that. He was certain he could borrow enough money for Alex's legal fees, as long as he got it back eventually.

"We have to find out if we can use that money from 'Handsome,'" suggested Alex, referring to his father's inheritance.

"And there's questions about that too," said John Marvin. "They said some money that you paid to Daddy was not legitimate. I think it's safer to borrow than to pull out of retirement."

Always genial, Big Red soon made friends with several other inmates over poker and games of chess, but he was always on his guard against a possible snitch.

"I make a point not to have too much interaction with anybody," Alex told his sister, Lynn. "So they say, 'Well, he told me this . . . he said that.'"

But he made an exception for a one-legged trustee named Clarence, who did him favors in exchange for small bribes.

"He's an old guy in a wheelchair," Alex told John Marvin's wife, Liz. "He moves himself with his one leg. He's like the guards' little pet . . . and does all the running around. He does a lot for me. Twenty bucks means all the world to him."

Clarence arranged extra channels on his TV as well as sneaked in books, which were banned so that inmates couldn't use the paper to get high on K2, a synthetic marijuana some of the inmates smoked. He was now devouring books by his favorite authors, John Grisham, Pat Conroy, and James Patterson.

A lifelong hustler, Alex had easily adapted to jail, already gaming the system to his advantage. But instead of dealing in millions of dollars as he had on the outside, it was now for meager commissary items such as candy bars and soap.

"It would amaze you, the trade system in here," he told his brother Randy, "and how innovative these folks are and resourceful with so little.

I'll have to tell you about it later and not on the phone, because I know they listen to every single phone call I make."

Inmates were only allowed $60 a week to be deposited into their commissary accounts, so Alex had either Liz or Lynn put an additional $60 a week into another inmate's, Lucas's, account. Alex paid him a $15 commission and kept the extra money.

"Canteen is commerce," he explained to Buster in one call. "It's the trade and it really helped me last week. He doesn't get canteen so I give him some of the money and he orders canteen for me."

"It just looks a little weird," replied his son. "I just hope you're not doing anything you shouldn't be doing."

Alex was also gambling on NFL football games for meager canteen items, proudly boasting about his successes to Buster during jail calls.

"I had nine out of eleven games on Sunday on the pro games," he told him on December 1. "I missed the Steelers. The Eagles were three-and-a-half-point favorites over the Giants and they lost. But I had nine out of eleven . . . that's pretty damn hard!"

"Oh, yeah," said his son and he sighed.

"I won like six suets, four beef sticks, and a bunch of crackers . . . you know a bunch of canteen shit."

Alex had also bonded with a hardened criminal who had spent most of his life in prison and became a mentor for the former attorney and assistant solicitor.

"We really hit it off and I liked him," he told Liz Murdaugh. "He was always in trouble with guns but laid-back and very jail-smart. He taught me a lot about being in here that helped me."

Behind bars, he became obsessed with Buster reentering law school, after being expelled for plagiarism and low grades two years earlier. Prior to his arrest, Alex had orchestrated an elaborate plan for his son to be re-admitted to the South Carolina University School of Law. It involved paying a high-powered Columbia attorney, Butch Bowers, $60,000 to make it happen, half up-front and half if he succeeded.

"I'm not trying to bug you, babe," Alex told Buster in one call, "but you've got to get that thing reset with law school."

Buster promised to send an email to the dean of the SC University School of Law, William C. Hubbard, but Alex immediately picked up on his lack of enthusiasm.

"I hope you didn't think I was being short with you today," he told Buster. "I'm asking you to make that appointment at law school. I just don't want to bug you if you don't want to do it."

"Yeah," replied Buster, "I'm going to do it. It just hasn't worked out and probably, with the holiday coming up, probably won't. . . . I might not be able to sit down with Hubbard prior to that."

"I understand that, but just remember it's important. Do you follow what I'm saying?"

"Yeah, I do."

Then his father ordered him to make an appointment with the dean the first week of December, with a view to returning to law school next fall.

"Did you hear back from the dean?" he asked a few weeks later.

"No, sir," replied his son. "I'm checking my email every day."

"Okay, if you don't hear tomorrow . . . you might do a follow-up."

"Yeah, if I don't hear from them, I will definitely shoot a follow-up later this week."

"Tomorrow?" insisted his father.

"And if I don't hear from them," said Buster, "I might get in touch with Butch to see if [he can] call them and say that I've been trying to get in touch."

"All right," said Alex. "Was Butch paid all the money that he was owed . . . thirty grand up front and thirty [later]?"

"Yes."

"Call Butch late Friday afternoon," ordered his father, "and that way he can . . . call them first thing Monday morning."

Aware that all his jail calls were being recorded, Alex never mentioned Maggie or Paul, except to remind Buster to arrange headstones and make sure there were always flowers on their graves.

36

"I Was in the Throes of Withdrawal"

On Friday, December 9, six months after Maggie and Paul's murders, a state grand jury hit Alex Murdaugh with seven new indictments, with twenty-one new charges of stealing a further $1.3 million. This brought his total number of indictments to a dozen, with forty-eight separate charges of cheating his personal injury clients out of $6 million.

There were a further nine counts of breach of trust with fraudulent intent, seven counts of computer crimes, four counts of money laundering, and one count of forgery.

His newly named victims included: Randy Drowdy, the Estate of Blondell Gary, Christopher Anderson, Jordan Jinks, Jamian Risher, the Estate of Sandra Taylor, and Johnny Bush. All the money was alleged to have been laundered through his bogus Forge account with the Bank of America.

Four days later, Alex Murdaugh appeared from Richland County jail at a virtual bond hearing in front of Judge Alison Renee Lee. At the defense's request, the morning hearing was not public, and reporters could only take written notes. All video or audio recording devices were strictly prohibited.

Dick Harpootlian told Judge Lee that his client had now agreed to confess a judgment of owing $4.3 million to the Satterfield estate. He read out a statement from Alex Murdaugh, apologizing to Gloria Satterfield's entire family for his "financial transgression committed in connection with the wrongful death settlement" and all the "pain" it had caused her sons.

The defender said his client was not a flight risk, as he could no longer practice after being fired by his family law firm.

"This case has got a lot of notoriety," said Harpootlian, "and Your Honor, you'd have to be living in a different world to not know this has been written about [and] blogged about. This case has intrigued a number of people in the blogosphere."

He urged the judge not to be influenced by the case's notoriety in setting bond, adding that he believed his client deserved to be released on his own recognizance, meaning he would not have to pay anything.

"There are those who would indicate because he has fallen so far from grace that he should be punished by a high bond and kept in jail," observed Harpootlian. "We'd ask you to release him on a reasonable bond with house arrest [and] electronic monitoring."

Then Alex Murdaugh addressed the court for the first time since his arrest, knowing that he was not being recorded. Although he had spent much of the virtual hearing with his head down and eyes closed, he seemed unusually animated for his impassioned eight-minute mea culpa.

"Your Honor," he began. "Please understand that there may be concern over whether I'm a danger to myself, based upon my actions on Saturday, September the fourth."

Murdaugh told the judge that the day before the shooting, he had met with his brother Randy and another PMPED partner after being confronted about stealing money from the law firm.

"I divulged to them that I had an opioid addiction that I had concealed for twenty years," he explained. "Things were moving really quickly and really negatively. My world was caving in. I was in the throes of withdrawal, as I had not taken opiates as I had for so long."

He said he was still grieving the murders of Maggie and Paul, and knew that everyone he cared about would be hurt when they learned what he had done.

"I knew that this news was going to humiliate me," he said. "Humiliate my son, who's trying to be a lawyer . . . and deserves none of what he's gotten. I knew it would humiliate mine and Maggie's family, who's very proud of me, [and] my family's legacy, which I know I've tarnished badly."

He told the judge that since the murders he had tried to maintain a close relationship with Buster, worried that this would alienate him.

"All of this was crushing to me," he explained. "I was in a very bad place due to the withdrawals. I made a terrible decision that I regret, that I'm sorry about and frankly that I'm embarrassed about."

He said that after thirty-eight days of inpatient drug treatment he was drug free and his life had changed dramatically.

"My head is straighter," he said, "and I'm thinking clearer than I have in a long time. I've been exercising. What started out as just trying to break the monotony has turned into several hours a day of exercising."

Now that he had kicked his twenty-year opioid addiction, he was back to defense attorney Harpootlian and feeling better than he had in years.

"I've been humbled and surprised by the outpouring of love and support I have received," he judge. "I want to be there for my son. I want to deal with these charges appropriately and head-on."

He then appealed to the judge to free him on his own recognizance, saying he was committed to "being [his] best self" in order to avoid a relapse.

"I guess in conclusion, Judge," he told her, "I'm not a danger to myself, and I look forward to the opportunity to hopefully try to begin working to put all this behind me. Thank you for letting me speak with you."

Firing back, prosecutor Creighton Waters pointed out that the defendant's "significant personal family assets" posed a flight risk, as he was already facing forty-eight charges of defrauding his clients out of $6.2 million, with many more expected.

"Some of the victims have claimed a backlash," he said. "One victim was called 'a snitch,' and people are afraid to come forward. And indeed for others to come forward they need, I believe, to see a strong message about how serious that the system is taking these particular charges, regardless of the name that this man carries and the family prestige that he carries."

Waters told the judge that the defendant had "preyed" on the "most trusting and most vulnerable," exploiting the Murdaugh family influence and power in the community, which heightened the dangers he still posed.

He asked the judge to set a $4.7 million bond, representing $100,000 for every felony Murdaugh stood charged with.

Judge Lee expressed doubts about releasing Murdaugh on bond, but under the law, she would have to set one.

"I'm a little reluctant," she explained, "but I'm obligated by state law and the constitution."

She then set a $7 million cash bond, to be paid in full. She also set bond conditions that Alex be under house arrest and wear a GPS monitoring device, surrender his passport, be subject to random drug tests, and receive mental health and substance abuse counseling.

Defense attorney Harpootlian observed that even the SC Attorney General's Office had not asked for a bond that high, and vowed to appeal.

After the hearing, he said it would be impossible for his client to come up with $7 million.

"He's impecunious," he said. "He's locked down and got no money. This is tantamount to no bond."

On December 29, Peters, Murdaugh, Parker, Eltzroth & Detrick restructured and dropped the name "Murdaugh," to become the Parker Law Group, LLP. It was a huge body blow for the Murdaugh family legacy law firm, founded in 1910 by Randolph Murdaugh Sr.

According to a PMPED press release, the new firm would remain at 101 Mulberry Street East in Hampton, and had been renamed to honor partner Johnny E. Parker for his fifty years of outstanding service. It noted that Parker was the only surviving partner left from the original PMPED name.

"We're grateful to Johnny Parker for his dedication and leadership of our firm," said partner Ronnie Crosby. "It's an honor to name our firm after one of South Carolina's most accomplished and respected lawyers."

Crosby also confirmed that Alex Murdaugh's brother Randy would remain at the new Parker Law Group as one of eight partners.

"Our firm is a collection of talented and dedicated attorneys," Parker told *The Hampton County Guardian*. "While this firm may bear my name, it's made up of a team of attorneys and employees who put their energy into achieving the best results for our clients."

John Marvin broke the news to Alex in a jailhouse phone call.

"The law firm's been dissolved and they're re-forming under a new name," he told Alex.

"I didn't know anything about that," replied Alex. "What is that?"

"Just because of all the negative publicity, and all of the stuff they're going through."

"What is the new name?"

"It's going to be operated under the Parker Law Group."

"The what?" asked Alex incredulously.

37

"He Stole Every Dime I Had"

At the dawning of 2022, America was riveted by the Murdaugh family saga, a true-life Greek tragedy playing out right in front of their eyes. It was the most intriguing crime story for years, and the public's appetite was insatiable. Thousands of social media sleuths worldwide had their own theories of what had really happened that June night at Moselle, and the name "Alex Murdaugh" was now one of the most Googled subjects in America.

But the big question still remained of whether Alex had murdered Maggie and Paul, and Hampton locals all had their own opinions.

Sam Crews III believed the double homicide was directly tied to the upcoming Beach civil hearing, where Alex would have been ordered to reveal all his financial information.

"I don't want to say that Alex did it," said Crews, "but I think getting rid of Paul was going to make his life a lot easier. When you lay down with dogs, you're going to get up with fleas, and Alex was laying down with too many dogs."

Longtime Hampton business owner Kim Brant, who knew the Murdaugh family well, theorized that Alex's father had orchestrated the murders from his deathbed to protect his family's name and legacy.

"I believe Randolph III put a hit on Paul," she explained. "He was dying and he could not leave that mess for the rest of the family, because he knew it was only going to get worse."

Then in early January, *FITSNews* news director Mandy Matney reported that SLED investigators had found physical and forensic evidence directly linking Alex Murdaugh to both murders. Her sources inside the investigation called the mounting evidence against Alex "substantial and serious."

SLED officials declined to comment on the report, citing an ongoing investigation.

The first week of January, Alex Murdaugh's attorneys filed a seventeen-page motion for bond reduction and a new hearing. They argued that the $7 million bond set was unreasonable and "tantamount to no bond at all," claiming their client had less than $10,000 in his two Palmetto State Bank accounts.

"Mr. Murdaugh does not have seven million dollars or anything close to that amount," read their motion. "Mr. Murdaugh is a man who cannot pay his phone bill."

This became a running joke with Alex in his jail calls, where he complained that even Bernie Madoff, who stole around $65 billion in the largest Ponzi scheme in history, was released on bail.

"Have you got my bond posted yet?" he asked John Marvin.

"Yeah, I'm writing them a check as we speak," quipped his brother.

"Ain't that some shit," said Alex.

On Tuesday, January 4, 2022, Palmetto State Bank CEO Russell Laffitte was placed on administrative leave by the bank's board of directors, composed mainly of his family. Three days later, he was fired from the bank his family had owned and run for seventy years. An investigation was immediately launched to examine all of Laffitte's bank dealings involving his lifelong friend, Alex Murdaugh.

"Palmetto State Bank has permanently severed the employment of Russell Laffitte," said bank president Jan Malinowski. "The bank and its board of directors remain fully committed to their customers . . . and the communities Palmetto State Bank serves."

A bank spokesman said that Chad Westendorf, who had acted as personal representative for Gloria Satterfield's sons and later repaid his $30,000 fee, remained at the bank.

Six days later, circuit judge Alison Renee Lee held another virtual bond hearing to discuss the defense's bond reduction motion. Defendant Alex Murdaugh attended via Zoom from the Richland County Detention Center, wearing a black Covid mask, appearing to have a black eye and heavily bruised knuckles. The virtual ninety-minute hearing was held in public, although it could not be broadcast live.

There was much media speculation because one of Murdaugh's alleged victims, Lieutenant Thomas Moore, would be testifying.

Attorney John Lay, one of two court receivers now overseeing the Murdaugh finances, testified that the defendant had around $10,000 in his three bank accounts. There was also a retirement account with $2.2 million and various real estate holdings, which had been seized by the court. Lay added that Alex also stood to inherit his late wife Maggie's estate, including Moselle and the Edisto Beach house, and may be a beneficiary of his late father's estate.

Dick Harpootlian told the judge that his client had no available liquid assets to post bond, and could not even afford to pay a bondsman ten percent for a surety bond. He strongly disputed the prosecution's assertions at the previous hearing that his victims felt threatened and had been called "rats."

"My client is sitting in jail," said Harpootlian. "He hasn't been in a position to threaten anybody. Every word he says on the phone is being recorded . . . so I think that is bogus."

Harpootlian then attacked the heavy media coverage of the case, saying that all the negative publicity should not affect his client receiving a fair bond treatment.

"Your Honor, the problem with this case [is] what I would call the paparazzi view," he told the judge. "This thing has been ginned up so much in the press that it's denied Mr. Murdaugh the same kind of treatment anybody else in his position would get. Bernie Madoff stole $65 billion [and] his bond was $10 million and he made it."

Harpootlian claimed his client was being punished for being a Murdaugh, one of Hampton County's most "reputable, well-respected, and affluent" families.

Then prosecutor Creighton Waters stood up to argue against reducing the $7 million bond, calling the defendant a flight risk and a danger to the community.

"[This is] a unique case," he explained, "where we have a man from such a powerful family, from the heights of power and success in the legal profession here in South Carolina, who is facing these allegations. That tends to make one, in my experience, more dangerous and more unhinged than perhaps someone who's . . . been in this position before."

Waters refuted the defense's claim that no victims had been intimidated and threatened.

"We've had people tell us that they've faced a backlash," said Waters. "We've had a victim being called 'a snitch.' Another said over and over again that he's not worried for himself, but if he comes forward, what's going to happen to his wife and kids? That is the general theme that we have felt throughout this case, and it is indicative of the power that this man exercised."

He said many still struggled with thinking Alex Murdaugh had been their friend before he stole their money.

"And this, when combined with the power and influence of this family," said Waters, "the danger to the community is very palpable."

A furious Dick Harpootlian demanded to address these allegations before any victim testified.

"You can," said Judge Lee, "but I know you're going to have more to say once you hear the victims."

"Well, not really," answered Harpootlian, "I've heard them before. It's the same old song."

He told the judge that contrary to the prosecutor's claim that the Murdaugh family was so influential in Hampton County, they had not been charged.

"The guy sitting in front of you in the jail with the mask on," he told the judge, "is the only one who's charged with anything. He's not Don

Corleone. There's not some Mafia family out there. If there is, I challenge Mr. Waters to indict them."

Then Harpootlian attacked the prosecution for its "inability" to focus on the murders of Paul and Maggie.

"And they're attempting to distract from those murders," Harpootlian told the judge. "They're attempting to infer that somehow Alex Murdaugh was involved and use that as a way to heavy up on him. He was not involved and this is a total distraction. I apologize to the court for being somewhat emotional about this."

Then highway patrolman Lieutenant Thomas Moore appeared on the Zoom screen in full uniform from his police station to testify. He began by telling the judge how he'd gone to Alex Murdaugh because he'd heard he was "a good attorney," after being seriously injured while on duty in a snowstorm.

"I know Mr. Murdaugh as my attorney," he said. "A very nice man and very cordial. I never had any issues and would communicate with him on a regular basis.

"Now here's the problem. He treated me *that* nice and he stole every dime I had from the injury I incurred."

Lieutenant Moore testified that after being rear-ended, he'd undergone extensive back surgery costing around $250,000. After Murdaugh took his case, he expected a big settlement but waited and waited. When he finally received a check for $125,000, Murdaugh had him bring it into the PMPED office to be deposited in a special account until his workers' compensation case was fully resolved.

"And I was given bad legal advice," he told the judge. "The same day that I took the check [to his law firm] it was taken to another bank and cashed."

He said his chronic debilitating back condition was only getting worse, and he was only working to pay his medical bills and monthly expenses. He questioned how Alex Murdaugh was still able to afford two of South Carolina's most expensive lawyers if he was truly as broke as they claimed he was.

"I'm not up here to give the same old song and dance," he told the judge, alluding to Harpootlian's previous remark. "I'm up here to just give you my opinion as far as what's happened to me."

Then he asked Judge Lee not to set Alex Murdaugh free, as he was very intelligent and clearly dangerous.

"He's got a way of getting money," said Lieutenant Moore. "He's not dumb. He's a financial threat in my opinion as well as a physical threat. Would I be surprised if he or somebody related to him showed up at my house with a gun? Absolutely not."

He told the judge that if Murdaugh was released, he would either disappear or commit suicide.

"I think he's done as much harm as it is," said Lieutenant Moore. "I don't think we need to give him the opportunity to do any more until he goes to trial. And that's all I want to say, Your Honor."

At the end of the hearing, Judge Lee said she would consider the matter "under advisement," and then issue a written order with her decision.

The next day, an angry Randy Murdaugh called Alex about the hearing. He was especially concerned with the highway patrolman's testimony that he would be in danger if bond was granted.

"Were you in the courtroom when Tommy Moore said that he wouldn't be surprised if your family members would show up with a gun to shoot him?" asked Randy.

"Yeah," replied Alex.

"I'd like to know who the hell any of them are on the fricking list," said Randy. "Does he think Buster's going to show up? Or John?"

"I don't know," said Alex, and he sighed. "They were saying a bunch of stuff about people being threatened and the same old stuff. They're pretty good with all that rumor and innuendo. If someone's threatening somebody, then do something. Don't just come in here and say, 'Hey, there's all this stuff going on.'"

Soon after the bond hearing, the SC Supreme Court ruled that the defense's petition for a writ of habeas corpus was moot, as Judge Lee had set a $7 million bond after it was filed.

Then on January 18, Alex Murdaugh received more bad news when

Judge Lee denied his request to lower bail, leaving it at $7 million, with no ten percent cash option.

"After considering all the information provided," wrote the judge in her one-page decision, "this Court finds that the current bond is reasonable to assure his appearance in court as defendant remains a flight risk and potential danger to himself and community."

Attorney Jim Griffin said although he was "disappointed" with her decision, he respected it.

Two days later, on January 20, a state grand jury indicted Alex Murdaugh on four new indictments with twenty-one new counts of breach of trust with fraudulent intent and computer crimes. The new indictments accused Murdaugh of embezzling a further $2.65 million, bringing the total charges he now faced up to seventy-five for allegedly stealing $8.9 million. If found guilty on all criminal charges, Murdaugh now faced a potential term of 731 years in prison.

The unfortunate victims named in these new indictments were: the Estate of Hakeem Pinckney, Natarsha Thomas, and Arthur Badger. Many of these cases involved the recently fired Palmetto State Bank CEO Russell Laffitte as the victims' personal representative.

Soon after the new indictments came down, Russell Laffitte issued a statement that he had been "fully cooperating" with SLED investigators since the beginning and would continue to do so.

Attorney Justin Bamberg, who represented Hakeem Pinckney's family, told *The Washington Post* that Murdaugh had preyed on the poor Black families who had looked up to him.

"Alex gave them just enough money," he said, "so they would drop to their knees and say, 'Thank you, Jesus,' and took the rest."

The following Monday, Mark Tinsley filed six creditor's claims against Maggie and Paul Murdaugh's estate, totaling $65 million. It was a deft legal maneuver to prevent Alex Murdaugh from handing over Moselle and his other assets to family members and other beneficiaries before his creditors, such as former clients, were paid.

Two $25 million creditor's claims were filed in Colleton County Probate Court on behalf of the Beach family estate, two $5 million claims for Paul Murdaugh's ex-girlfriend Morgan Doughty, and two $2.5 million ones for Miley Altman.

As the personal representative of Maggie's estate, which included Moselle, John Marvin Murdaugh would have to settle any creditor's claims before his jailed brother could receive anything.

"[John Marvin] is not working with Alex or anyone else," his probate attorney said in a statement, "and will not make distributions of any sale proceeds to Alex or anyone else, until the court directs him who to pay."

On February 14, Morgan Doughty and Miley Altman became the final two boat crash survivors to file suit against the Murdaugh family and Parker's convenience store. Attorney Mark Tinsley filed motions into Hampton County Courthouse, ten days before the third anniversary of the boat crash when the statute of limitations ran out.

The new filing named Alex, Buster, John Marvin, and Randy Murdaugh in their respective roles as the personal representatives for Maggie's and Paul's estates.

They alleged that Alex and Maggie "condoned" and even "encouraged" Paul to drink to excess, "as evidenced by the fact she 'liked' social media posts" of their underage son imbibing alcohol. It also accused them of allowing Paul to drive vehicles and boats knowing he "was incompetent, unfit, and/or reckless based on his constant consumption of alcohol."

It also revealed for the first time that Paul had spoken to his mother on the phone shortly before the fatal crash.

"However," it stated, "she failed to stop Paul, despite knowing he was intoxicated after having paid for the alcohol he consumed earlier."

On February 15, the Murdaughs' Moselle hunting lodge was put up for sale at $3.9 million. The infamous site of the double homicide had now been rebranded as "Cross Swamp Farm," but there would be many legal hurdles to overcome before any sale, which a judge would have to approve.

The immense 1,772-acre property bordering the banks of the Salkehatchie River was described as "an unusually diverse habitat with varying forest types." It had over 2.5 miles of river frontage "offering freshwater fishing, kayaking, and abundant deer, turkey, and waterfowl."

The sales brochure stated that the 2011 custom-built 5,275-square-foot house with a large game room could easily double as a weekend hunting lodge sleeping up to fifteen people. It also had a 1,140-square-foot care-taker's house on the property, as well as twelve dog kennels.

On Wednesday, March 16, 2022, a South Carolina grand jury indicted Cory Fleming on eighteen criminal charges, with four new ones against Alex Murdaugh, for their alleged roles in the Gloria Satterfield insurance scam.

In the forty-four-page indictment, they were jointly charged with crim-inal conspiracy. Fleming was also charged with three counts of making false statements and misrepresentations, seven counts of breach of trust with fraudulent intent, six counts of money laundering, and one count of computer crime.

The new superseding indictment charged Murdaugh with a further three counts of obtaining signature or property by false pretenses, three counts of money laundering, three counts of computer crime, and three counts of making a false statement or representation.

After the indictments went public in a press release from the SC Attor-ney General's press office, Cory Fleming's attorney Deborah B. Barbier issued a statement on his behalf.

"Mr. Fleming is deeply disappointed in the decision of the Attorney Gen-eral's Office to seek criminal charges against him," it read. "Mr. Fleming is yet another casualty of the host of crimes perpetrated by Alex Murdaugh."

The next morning, Cory Fleming appeared before Judge Alison Lee, who granted him a $100,000 surety bond with a ten percent cash op-tion. She set conditions that he surrender his passport, not leave South Carolina without court permission, and have no contact with Alex Murdaugh.

February 23, 2022, marked the third anniversary of Mallory Beach's death and the boat crash that had plunged the Murdaugh family into the abyss. It was also the day that a dozen jailhouse recordings of Alex Murdaugh's calls to his family first aired on the popular *Murdaugh Murders* podcast.

A month earlier, reporter Mandy Matney had filed a Freedom of Information Act (FOIA) request for the Alvin S. Glenn Detention Center inmate's phone calls and it was approved. The first calls released were between Alex and his son Buster, brothers Randy and John Marvin, his sister-in-law Liz, and his sister, Lynn.

Alex received no in-person visitations because of COVID-19 restrictions in the jail, where only video conferencing was allowed. In a five-month period from October 2021 to May 2022, he made almost two hundred calls.

They clearly demonstrated for the first time the Murdaugh family dynamic and Alex's desperate need for control. He discussed finances and protecting the family assets with his brothers, and made small talk with his sister about him "rotting away" in jail. He was continually reminding them to keep topping up his two $60-a-week commissaries, complaining he only "ate canteen" because the jail food was inedible.

In his increasingly fraught calls to Buster, he chided his son for not being proactive enough about getting readmitted into law school, but always ended the calls by saying how much he loved him and how proud he was. Buster, on the other hand, did not condone what his father had done.

"I understand that you've done some illegal shit," he told him in one call, adding that investigators couldn't just "turn a cold shoulder to the laws of the United States."

"Allegedly done illegal stuff," quipped Alex, chuckling. "I'm kidding . . . it is what it is."

On March 1, Dick Harpootlian and Jim Griffin filed a federal lawsuit in US District Court in South Carolina to prevent any further calls going public, citing the federal wiretapping statute. It stated that although inmates were made aware that every call would be monitored and recorded, they were not told it would go public.

Alex was clearly rattled, and from then he made far fewer calls than he had done before.

"I'm trying not to call a lot right now until they get this thing resolved," he told Buster. "Jim and [Dick] are working on getting all this stuff straight with the phones, and hopefully I'll be talking to you more regularly."

In mid-April, as local media outlets filed motions to access the jail calls, Richland County announced that it was not releasing any more until a judge could rule on the matter. Then on June 10, US district judge Cameron McGowan Currie agreed to release a further two hundred calls, a major defeat for Murdaugh and his defense team.

It is believed that Alex then started routing calls that he didn't want monitored as three-way calls through his attorney's office phone, so that they would be covered by client-attorney privilege.

38

"THE SCOPE OF MURDAUGH'S DEPRAVITY IS WITHOUT PRECEDENT"

The last week of March, John Marvin Murdaugh broke his silence to give interviews to *The Island Packet* and *Post and Courier* newspapers. It is unknown whether he was paid for the interviews, but earlier he had discussed selling his story with Alex in a jailhouse call.

"There's going to be some people that want to pay for books or interviews," he told Alex the previous November. "Do you know of a media-style attorney, somebody that could handle it in a proper manner, so it's not exploited by anybody?"

"I have no idea," replied Alex. "I just don't know anybody in South Carolina that really specializes in that kind of stuff."

Now, in an attempt to repair some of the damage done to his family, the youngest Murdaugh brother went public to answer a wide range of questions. But he refused to discuss Maggie and Paul's murder, saying it was just too painful.

"I want the truth to get out there," he told *Island Packet* reporter Kacen Bayless during a two-hour interview at his equipment rental business. "I know he did some things. I'm embarrassed for what he's done. I feel so bad."

John Marvin said he couldn't comprehend why his brother would rob clients, since he was making so much money.

"I believe when the time is right, he's going to fess up," said John Marvin. "And if he's been charged with things he didn't do, he needs to say that."

He denied that the family had known anything about Alex's alleged drug addiction and financial shenanigans, saying they would have taken immediate action if they had.

"If [we] had suspected," he said, "I think any of us would step up to the plate and sit down and talk."

Questioned about the ongoing murder investigation, in which Alex remained a person of interest, John Marvin said he and his brother Randy had been interviewed "multiple" times by SLED investigators.

Asked straight out if he thought Alex had killed his wife and son, John Marvin appeared to hedge.

"No, I do not believe he did," he replied. "Is it possible that he could have? Well, I guess anything's possible, but I don't believe it. [I'm] certain that he did not. That is my belief and I truly believe that to my core. But I also understand that . . . maybe I don't know things. Maybe SLED knows a lot more than I do."

Alex Murdaugh was becoming increasingly despondent in jail. He repeatedly asked Buster if Maggie's parents and sister, Marian Proctor, wanted to talk to him, as he hadn't heard from them since his arrest almost six months earlier.

"Honestly speaking," he asked Buster, "do you think Grandma and Pappa T would rather not talk to me while I'm in here?"

"I don't know what to tell you, Dad," said Buster. "It's not like I sit down and talk to them about it, so I don't really know their position."

Buster said that they must be "embarrassed," with all the sensational coverage on television and in the press.

"Yeah," sighed his father. "I know they're having a hard time and I understand. Truthfully, do you think they are at a place where they feel like talking to me, or do you think they're too upset?"

"I don't know," said Buster. "I know they're upset."

"Well, will you find that out point-blank?" he ordered. "I won't bother them if they need more time."

"All right," replied his son.

"So tell them that I'd like to [talk to them] but I totally understand if they're not ready. Is that a deal?"

"All right."

On April 9, two days before Buster's twenty-sixth birthday, his father trust called sounding very emotional.

"I just want to call you to say I'm sorry," he said, breaking down. "All those memories of yours and Paul's birthdays are about to kill me."

Five days later, Alex called to see how Buster was coping on Paul's birthday, checking whether he was going to Hampton Cemetery to put flowers on his brother's grave.

Through a third party, Alex had also arranged a birthday party for his dead son at the Shem Creek Bar in Charleston Harbor, giving Buster a list of Paul's friends to invite.

"I think you'll be happy to know," Buster told his father, "that a bunch of those boys down in Charleston are all going tonight. It's kind of like a commemorative thing."

"I appreciate you doing that very much," said Alex. "Did you get all of them that were on that list?"

"No, not in its entirety," replied his son. "The ones that I didn't get on the phone I texted and people have been posting stuff on social media all day. So everybody knows."

That same day, a South Carolina grand jury secretly indicted Russell Laffitte on a slew of financial charges, hitting Alex Murdaugh and Cory Fleming with a barrage of new ones. The charges were all contained in three superseding indictments, two of them focusing on the Hakeem Pinckney case and the other on Arthur Badger, whose wife, Donna Hay, had died in a 2011 car accident.

Laffitte now faced twenty-one charges dating back to 2011, carrying up to 170 years in prison if convicted.

Alex Murdaugh faced an additional four charges, raising his grand total to fifteen separate indictments with seventy-nine charges, representing

$8.4 million allegedly stolen from his victims. Fleming's five new charges brought his to twenty-three.

Laffitte, fifty-one, was now accused of conspiring with Murdaugh to steal almost $660,000 held in a settlement trust belonging to the Hakeem Pinckney estate, and $350,245 from Hakeem's cousin Natarsha Thomas's trust at Palmetto State Bank. They were also both charged with conspiring to embezzle $1.1 million that Laffitte had issued Murdaugh from a client's account to repay loans.

In another superseding indictment, Murdaugh and Fleming were accused of misappropriating $89,133 from the Hakeem Pinkney estate settlement trust, which had been legally represented by Fleming. Murdaugh's former law school roommate was also accused of using more than $8,000 of Pinckney estate money to hire a private plane to fly Murdaugh and another friend to the 2021 College World Series in Nebraska.

Before he surrendered, Russell Laffitte's attorney Bart Daniel said his client had been "fooled by Alex Murdaugh and taken advantage of."

On May 6, Laffitte appeared at a virtual bond hearing in front of circuit judge Alison Lee, wearing a green detention center jumpsuit. His wife, Susie, appeared from defense attorney Bart Daniel's office to support him.

Prosecutor Creighton Waters told Judge Lee that the defendant had granted his friend Alex Murdaugh $1.8 million of loans that were "off the books." He described how disbursement checks from a client trust account would be made out to Palmetto State Bank. Murdaugh would then take them to Laffitte, who converted them for his personal use.

"Why would Mr. Laffitte allegedly do that?" asked Waters. "Well, he was a loan officer who had given a whole lot of loans to Alex, the bank had a lot of exposure and Mr. Laffitte is the officer responsible for those loans."

Waters explained that Murdaugh was always hard up, despite his legitimate earnings as a lawyer.

"[He] had to beg, borrow, and allegedly steal to stay afloat," explained Waters. "An important cog in that hamster wheel, constantly spinning, was his friend at Palmetto State Bank . . . Russell Laffitte."

The prosecutor added the two had been friends for many years and came from "very prominent families in Hampton County."

Defense attorney Bart Daniel denied his client was a flight risk, saying he was fully cooperating with authorities.

Judge Lee granted Russell Laffitte a one-million-dollar bond with a ten percent option, ordering him to remain under house arrest with GPS monitoring. She also froze all his assets, as he had recently put his Varnville house up for sale, until an agreement could be reached by both sides about protecting the money while his criminal case was pending.

Within hours, Russell Laffitte had posted bond and was back at home under house arrest.

Sunday, May 8, was Mother's Day and Alex Murdaugh called his sister, Lynn, to wish her a happy Mother's Day and see how their ailing mother was doing.

"Her memory is shot," said Lynn. "She doesn't know where she is or who she is or anything else. It's tough."

Alex was obsessed with Buster going to Hampton Cemetery to place flowers on his mother's grave. The previous day he had asked his sister-in-law Liz to prod him.

"Buster's going to Hampton tomorrow to the cemetery," he told her. "Make sure he takes flowers."

"I will," Liz dutifully replied.

He then called Buster with instructions to arrange a Mother's Day conference call with Maggie's family, whom he had still not spoken to since his incarceration.

"I'm trying to call tomorrow," he told Buster, "and get a three-way with Grandma, so I can tell her happy Mother's Day."

"Okay," replied his son.

He said that if he hadn't called by 8:00 P.M., because the jail was so short-staffed, Buster should text Maggie's mother, Kennedy, and sister, Marian, to wish them a happy Mother's Day on his behalf.

When he reminded Buster to put flowers on his mother's grave, his son said that Maggie's family had already ordered a floral arrangement from her favorite Hampton florist, Nix. He and Brooklynn would also bring flowers to the cemetery.

"And I want you to put some for me too," said Alex. "She'd like that."

The first week of June, nine months after SLED had opened an investigation into her death, investigators announced that Gloria Satterfield's body would be exhumed for an autopsy to see exactly what had caused her death. The Satterfield family had reluctantly agreed.

"This is a complex process that will take weeks, not days," said a SLED spokeswoman. "The investigation is still active and ongoing. As such, no additional information . . . is available at this time."

Satterfield family attorney Eric Bland confirmed that the family had given its permission, and it would be done in a respectful fashion.

"I guess SLED wants to rule out foul play," said Bland.

Tuesday, June 7, marked the first anniversary of Maggie and Paul Murdaugh's savage murders, and SLED was still keeping a tight rein on the investigation. Alex Murdaugh, incarcerated since October, was officially still a person of interest. To many, the investigation was frustratingly slow and seemed to have ground to a halt.

The South Carolina news blog *FITSNews* had covered the case from every angle since the very beginning. In late April, it had reported that "high-velocity impact spatter" had been found on a shirt Murdaugh had been wearing on the night of the killings, forensically linking him to the murders. A source inside the investigation revealed there was also evidence that Alex had lured Maggie to Moselle to visit his ailing father on the night of her death.

"There is a 'mountain of evidence' implicating Alex Murdaugh in the crimes," the blog reported.

SLED Chief Mark Keel, who was leading the double homicide investigation, said it was "still very active," refusing to elaborate further.

A week later, the South Carolina Supreme Court's Disciplinary Office announced it was revoking Alex Murdaugh's law license, citing "overwhelming evidence" that he had robbed his clients of millions. Murdaugh, through his attorneys, waived his right to contest it, as it would have meant appearing in person in front of the SC Supreme Court.

A recent lawsuit, lodged in federal court by the Nautilus Insurance Company against Alex Murdaugh and others to recoup the money from Gloria Satterfield's wrongful death suit, was particularly scathing.

"The scope of Murdaugh's depravity is without precedent in Western jurisprudence," it stated.

In mid-June, there was finally some good news when Gloria Satterfield's sons announced they were starting a charity in her honor. At a press conference in Hampton, the Satterfield family announced "Gloria's Gift Foundation," created to provide needy local families with special gifts and meals at Christmas.

It would be set up as a nonprofit foundation and funded out of the now more than $7 million in settlements from the civil suits, as well as from Alex Murdaugh's recently signed $4.3 million confession of judgment, admitting full liability.

"After having fought the good fight for justice," said Gloria's sister, Ginger Hadwin, "we chose to make sure that Gloria's lasting legacy will not be that of a victim, but will be as a champion of love and charity."

On June 23, a South Carolina state grand jury indicted Alex Murdaugh and Curtis Smith on drug charges. They were both accused of conspiracy to manufacture, distribute, and possess oxycodone.

Smith also faced four counts of money laundering and three counts of forgery, as well as charges of trafficking methamphetamine and unlawful possession of marijuana.

It was alleged that Murdaugh had written almost 450 checks to his distant cousin over an eight-year period, totaling more than $2.4 million.

The indictment stated that Murdaugh, Smith, and "other persons known and unknown to the Grand Jury" had conspired together to purchase and distribute "illegally obtained narcotics."

Smith, just a week away from his sixty-second birthday, was arrested at his Walterboro home and booked into the Colleton County Detention Center.

On Tuesday, June 28, the fifteen-page indictment was unsealed and Smith appeared at a noon bond hearing at the Richland County Courthouse wearing leg irons and hand restraints, his greasy blond hair falling past his shoulders.

Prosecutor Creighton Waters told Judge Clifton Newman that the defendant now faced charges, carrying a maximum of 122 years in prison.

"[It was] a long-standing conspiracy in which Mr. Smith was providing and distributing pills in large numbers to Mr. Murdaugh," Waters told the judge. "The investigation has revealed that these millions of dollars did go to facilitate this oxycodone distribution network that Mr. Smith was a big part of. There was also a substantial amount of cash unaccounted for . . . and I would ask for a $350,000 surety bond for Mr. Smith."

Defense attorney Jarrett Bouchette argued that Smith's only income was from disability, so he qualified for the indigent defense program.

"We have someone who has a minimal criminal record and very limited means," said Bouchette. "Given his health, given everything else, a $350,000 bond would seem greatly excessive."

Then Judge Newman asked Smith if he had anything to say before he decided bond.

"Your Honor, I got pulled into it, not by choice," he told the judge. "I don't have any money. Alex Murdaugh got it all; I didn't get none of it. All I have is the disability I live off of and that's it."

He added that he lived in a modest house and looked forward to clearing his name.

Judge Newman said that due to the very serious nature of the conspiracy charges with Alex Murdaugh, he was setting a $250,000 surety bond. If Smith made bond, he would be put under house arrest with GPS monitoring and subject to random drug tests.

Smith spent the following week in the Alvin S. Glenn Detention Center, where Alex Murdaugh had been residing since October, before making bond and being released.

39

"IT ALL CAME BACK TO ALEX MURDAUGH"

Early Tuesday morning, July 12, SLED agents met with the Murdaugh and Branstetter families to warn them that Alex was about to be indicted for Maggie and Paul's murders. It was a courtesy call to prepare the families before murder indictments went before a grand jury.

The agents told the stunned family members that they believed Alex had acted alone, using a rifle and a shotgun, and did not have an accomplice.

Though the dramatic meeting at John Marvin's home proceeded behind closed doors, it was quickly leaked to the media. *FITSNews* was the first to break it with the headline, "Murdaugh Murders: Charges Coming Against Alex Murdaugh."

"If our sources are correct," it read, "the evidence they are relying upon will (as expected) implicate disgraced 53-year-old attorney Alex Murdaugh in the brutal slayings of his wife and younger son last spring."

A few minutes later, the story was updated to report that SLED investigators had been spotted leaving John Marvin's home after telling both families about the murder charges.

As soon as news of his brother's impending indictment broke online, John Marvin confirmed it was true.

"The entire family has been consistent that regardless of what goes on, we want the truth," he told reporters. "We seek justice and we want the truth."

A SLED spokeswoman declined to comment except to say that the investigation remained "active and ongoing."

That afternoon, Jim Griffin issued a statement acknowledging that law enforcement had advised the family it would be seeking murder indictments.

"We won't have any comment until charges are actually brought against Alex," he said.

The Murdaugh family law firm PMPED, now rebranded as the Parker Law Group, also issued a statement, calling the news "sad and upsetting" but saying that justice must be served.

"Our thoughts turn to Maggie and to Paul whom we loved and who we miss," it read. "We ask for our judicial system to act swiftly and to bring a conclusion to this heinous situation."

A few hours later, the South Carolina Supreme Court officially disbarred the fifty-four-year-old from ever practicing law again in the state.

"[We] conclude from the public record that Respondent's untruthfulness and misconduct," read its formal decision, "resulted in significant harm to clients and demands his removal from the practice of law."

Two days later, a Colleton County grand jury indicted Richard Alexander Murdaugh on two counts of murder and two counts of possession of a weapon during the commission of a violent crime—allegedly shooting Maggie and Paul.

In a joint press release, SC Attorney General Alan Wilson and SLED Chief Mark Keel said that because it was still an active investigation and now a pending court case, they could not comment on specifics.

"Over the last thirteen months," said Chief Keel, "[we] have worked day and night to build a case against the person responsible for the murders of Maggie and Paul and to exclude those who were not. At no point did agents lose focus on this investigation. Today is one more step in a long process for justice for Maggie and Paul."

Minutes after the grand jury indictments were unsealed, attorneys Dick Harpootlian and Jim Griffin issued an official statement on behalf of their client.

"Alex wants his family, friends, and everyone to know that he did not have anything to do with the murders of Maggie and Paul. He loved them more than anything in the world."

They accused SLED and the attorney general of a rush to judgment, deciding Alex was guilty from day one.

"Alex did not have any motive whatsoever to murder them," it stated. "We are immediately filing a motion for a speedy trial. We are requesting that the Attorney General turn over all evidence within thirty days as required by law and we demand to have a trial within sixty days of receiving that evidence."

The long-awaited breakthrough in the Murdaugh murder investigation made headlines from coast to coast, with cable news stations breaking into their regular scheduling to air special reports. CNN reported a source inside the investigation had confirmed that blood spatter had been found on Alex's clothing. NBC's *Today* show revealed that Paul's time-stamped cell phone video directly linked Alex to the killings, contradicting his previous alibi of being with his dying father.

Although many Hampton locals had long suspected Alex Murdaugh of committing the horrific murders, there was still shock and surprise at his indictment.

Patricia Moore, who owns Spinbad Church Supply on Lee Avenue, had always considered Alex Murdaugh as Hampton's own "Andy Griffith" for his affable personality.

"To hear a parent kill a child, their own child, that's crazy," she told *The Daily Beast*. "To know that he had that sinister side that has gone back a while—that's scary."

Moore said that, like most of Hampton, she had turned to Alex for help at one time or another and he had always come through.

"When you get in trouble, you go to the Murdaughs," she said. "If they like you, you don't have anything to worry about."

And Hampton locals were fed up with the constant media spotlight on their tiny town since the double homicide thirteen months ago.

"You'd never heard of Hampton until this," said Nix Florist manager

Angie Dempsey, who used to serve Maggie Murdaugh. "[Now it's] 'Oh, that's where the murders happened.' I can't wrap my head around it. I'm in total disbelief that you can take a gun and kill someone you profess to love."

The following Wednesday morning, July 20, Alex Murdaugh was driven ninety miles from the Alvin S. Glenn Detention Center to the Colleton County Courthouse in Walterboro for his bond hearing. He arrived at the courthouse in his navy blue jail garb and prized pink Nike sneakers, which he had boasted to family were much sought after in jail.

He was almost unrecognizable with his distinctive red hair shaved off, and a massive weight loss over his nine months of incarceration.

An hour later, he was led into the courtroom in handcuffs and leg irons, having changed into a white linen shirt and khaki pants brought in by his legal team. Ironically, a portrait of the defendant's grandfather, Randolph "Buster" Murdaugh, hung on the rear wall of the historic courtroom, where he had successfully tried many murder cases during his long career as solicitor.

The second-floor courtroom was packed with reporters, photographers, TV news crews, and law enforcement. Although Maggie's family were not present, they were watching the proceedings on a live stream.

Prosecutor Creighton Waters told the hushed court that the defendant had been indicted by the Colleton County grand jury for the murders of Maggie and Paul Murdaugh, and two counts of possession of a rifle and shotgun respectively.

"Your Honor," said Waters, "it's my understanding at this time that the defense would request a formal arraignment, but waive reading of the indictments."

Murdaugh stood up and removed his white mask.

"Richard Alex Murdaugh, please raise your right hand," said the prosecutor. "Do you waive reading of the indictments?"

"Yes, sir," he replied, lifting his right hand as far as he could with the handcuffs attached.

"What say you, Richard Alex Murdaugh, are you guilty or not guilty of the felonies of which you stand indicted?"

"Not guilty," he replied.

"How shall you be tried?"

"By God and my country," answered Murdaugh resolutely.

Then the prosecutor thanked all the SLED agents for their "long and arduous" thirteen-month-long investigation.

"As we explored every possibility," he told the judge, "it all came back to one person, and that is Alex Murdaugh."

The prosecutor said the eighty-one counts of white-collar fraud, drugs, and other crimes the defendant now faced explained the murders.

"A lot of that provides the background and the motive for what happened on June 7, 2021," he told the judge.

Then Harpootlian asked Judge Newman to seal all motions for the murder case so they wouldn't become public.

"We're trying to get a fair trial for our client," he told the judge, "and not try it in the media but try it in this courtroom."

Judge Newman asked what parameters a proposed gag order would take.

Waters said it would only cover "extrajudicial comments to the press," but all court hearings should be in public.

Harpootlian complained that somebody inside the investigation was leaking information, creating a "constant churning" of the case in the media.

Judge Newman then asked both sides to prepare a proposal for him to review, saying he "typically disfavors" gag orders.

"I just want it clearly understood," said the judge, "that it's a public matter with a public trial. I want to make it clear that we will not have any private motion hearings. Public matters will be public."

Then Harpootlian said the defense had filed a motion for a speedy trial.

"We'd like to get this matter before a Colleton County jury as quickly as possible," he told Judge Newman. "Mr. Murdaugh believes he is innocent, and that the killer, or killers, are still at large. He wants to put this behind him and go after real killers."

At the end of the eighteen-minute hearing, the judge denied bond, saying he would give a written decision regarding a gag order under advisement.

After the hearing, Dick Harpootlian and Jim Griffin swept past two dozen reporters who fired questions at them about their client.

"I'm gagged," Harpootlian told them as he headed toward his car.

That same day, a federal grand jury indicted Alex Murdaugh's banker friend Russell Laffitte with conspiracy, wire fraud and bank fraud, and misappropriation of bank funds. The five-count indictment accused the former CEO of Palmetto State Bank and "the Bank Customer," presumed to be Alex Murdaugh, of defrauding four personal injury clients from July 2011 onward. The federal charges carried up to thirty years in prison.

Although only identified by their initials, the victims were Hakeem Pinckney, Arthur Badger, and Hannah and Alania Plyler. These were the first federal charges to be filed, but many more were expected, since the FBI had joined the Murdaugh investigation the previous September.

"We intend to vigorously fight the charges at trial," one of Laffitte's attorneys, Bart Daniel, told a reporter.

A week later, Laffitte pleaded not guilty to the charges in US District Court in Charleston, at a bond hearing attended by one of his alleged victims, Alania Plyler-Spohn, whose mother and brother were killed in a car crash in 2005; she was now a married mother of twins. Laffitte's wife, Susie, and their children were in the public gallery to show support.

Laffitte's other defense attorney, Matt Austin, complained to Judge Molly Cherry about the "overwhelming publicity" surrounding the case, saying his client didn't believe he had committed a crime.

Judge Cherry set Laffitte's bond at $500,000, requiring him to post $25,000 up front. She also set conditions that he surrender his passport, not have firearms in his house, and wear a GPS ankle monitor, which he already had to do as part of his one-million-dollar South Carolina state bond.

After the bond hearing, Alania Plyler-Spohn told reporters she had come to the courtroom to confront Laffitte, whom she had once trusted as a father figure before he had betrayed her.

"We're not these little girls anymore that he took advantage of," she said.

On August 16, a state grand jury indicted Alex Murdaugh on nine additional charges of stealing money from his brother Randy and his former family law firm of PMPED. He was now facing a total of eighteen indictments, representing ninety charges, that he had stolen almost $9 million from a dozen personal injury clients.

The new round of charges alleges that he had embezzled $121,358 from Randy, after mistakenly receiving a loan repayment meant for his brother and then cashing it himself. He was also accused of siphoning $175,200 from PMPED cases into his Bank of America Forge account.

There were also two new suspects mentioned in the indictments, whom law enforcement believed were part of Alex Murdaugh and Curtis Smith's elaborate drug-trafficking and money-laundering ring. Spencer Anwan Roberts and Jerry K. Rivers were both tied into the labyrinthian Murdaugh case by SC Attorney General's Office prosecutor Creighton Waters at separate bond hearings.

In mid-August, thirty-four-year-old Spencer Roberts appeared in front of Judge Clifton Newman, accused of obtaining $20,000 in COVID-19 unemployment funds under false pretenses.

Waters told the judge that Roberts was "part of the investigation down in the Lowcountry," alluding to the ongoing Murdaugh investigations.

"Roberts received downstream a substantial number of checks," he told the judge, "allegedly originating from Alex Murdaugh."

Prosecutors believe that Murdaugh had headed a sophisticated drugs pipeline, giving checks of money stolen from personal injury clients, always under $10,000, to Curtis Smith, who cashed them. He then handed the cash to Spencer Roberts in exchange for drugs, which he gave Murdaugh.

"This is an ongoing investigation," said Waters. "There is a lot more being explored and that is to include a substantial amount of drugs."

Judge Newman set Roberts's bond at $200,000 with the condition of GPS monitoring and house arrest.

Later that day, Curtis Smith had his bond revoked by Judge Newman and was sent back to the Alvin S. Glenn Detention Center, after Waters said he had lied by claiming he had no money when he actually had $58,000 in a bank account.

A few days later, at a bond hearing for Jerry K. Rivers, accused of hiding another person's cell phone during a law enforcement search, Prosecutor Waters said Rivers was "very much" involved in Alex Murdaugh's ongoing money-laundering and check-cashing investigations.

"[Rivers is] one of the individuals downstream from Alex Murdaugh," the prosecutor told Judge Newman, "who received substantial amounts of checks . . . the high figures for Mr. Rivers."

Waters told Judge Newman that $89,000 worth of checks originating from Murdaugh was given to Rivers in 2021 alone by Curtis Smith to cash.

"These are very serious charges," said Judge Newman, setting Rivers a $150,000 surety bond.

On Monday, August 29, Alex Murdaugh appeared in Colleton County Court for a hearing, after defense attorneys accused the prosecution of leaking damaging information about the murders and withholding discovery. Two weeks earlier, Harpootlian and Griffin had filed a "motion to compel," to force the state to turn over all the evidence against their client, after the Attorney General's Office would only release it under protective orders, so it wouldn't be made public until trial.

Wearing a red-and-blue checked long-sleeved shirt and shackled at the waist and wrists, Murdaugh was now completely bald.

The fifty-two-minute hearing got off to a contentious start with Dick Harpootlian interrupting prosecutor Creighton Waters and accusing him of "trying to hijack this proceeding."

"Your Honor, I'm not done," Harpootlian told Judge Newman. "I'm sorry if I appear upset, but every time we turn around, they are trying to hide something. I don't trust the state to follow the rules."

Waters told the judge that he did not "play games," and only wanted to try the double murder case once and not twice on appeal.

"I don't play fast and loose!" he said angrily. "I have not leaked any information and I am not aware of any leaks. This case is unique and it is unprecedented in South Carolina history, in as much as it combines violent crime with alleged corruption of someone with a law license on a scale that is somewhat inconceivable."

Previously, the defense had subpoenaed four SLED investigators to testify at the hearing, but Judge Newman refused to let any of them take the stand.

Under the protective rules the state wanted, the defendant would only be able to review evidence in jail with his lawyers in the room. Harpootlian said Alex's Richland County Detention Center only allowed one-hour visitations every other day.

"Mr. Murdaugh, who is a lawyer, can help us if he has time to review it in his cell," Jim Griffin told the judge. "He does not want to see crime scene photos, Your Honor. That's the last thing in the world he wants to see."

"He *was* a lawyer," Waters wryly observed, noting that there is "unique media interest" in the case. "This information is worth over a million dollars to unscrupulous hands."

Judge Newman ruled that all discovery must be turned over to the defense, while ordering a temporary order restricting any release or sharing of the evidence improperly.

"This is a case that cries out for a protective order," said the judge. "The court has an . . . obligation to avoid the creation of a carnival-type atmosphere in a case of this nature, and I will do all I can to limit that."

Prosecutors and the defense are now busily preparing for Alex's upcoming murder trial, presently scheduled for January 2023.

40

THE TRIAL

At 9:30 A.M. on Monday, January 23, 2023—almost six hundred days after the brutal murders of Maggie and Paul—a smiling Alex Murdaugh was led into the Colleton County Courthouse in Walterboro to stand trial. He was almost unrecognizable from his last court appearance in December, with his graying red hair now grown back and perfectly groomed. Dressed in a starched white dress shirt and navy blazer, he looked every inch the successful lawyer he had once been.

His grandfather's portrait, which had adorned the courtroom's rear wall for decades, had been removed on the orders of Judge Clifton Newman. One can only speculate what the late Randolph "Buster" Murdaugh Jr. would have to say about Alex's fall from grace.

Several hundred journalists had descended on the tiny town, and a media overflow room had been set up in the nearby Walterboro Wildlife Center. Court TV would carry the trial live, supplying a pool of network and local TV stations that would stream it from gavel to gavel.

With so few restaurants in Walterboro, a battalion of food trucks had set up in the town square, alongside half a dozen portable toilets in a nearby parking lot. To capitalize on the murder trial, the shabby two-star Hampton Inn had raised its rates to as much as $374 a night. But the defense team, led by Dick Harpootlian and Jim Griffin, had taken over the luxurious five-hundred-acre Eden at Gracefield wedding venue, costing a staggering $20,475 a week.

Two months earlier, Russell Laffitte had been convicted of six federal criminal charges, including misappropriation of bank funds. The disgraced former CEO of Palmetto State Bank, who was appealing, would loom large in the Murdaugh trial for his alleged role in Alex's illicit dealings.

Charged with the first-degree murders of Maggie and Paul, as well as two charges of possessing a weapon during the commission of a violent crime, if convicted, Alex, now fifty-four, faced thirty years to life in prison. These were on top of the ninety-nine other criminal charges he faced after the murder trial.

More than nine hundred potential Colleton County jurors had received questionnaires to see if they were eligible to serve. Over the next two and a half days, they would be whittled down to a jury of eight women and four men with six alternates.

On Wednesday afternoon, lead prosecutor Creighton Walters stood up to deliver his dramatic opening speech to the jury as Alex's son Buster, sister Lynn Goettee, and brothers Randy and John Marvin watched from the public gallery. The prosecutor began by vividly describing how on June 7, 2021, at around 8:50 P.M., the defendant had shot his own twenty-two-year-old son with two shotgun blasts before executing his wife with a 300 Blackout semiautomatic assault rifle.

"Pow! Pow!" shouted Waters, as the jury looked on intently. "They were shot at close range and did not have any defensive wounds. You are going to see what he did to Maggie and Paul. It's going to be gruesome. There's no other way around it."

Armed with a purely circumstantial case, Walters then laid out a detailed timeline of how the state believed Alex had committed the murders and set up his alibi.

"It's complicated. It's a journey. There's a lot of aspects to this case," he told the jury. "But like a lot of things that are complicated, we start to put them all together, piecing together like a puzzle—all of a sudden a picture emerges."

He also revealed for the first time that a Snapchat video on Paul's iPhone, taken at the kennels five minutes before the murders, had Alex's voice on it. From the beginning, Alex had claimed to have last seen Paul and Maggie several hours earlier at dinner.

In his opening statement, Dick Harpootlian accused inept SLED investigators of a rush to judgment that his client was guilty, without ever bothering to investigate other potential suspects.

"Alex was the loving father of Paul and the loving husband of Maggie," Harpootlian told the jury as Alex sobbed into a folded tissue at the defense table. "He didn't kill, butcher, his son and his wife, and you need to put out of your mind any speculation that he did."

On Thursday morning the prosecution called its first witness, Sergeant Daniel Greene of the Colleton County Sheriff's Office, who was first on the murder scene after Alex's hysterical 911 call.

The jury then viewed Sergeant Greene's bodycam video showing his first interaction with the defendant, who immediately said the killings were a result of the 2019 boat crash that killed Mallory Beach.

"My son was in a boat wreck," he told the officer. "He's been getting threats. I know that's what it is."

In Harpootlian's cross-examination, Sergeant Greene conceded that the first responders did not wear protective gowns or booties to preserve the crime scene.

"Did they put anything to insulate themselves from contaminating the scene?" asked Harpootlian.

"No," answered Greene, admitting that this was not normal procedure for the Colleton County Sheriff's Office.

The state then called a succession of first responders to the Moselle double homicide crime scene, who described different aspects of it to the jury.

On Friday—the fifth day of the trial—the state called its seventh witness, Detective Laura Rutland of the Colleton County Sheriff's Office. She testified that Murdaugh said he tried to turn over Paul's bloody body to check for a pulse, although his white shirt and shorts appeared freshly laundered with no signs of blood.

Then the jury were shown Alex Murdaugh's first videotaped interview in a police car at 12:57 A.M. on September 8, 2021. Murdaugh, who was in the front passenger's seat, was interviewed by SLED lead investigator David Owen, with Detective Rutland and Alex's personal attorney Danny Henderson in the back.

Frequently breaking down in tears, he claimed to have woken up from a nap and gone to visit his mother, returning to Moselle to find Paul and Maggie shot dead. He never mentioned being with them in the kennels just prior to their murders.

On Monday, January 30, SLED Senior Special Agent Jeff Croft took the stand as the jury viewed Alex Murdaugh's second videotaped interview from January 10, three days after the killings. At one point he broke down crying, appearing to admit to the killings.

Prosecutor Waters then paused the video and asked Croft to repeat what the defendant had said.

"It's just so bad," said Croft, as Murdaugh shook his head. "I did him so bad."

In his cross examination the next morning, Jim Griffin insisted that his client had actually said, "They did him so bad." He then replayed the audio, first at normal speed and then at one-third speed, which failed to make it any clearer.

"Are you one hundred percent confident that Alex said, 'I did him so bad' and not 'They did him so bad?'" asked Griffin.

"I am one hundred percent confident in what I heard and what I testified to," Croft replied.

Cell phone records and firearms took center stage on Tuesday afternoon. Custom gunmaker John Bedingfield, who was also Alex's second cousin, testified that he built three assault-style rifles in 300 Blackout caliber for him. Lead prosecutor Creighton Waters emphasized that 300 Blackout cartridges found at the murder scene matched similar ones scattered around Moselle, indicating it was a family weapon that had killed Paul and Maggie.

Lieutenant Britt Dove of SLED's computer crimes division then testified about his analysis of Alex's, Maggie's, and Paul's iPhone data. The last text messages Maggie read were before 8:49 P.M. on June 7, including a text from John Marvin Murdaugh about visiting her terminally ill father-in-law in hospital. Following that, Maggie received several phone calls and texts from Alex.

"Going to check on M. Be right back," Alex texted her at 9:08 P.M., a few minutes after prosecutors believe she was killed.

"Call me babe," was his final text, sent at 9:47 P.M., twenty minutes before he dialed 911 to report the murders.

On Wednesday, the state called its star witness, Rogan Gibson, one of Paul's best friends.

Minutes before his murder, Paul had called Rogan from the Moselle kennels as he was worried about Cash, Rogan's pet puppy being boarded there. Rogan asked Paul to take a video of the dog's injured tail so he could show it to a vet friend of his as the cell phone service was cutting out.

Gibson later told investigators that during the call he had heard two other voices besides Paul's in the background; one was "Miss Maggie," and he was positive the other was "Mr. Alex."

Then Creighton Waters dramatically played Paul's smoking gun video, shot at 8:44 P.M. at the kennels the night of the murders, and discovered almost a year later on his iPhone.

"Quit, Cash. Come here," Paul is heard saying as he corrals Cash.

"Hey, he's got a bird in his mouth," says Maggie loudly, referring to her pet lab, who had caught something in his mouth.

"It's a guinea," says Maggie.

"It's a chicken," Paul says, trying to calm down Cash.

"Come here, Bubba!" shouts the distinctive male voice. "Come here, Bubba!"

After hearing the video, Rogan testified he was "one hundred percent" certain the third voice belonged to Alex Murdaugh.

In cross-examination, Jim Griffin asked Rogan about his relationship with Maggie Murdaugh.

"She was like a second mother to me," he replied. "Always took care of me. Treated me as one of hers."

"Was there any circumstance that you can think of, knowing them as you do, that would lead [Alex] to brutally murder Paul and Maggie?" asked Griffin.

"Not that I could think of," Gibson replied.

The state's next witness, Will Loving, testified that he had received a Snapchat video from Paul about an hour before his murder, showing him and his father driving around the Moselle property. In it Alex was wearing a light blue short-sleeved button-down shirt and khaki pants, which have never been accounted for.

Then Waters played the video found on Paul's iPhone from the kennels. Loving was one hundred percent sure it had Alex's voice on it.

On Thursday morning—the ninth day of the trial—the defense suffered a major defeat when Judge Newman ruled that the Murdaughs' alleged financial crimes may be admissible, as Jim Griffin had opened the door by asking Gibson for reasons why Alex might want to kill his wife and son.

"That turned cross-examination of the witness," explained Judge Newman, "from dealing with specific issues in the case to having him testify as a character witness for Mr. Murdaugh."

The judge then embarked on a trial-within-a-trial to decide whether the jury could hear about the defendant's "bad acts." Over the next several days, Creighton Waters called a stream of witnesses, including Alex's friends, PMPED colleagues, as well as his personal injury victims, to testify about his financial misdeeds.

And finally, after hearing from seven witnesses without the jury present, Judge Newman ruled that the defendant's alleged financial misdeeds were admissible.

"The looming exposure of financial crimes provided motive for the murders," said the judge, "and is evidence of malice, an essential element of the crime of murder."

On Monday, February 6, the trial entered its third week as the state called Mushelle "Shelly" Smith, who was caring for Libby Murdaugh on the night of the murders. She nervously testified that just after 9:00 P.M., Alex had suddenly arrived at his parents' Almeda house, staying fifteen to twenty minutes. She noted that it was very unusual for him to visit his mother that late, and he was "fidgety."

Then that following Sunday, after his father, Randolph's, funeral, Alex told Shelly that if she was interviewed by investigators she should say he had spent thirty to forty minutes at the house, twice as long as she remembered. He then offered to pay for her upcoming wedding.

Several days later, Alex turned up at his mother's house at 6:30 A.M., carrying a "balled-up" blue tarp with something inside it. He had carried it upstairs and then left. Weeks later Smith would tell this to investigators, who searched the Almeda house and discovered an extra-large blue rain jacket in a second-floor closet, which tested positive for high levels of gunshot residue.

Under Griffin's cross-examination, Smith described the Murdaughs as "a good family," saying she "loved working there."

On Tuesday, jurors learned how Alex Murdaugh had stolen millions from PMPED, leading to the law firm his great-grandfather had founded closing down. Its former chief financial officer Jeanne Seckinger, who had confronted Murdaugh about $792,000 in missing funds the day of the murders, could barely conceal her distaste.

"Did you really know Alex Murdaugh?" asked Waters.

"I don't think anybody really knew him," she replied.

Later, as Alex Murdaugh chewed tobacco at the defense table, his former law partner and close friend Ronnie Crosby fought back tears as he fondly remembered Paul. He testified that Alex had assured him and the other law partners that he had never been at the kennels that fateful night.

Waters then played him Paul's damning cell phone video, asking whose voices he heard.

"Those are the voices of Paul Murdaugh, Maggie Murdaugh, and Alex Murdaugh," Crosby replied.

On Wednesday morning—the thirteenth day of the trial—Alex Murdaugh's longtime PMPED paralegal Annette Griswold testified against her former boss.

"I refer to Alex as the Tasmanian Devil," she told the jury. "He has always been hard to sit still and get answers from. He was rarely there and when he was, the door was closed."

Griswold told the jury how Alex would correct her when she made out checks to the legitimate Forge Consulting, having her change them to his fake Forge account. Eventually she had become suspicious about missing fees and told Jeanne Seckinger, who'd launched an investigation.

After the murders, she testified, the firm had gone into "mama bear mode" for Alex. It wasn't until early September that she had found another suspicious check, leading to Murdaugh's firing and staged roadside shooting.

"I was hurt. I was angry," she told the jury. "He's been lying this whole time."

Just before lunch Colleton County Courthouse received a bomb threat, and Judge Newman calmly announced that the court had to be evacuated. After a thorough search of the courthouse by SLED, the Murdaugh trial resumed at 3:00 P.M. without a word of explanation to the jury.

On Thursday, Alex Murdaugh's best friend, Chris Wilson, took the stand and explained how in early 2021 they had worked on a personal injury case together and won a $5.5 million award. But instead of sending the $792,000 fee to PMPED, Alex had instructed him to make the checks out to him personally, and Wilson had complied.

"I've known him for thirty years," said Wilson, "and didn't have any reason not to trust him."

After PMPED became suspicious about the missing fee, Murdaugh had attempted to cover it up by borrowing money and wiring $600,000 to Wilson. Murdaugh asked Wilson to send the full fee amount to PMPED and loan him the remaining $192,000, which Wilson had done from his own pocket.

Wilson testified that on September 4, 2021, the day after Murdaugh had been fired from his family's law firm, they met at his mother's house and Murdaugh had admitted to a twenty-year opioid addiction and stealing millions.

"He broke down crying," said Wilson. "He said, 'I have a drug problem . . . I shit you up. I've shit a lot of people up.'"

It was directly after this conversation that Murdaugh asked Curtis Smith to meet him on the Old Salkehatchie Road and kill him.

On Friday morning, Blanca Turrubiate-Simpson, the Murdaughs' longtime family housekeeper, testified that prior to her murder, Maggie had been worried about the civil boat crash lawsuit and the huge damages she and Alex were facing. She also told Blanca that Alex was lying to her about the lawsuit and keeping things from her.

"Maggie was crying," Blanca told the jury, "and said, 'We don't have that kind of money. If I could give them everything I've got and make it go away, I will. We'll start over. I just want it gone.'"

She also testified that Alex had wanted Maggie to come to Moselle the night of the murders, and although Maggie was reluctant to go she had finally agreed.

Blanca then became the fifth person close to the Murdaugh family to identify Alex's voice on Paul's kennel video, and there would be plenty more to come.

On Monday, February 13, two jurors came down with COVID-19, and the prosecution and defense both suggested delaying the trial in case of a jury room outbreak. Judge Newman ordered the trial to proceed with two alternate jurors chosen at random to replace them.

As the trial entered its fourth week, the state called a procession of computer, blood spatter, DNA, firearms, crime scene, and medical experts. The defense's aggressive cross-examination emphasized how the investigation had been sloppy by failing to photograph evidence properly, take fingerprints, or collect and test blood.

On Tuesday, Maggie Murdaugh's older sister Marian Proctor took the stand to testify against her brother-in-law. In revealing testimony she said she was aware of Alex's drug addiction and how Maggie called Paul her "little detective," as he "was always looking to make sure his dad was behaving."

Just hours before the murders, Marian had encouraged Maggie to go to Moselle as Alex had requested, as he "really wanted her to come home that night."

Prosecutor Waters then asked if she had pressured Maggie to go.

"I did," Proctor replied, bursting into tears.

She had also wondered why Alex appeared unconcerned about finding the killers, unlike the rest of the family.

"He never talked about it," she told the jury. "It was odd. We were sort of living in fear because we thought this horrible person was out there."

She said her whole perception of Alex changed after his firing from PMPED and botched suicide attempt.

Then, without the jury present, Marian revealed that her sister had suspected Alex of having an affair in 2007 and had kicked him out of the house. Although they had put it behind them, it still bothered Maggie, who would bring it up from time to time. Judge Newman ruled that the jury could not hear about the suspected affair as it was too long ago.

In cross-examination, Jim Griffin asked if Maggie was happy in her marriage.

"It was good," replied Proctor. "It wasn't perfect, but Maggie was happy."

On Wednesday morning, the state called SLED lead investigator Special Agent David Owen, who would spend the next day outlining the investigation. It would all lead up to the jury watching his third interview with the defendant on August 11, 2021, three months after the killings.

At the end of the friendly ninety-seven-minute interview, Owen told Alex that he had a few more questions.

"Did you kill Maggie?" he asked.

"No," Alex replied, taken by surprise. "Did I kill my wife? No, David."

"Do you know who did?"

"No, I do not know who did."

"Did you kill Paul?"

"No, I did not kill Paul."

"Do you know who did?"

"No, sir. I do not know who did," replied Alex defiantly. "Do you think I killed Maggie?"

"I have to go where the evidence and the facts take me," replied Agent Owen. "And I don't have anything that points to anybody else."

In cross-examination, Jim Griffin asked Agent Owen if he'd ever investigated Alex's alleged drug dealer Curtis "Eddie" Smith as a possible suspect for the murders. This led to Judge Newman reversing his previous decision to disallow any evidence about the September 4, 2021, roadside shooting involving Smith. It was another major setback for the defense.

"The state is entitled to explore the relationship between the defendant and Smith," ruled Judge Newman. "The defense decided to go right there, as if they could dance through fire without getting burned."

On Friday the state called its sixty-first and final witness, SLED agent Peter Rudofski, who presented a detailed forty-three-page timeline he'd prepared of Alex's, Maggie's, and Paul's movements on June 7, 2021. Using text messages, phone calls, cell tower pings, step counts, and GPS coordinates, as well as General Motors' OnStar data from Murdaugh's car, Rudofski laid out a compelling case against him for the jury.

It showed that his 2021 Chevrolet Suburban left Moselle for his mother's house in Almeda at 9:07 P.M., about twenty minutes after investigators believe he committed the murders, passing the exact spot where Maggie's phone was later found. He had then sped up, hitting speeds of up to seventy-four miles per hour during the fifteen-minute drive to Almeda.

He parked around the back of his mother's house at 9:22 P.M., before leaving again at 9:43 P.M. for the return drive to Moselle, reaching eighty miles per hour on the narrow two-lane rural roads.

He arrived at 10:05 P.M., driving straight to the kennels, where he dialed 911 just seventeen seconds later.

Then, just before the state rested its case, Rudofski showed the jury a damning text Paul Murdaugh had sent his father on May 6, 2021, just a month before the murders.

"When you get here we have to talk," it read. "Mom found several bags of pills in your computer bag."

That same day, Maggie scoured the internet to identify oxycodone pills she had found, and three weeks later, on May 26, she searched again for other pills.

In cross-examination, defense attorney Phil Barber produced a text Alex had sent Maggie on May 7, the day after she apparently confronted him.

"I am very sorry that I do this to all of you," he read. "I love you."

41

"WHAT A TANGLED WEB WE WEAVE"

Monday, February 26, was Presidents Day, so the defense began its case in earnest the next day, calling the defendant's surviving son, Buster, to the stand. Gently questioned by Jim Griffin, Buster, who had attended every day of the trial with his girlfriend, Brooklynn White, testified that his father had been "destroyed" and "heartbroken" after the murders.

Questioned about his father's opioid addiction, Buster, now twenty-six, said the family knew about it, and he had unsuccessfully undergone drug rehab around Christmas 2018. His mother and Paul would confront him when they found pills, and he was always apologetic.

"Was there any violence in the family?" Griffin asked.

"No, sir," replied Buster.

Murdaugh smiled approvingly during his son's testimony, patting him on the hip as he walked out of the courtroom.

For the next several days, the defense called a stream of highly paid experts to bolster its case. Forensic engineer Mike Sutton testified that he had analyzed SLED's crime scene photographs and recently visited the Moselle kennels to study the trajectories of the bullets that had killed Paul and Maggie. He found it "very unlikely" that the six-foot, four-inch defendant could have fired the shots, as by his calculations the shooter was just five feet, two inches tall.

The defense also called Murdaugh's longtime friend and former PMPED law partner Mark Ball, who testified of his concern at seeing more than a dozen people walking around the chaotic murder scene when he arrived.

"Two people have been gunned down," he said. "Where does the crime scene start and stop?"

Ball told the jury he had known Alex for thirty-four years and had always seen him as a loving husband and father. But after Alex's firing from the law firm for stealing millions and subsequent suicide attempt, Ball's opinion had changed.

"He was pretty good at hiding who he really was, wasn't he?" asked Prosecutor Waters.

"Obviously," replied Ball.

On Thursday morning, February 23, the defense called its eleventh witness, Richard Alexander Murdaugh. There was a collective gasp in the courtroom as the defendant confidently strolled up to the stand against his defense team's advice.

Murdaugh now freely admitted lying to law enforcement about being at the kennels prior to the murders, blaming his opioid-induced paranoia.

"Oh, what a tangled web we weave," he tearfully explained, quoting the seventeenth-century English poet Sir Walter Scott. "Once I told a lie— then I told my family—I had to keep lying."

But he vehemently denied shooting "Mags" and "Paul-Paul," as he would constantly refer to them.

Alex told the jury that he had become addicted to oxycodone after knee surgery more than twenty years ago, stealing millions of dollars from his clients and family law firm to feed his raging drug addiction. He claimed he spent up to $60,000 a week on pills, frequently taking more than two thousand milligrams of oxycodone a day.

"Opiates gave me energy," he explained.

After being confronted on June 7, 2021, about $792,000 in missing fees, he claimed not to have been unduly concerned.

"Did you believe your financial house of cards was about to crumble?" asked Griffin.

"Absolutely not," Murdaugh replied.

Then, in a new version of the events of that fateful night, Alex said that after dinner Maggie had wanted him to go down to the dog kennels with her and Paul. He had initially refused as he was freshly showered and it was hot outside. But eventually he changed his mind and went in a golf cart.

While at the kennels, he had pulled a chicken out of Bubba's mouth before returning to the main house to cool down and have a short nap. Then he had left to visit his mother in Almeda, who was suffering from late-stage dementia.

He had arrived back at Moselle at around 10:00 P.M., thinking it strange that Maggie and Paul weren't there, so he went to the kennels to look for them.

"What did you do when you drove down to the kennels?" asked Griffin.

"I saw what y'all have seen pictures of," replied Murdaugh. "I'm not exactly sure what I did, but I know I got out of my car. I know I ran back to my car, called 911."

He said he had "gone back and forth" between the bodies while on the phone to the 911 dispatcher.

"My boy's lying facedown," he sobbed. "I could see his brain laying on the sidewalk. I tried to turn him over, tried to grab him by the belt loop and tried to turn him over."

In a scathing five-hour cross-examination, which stretched well into Friday, Creighton Waters accused Alex of acting above the law by freely displaying his 14th Circuit assistant solicitor's badge and installing blue police lights on his car.

Waters then dropped a large stack of papers onto the lectern, relating to some of the clients Alex had robbed blind.

"You had to sit down and look somebody in the eye," Waters told the defendant, "and convince them that you were on their side, when you were not, correct?"

"I misled people that trusted me," Murdaugh admitted. "I did wrong. I stole their money."

Then, using the prosecution's minute-by-minute timeline, Waters took Alex through the night of the murders, showing the jury how preposterous his new story was.

"You had to sit in this courtroom," he told the defendant, "and hear your family and your friends . . . come in and testify that you were on that kennel video, so you—like you've done so many times over the course of your life—had to back up and make a new story that kind of fit with the facts that can't be denied. Isn't that true, sir?"

No, sir," Alex replied indignantly, "that's not true."

At the end of his eviscerating cross-examination, Waters looked Murdaugh in the eye and asked him point-blank, "Mr. Murdaugh, are you a family annihilator?"

"You mean, did I shoot my wife and son?" replied the defendant. "No."

After the defense rested its case the following Monday, February 27, the state called six rebuttal witnesses. Then on Wednesday, March 1, the jurors visited Moselle to view the murder scene firsthand.

On their return, Creighton Waters stood up to deliver his three-hour closing argument, summarizing the state's highly complex circumstantial case.

"Only one person had the motive, the means, and the opportunity to commit these crimes," he told the jury, pointing straight at the defendant, "and whose guilty conduct after these crimes betrays him."

He described the June 7, 2021, "gathering storm" of Murdaugh's accelerating thefts, compounded by the upcoming boat crash hearing that threatened to reveal his finances, and being accused by his law firm of stealing money as the last straw.

"The hounds were at the gate," said Waters. "The pressures on this man were all reaching a crescendo. This was nothing like he's ever experienced. He'd always been one step ahead of the game."

The most damning evidence, said Waters, was Paul's Snapchat kennel video, which totally blew apart Alex's alibi.

"Why would a loving husband and father lie about that, and lie about it so early?" he asked the jury. "[The defendant] was forced to do what he's done all the time, come up with a new lie when he's confronted with evidence he cannot deny. That's because all those witnesses sat there and said, 'That's him. He was there.'"

He warned the jury not to be fooled by the defendant, like his friends and family had been in the past, and give a voice to Paul and Maggie.

On Thursday morning, Jim Griffin gave his two-and-a-quarter-hour closing argument, focusing on the investigation's shortcomings.

"SLED failed miserably in investigating this case," said Griffin. "On behalf of Alex, on behalf of Buster, on behalf of Maggie, and on behalf of my friend Paul, I respectfully request that you do not compound a family tragedy with another."

Finally, in an hour-long passionate rebuttal, prosecutor John Meadors told the jury that ultimately it had been Maggie's little detective, Paul, who had solved the murders from the grave with his kennel video.

Just before 4:00 P.M., after Judge Newman had charged the jury, they retired to the jury room to begin deliberations.

Less than three hours later, at 6:41 P.M., the jury forewoman sent a note to Judge Newman that they had reached a verdict. Then Alex Murdaugh was brought back into the courtroom to hear it read out by Colleton Court clerk Rebecca Hill. Buster and Lynn Goattee sat in the public gallery.

It was a unanimous verdict finding Richard Alexander Murdaugh guilty of all four charges in the murders of Maggie and Paul. As each verdict was read out, the defendant stared at the table, displaying no sign of emotion.

Immediately, the defense team asked Judge Newman to declare a mistrial. He refused, making no secret of his feelings about the jury's decision.

"The evidence of guilt is overwhelming," he declared," and I deny the motion."

Newman then set sentencing for 9:30 A.M. the next morning, as court security handcuffed Murdaugh. As he was led out of the courtroom, he mournfully turned toward his son and mouthed something. Buster looked away, avoiding his father's gaze.

On Friday morning, a shackled Alex Murdaugh was brought into court, his tailored jackets and dress shirts replaced by a tan-colored Colleton

County Jail jumpsuit. His son Buster and siblings John Marvin and Lynn sat pensively in the public gallery.

Dick Harpootlian informed Judge Newman that although the defense had no comments, his client wished to address the court.

"I respect this court, but I'm innocent," declared Murdaugh. "I would never under any circumstances hurt my wife, Maggie, and I would never under any circumstances hurt my son Paul-Paul."

"And it might not have been you," said Judge Newman, who had lost his forty-year-old son, Brian, to a heart attack several weeks before the trial. "It might have been the monster you become when you take fifteen, twenty, thirty, fifty, sixty opioid pills. Maybe you become another person. I've seen that before."

Judge Newman then spoke at length about the Murdaugh family's storied legal legacy that overshadowed the case.

"Over the past century, your family, including you, have been prosecuting people here in this courtroom," said the judge, "and many of them have received the death penalty, probably for lesser conduct.

"You have practiced law before me [and] it was especially heartbreaking for me to see you go from being a grieving father who lost a wife and son to being the person indicted and convicted of killing them."

He told Murdaugh that he would have to wrestle with his conscience for the rest of his life.

"Within your soul, you have to deal with that," the judge told Murdaugh. "And I know you have to see Paul and Maggie during the night times when you're attempting to go to sleep. I'm sure they come and visit you."

"All day and every night," replied Murdaugh.

"They will continue to do so."

Judge Newman then asked Alex about the expression he had used on the witness stand.

"A tangled web we weave," repeated Murdaugh.

"What did you mean by that?" asked the judge.

"It meant when I lied, I continued to lie."

"And the question is, when will it end?" Newman asked. "This ended already for the jury because they've concluded that you continued to lie and lie throughout your testimony."

Then Judge Newman sentenced Alex Murdaugh to the maximum punishment under South Carolina law of two consecutive life sentences for the murders of Maggie and Paul and ordered Murdaugh to be taken away.

EPILOGUE

The previous May, Alex Murdaugh had celebrated his fifty-fourth birthday behind bars at the Alvin S. Glenn Detention Center. Birthdays had always been a big thing in the Murdaugh family and Alex's only known call that day was to his surviving son, Buster, who seemed more distant than ever. Over the last few weeks, they had rarely spoken and when they had Buster always seemed in a hurry to get off the phone.

The subject of him going back to law school was now rarely mentioned and seemed to be on the back burner.

When Buster received the call, he was pulling into a car wash and sounded highly uncomfortable. After a few minutes of uneasy small talk, with Buster failing to mention his birthday, Alex struggled to make conversation by asking how his chronic eczema was doing.

"It's good," replied Buster, somewhat taken aback. "I mean I still get the shots and everything."

"You know what today is, don't you?" Alex finally asked.

"Yeah," replied Buster half-heartedly. "Happy birthday."

"It ain't no big deal, I promise you." Alex sighed as if the air had been let out of his balloon.

"Will they get you a honey bun with a candle in it?" asked Buster sarcastically, as his father made an excuse to end the call.

As Alex Murdaugh came to terms with spending the rest of his life behind bars, his uncomfortable birthday conversation with his only surviving son must have haunted him, knowing full well that his family's chickens had finally come home to roost. He had banked on Buster reentering law school, but the University of South Carolina School of Law appeared not to want anything to do with the Murdaughs, after all the horrendous publicity of the last few months.

The once-powerful Murdaugh dynasty had ruled the swampy Lowcountry for more than one hundred years, thriving on the deeply embedded corruption that had gone unchallenged for generations. Over the years, the whole Palmetto State system had become infected with unscrupulous politicians, police officers, and judges; everybody greased each other's hands to turn a profit at the expense of someone else, usually the poor and needy.

It's no surprise that after Alex's high-profile downfall, so many other local powerbrokers started falling like dominoes, with many more expected to do so as the various criminal investigations unspool.

The five swampy counties that make up the 14th Judicial Circuit had been like the Wild West since the very beginning. Everybody had a price and justice could be bought and sold. Ironically it would take the labyrinthian Alex Murdaugh case, with all its alleged murders and millions of dollars of fraud, to finally shine a spotlight on all the wrongdoings for a shocked world to see.

Many locals, who had reluctantly lived with the malaise all their lives, as their parents had, and their parents' parents had, are now praying that, because of Alex Murdaugh, things might change for the better with the Lowcountry finally entering the twenty-first century.

ACKNOWLEDGMENTS

With the Atlantic Ocean on one side and the steamy Savannah River on the other, South Carolina's Lowcountry is a fascinating throwback to a bygone age. Packed with lush green swamplands, winding creeks, and Spanish moss vines, it encompasses five sprawling counties making up the easternmost part of South Carolina.

There's water everywhere with a myriad of tiny islands where pirates, moonshiners, and bootleggers once smuggled liquor before moving into the more lucrative drug market.

The Murdaugh family ruled the fabled Lowcountry with an iron hand for more than a century, literally laying down the law and lining their pockets at the same time. Now Alex Murdaugh, whose great-grandfather Randolph Murdaugh Sr. spawned the powerful legal dynasty more than a hundred years ago, stands accused of murdering his wife, Maggie and son Paul, as well as stealing almost $10 million from his unwitting victims. He is a modern-day Blackbeard, the infamous seventeenth-century pirate who plundered the original American thirteen colonies, including South Carolina.

How one of the Palmetto State's most respected and honored families crashed and burned is a fascinating story, with endless twists and turns and new developments happening daily. It is a twenty-first-century Greek tragedy that has played out in real time as the world watches aghast.

In recounting Alex Murdaugh's dramatic fall from grace, I have used personal interviews, police records, and Alex's own highly revealing jailhouse phone calls to his family, which provided a real insight into his true character. Whether or not Alex is a sociopath is not for me to say, but in all the true crime books I have written, I have never come across anyone as dark and totally devoid of conscience as he appears to be.

"Now here's the problem," said one of his unfortunate victims, highway patrolman Lieutenant Tommy Moore. "He treated me *that* nice and he stole every dime I had."

In late October 2021, I flew to Columbia, South Carolina, to attend the Standing For Stephen Smith fundraiser at the Capital Club, where I met Stephen's mother, Sandy, twin sister, Stephanie, and Aunt Pam Chaney. They shared stories with me about Stephen and their valiant six-year fight to have his case reopened by the South Carolina Law Enforcement Division (SLED).

There are so many people I am indebted to in making this book possible, and several wished to remain anonymous for their own protection, because the Murdaughs still exert much power in Hampton County.

I would especially like to thank Kim Brant and Sam Crews III for their invaluable help and background on Hampton County and the Murdaugh family. They were always there to answer my questions and put things in perspective, helping me understand how things worked in Hampton.

Many thanks are also due to Barbara and Gil Allen, who patiently pointed me in the right direction with invaluable help and encouragement from the very beginning.

I am also indebted to Jared "Buzzard" Newman, Chrissy Cook, Bonnie Crone, Trey Crosby, Ernestine Glynn, LaClaire Laffitte, Ron Stavac, Henry Philpott, Griffin Siegel, Jvonndra Brooks-Creech, and Edward Helmore.

As always, much gratitude is due to Charles Spicer and Sarah Grill of St. Martin's Press, who helped me see the wood from the trees in honing down the manuscript. I'm especially indebted to Jane Dystel and Lauren Abramo of Dystel, Goderich & Bourret Literary Management, who have always been there for me with their literary wisdom and encouragement.

Thanks also to Gail Freund, David Bunde, Barry and Charlene Eisenkraft, Martin Gould, Debbie, Douglas, and Taylor Baldwin, and Gurcher.

INDEX